KIYONORI KIKUTAKE

BETWEEN LAND AND SEA

KIYONORI KIKUTAKE

BETWEEN LAND AND SEA

Edited by Ken Tadashi Oshima

Harvard University
Graduate School of Design

Lars Müller Publishers

NOTE:
Japanese personal names within this volume are listed family name first, given name second.

Marine City 1960
Marine City 1963
Aquapolis 1975

FOREWORD

I feel fortunate to have met Kikutake Kiyonori. I still have a vivid memory of our first meeting, graciously made possible by Itō Toyoo. The taxi let me off in a relatively anonymous street like many others in Tokyo, with its convenience stores and cafes, and from there I climbed a steep small side street to find two very different manifestations of the architecture of Kikutake: the famous Sky House and his more recent office and residence. The buildings are placed diagonally across from one another, and if you didn't know better, you wouldn't think they were the work of the same architect.

Itō Toyoo worked for Kikutake when he began his architectural career, and during that first meeting it was clear that he not only felt indebted to the old master but was very fond of him too. Indeed, it was hard not to like Kikutake-san, who was quick to smile and spoke gently.

We sat down at a table in the corner of the office building, joined by Mrs. Smith Kikutake, the Hawaiian-born wife of Mr. Kikutake. All around us were books and models and drawings. As much as an office, this was a storage space, a repository for a whole life's work—so many items, each invested with ideas for a particular project or site. A young assistant brought us many folders of drawings documenting project after project.

The architect of these projects sat with us, talking and laughing, but he was already in a mausoleum dedicated to his work—a modern building that was full of light and transparency, but also dusty and aging gracefully. Everything in the building referred to the past, nothing to the future, not even the present.

Later, we crossed the street to visit the Sky House (1958), a single floor, 10 meters by 10 meters, raised from the ground on slender concrete piers. The overhang of the Sky House roof evokes something of the traditional, yet the feel of the interior is contemporary, sparsely furnished with sliding doors and windows all around. Almost empty, yet full of life, the house is a platform for living suspended amid its surroundings.

The two buildings, separated by only a few meters, yet so different in character, are in many ways emblematic of the constant tension between past and future in the work of Kikutake Kiyonori—a tension that now seems partly erased by the passage of time, perhaps in keeping with some inevitable metabolic process. Kikutake and his fellow Metabolists were mindful of modernist slogans and clearly produced a few of their own. Wishing to transcend the modernist stricture "form follows function," Kikutake emphasized instead the potential of space to continually adapt to changing functions in a way that is dynamic, seemingly biological, akin to a living organism.

The idea of architecture being responsive and adaptable, able to accommodate different functions at different times, is deeply inscribed in the history of architecture, with varying degrees of success. How can modern architecture, invariably made of solid materials like concrete and glass, be ever-changing? For Kikutake, the shift of emphasis from functionalist form to metabolist space also partly entailed a shift from the exterior form of the object to the interior spatial characteristics. In the Sky House, it is the character and qualities of the interior—its size, dimensions, orientation, and the relative scarcity of furniture—that provide the flexibility for alternative patterns of use. At the Sky House, he deployed a system of movable furnishings, called "movenettes," that could be responsive to the house's changing patterns of occupancy.

In terms of the image of the building, the Hotel Tōkōen in Tottori (1964) bears an uncanny resemblance to the Sky House. The main body of the building is made up of a substantial structural frame in concrete that in many respects is not dissimilar to structures we see under construction today, before the cladding is applied. But here, instead of cladding the structure, Kikutake leaves it exposed, inserting the functions of the hotel within the empty frame while keeping parts of the structure unfilled. The relationship between the structural frame that houses the hotel and the enclosures that accommodate its functions is revealed rather than covered by cladding. The gaps left within the open structure and the enclosed parts suggest opportunities for other activities to take place. Thus the possibility of a singular image for the building is resisted; as our eyes constantly move from part to whole, the structure becomes in the process the container of multiple functions.

A large tower containing the elevators and the stairs is placed on the outside of the hotel, linking the ground to the top of the building and beyond, the image reminiscent of an old clocktower. A small roof, in something not unlike the traditional *yosemune* style, sits like a cap on top of the whole structure. The building is at once a modern open-frame building, a giant Maison Domino, and an overscaled temple—a shrine. Even though the building was progressive for its time, somehow the architect seems to have been unwilling to let go of the image of a vernacular architecture that meant so much to him and to his work.

Conversely, the fascination with technology would play an increasingly important part in the imagery of projects like the Miyakonojō Civic Center, built a year later than the Sky House, and of course Kikutake's unrealized plans for the urbanization of the oceans. During the late 1950s and 1960s, there were numerous attempts to inhabit the ocean in ways that parallel that era's fascination with space exploration. Most of these experiments involved submerged vessels—such as the U.S. Navy's Sealabs, or Jacques Cousteau's Conshelfs—and were just as solitary as living in a space capsule.

Kikutake had witnessed the devastation brought about by World War II, as well as the dramatic increase in the population of Tokyo in its immediate wake. He argued that traditional patterns of agriculture were incapable of meeting the needs of an ever-growing population, and envisioned his Marine Cities as centers for aquaculture, producing and processing food from the sea, as well as harvesting energy from the ocean currents. The concept of floating megastructures was similarly proposed by Tange Kenzō in his Tokyo Bay Project of 1960, as a radical solution to housing and feeding the country's growing population.

The first step toward the Marine City (1963) was to be the construction of a factory on a floating platform, for the purpose of building many ocean cities that could be moved from place to place depending on the needs of the population. When no longer needed, these cities could also be sunk, submerged beneath the waves. Kikutake's water-based cities were intended to be nothing short of integrated, sustainable urban projects.

Kikutake wrote at length about his architectural and urban vision. He also tried to make his dream of urbanizing the oceans a reality by constructing full-scale fragments of his water-based structures. Unfortunately, nothing came of these ideas. Many years later we have only the gigantic offshore oil rigs to convey some sense of the form—but not the poetry—of his ideas.

Through its speculative and experimental nature, the work of Kikutake and his fellow Metabolists challenges us to think differently, more optimistically, about the possibilities for the future. Kikutake's conception of architecture transcended the idea of a mere service profession. He analyzed contemporary conditions and sought innovative design solutions that were both technologically advanced yet respectful of cultural traditions. Despite the sophistication of his ideas and the strange beauty of much of his architecture, in some ways his work remains unfinished; but this also means we have the chance to take on his mantle and seek a more aspirational path for architecture and for our creative responses to the future of the built environment.

Sadly, our plan to invite Kikutake Kiyonori to Harvard for the opening of the exhibition of his work never materialized due to his untimely death. But his dreams for architecture and urbanization continue to live in our minds, in our imagining of new ways of living and constructing the spaces we inhabit.

I would like to extend my gratitude to Ken Tadashi Oshima, for helping to curate the original exhibition and now this book, and thank everyone whose contribution has made this book possible. I am grateful also to Mrs. Smith Kikutake, for her unwavering support of this project, as well as the Kikutake family, and to Lars Müller and his team, who have been crucial in producing a book of outstanding quality, one befitting Kikutake.

Finally I would like to thank Itō-san for his friendship and for providing the introduction to Kikutake Kiyonori, who, I suspect, is smiling on us with encouragement for the future, wherever he is.

Mohsen Mostafavi
Dean and Alexander and Victoria Wiley Professor of Design
Harvard University Graduate School of Design

Tower-Shaped Community illustrated in "Ideas for the Reorganization of Tokyo City," 1959.

Sky House as presented at CIAM '59.

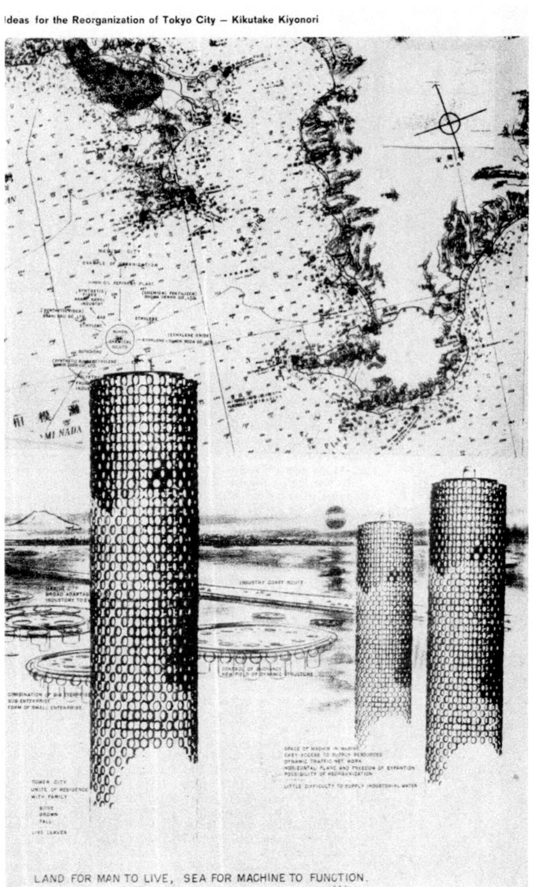

INTRODUCTION

TECTONIC VISIONS BETWEEN LAND AND SEA

Ken Tadashi Oshima

Kikutake exhibition space, Harvard University Graduate School of Design.

For more than half a century, architect Kikutake Kiyonori (1928–2011) pursued Metabolic architecture, embracing forces of renewal, recycling, and transformation. His broad vision spanned land and sea from domestic to urban scales—as expressed in the debut of his own Sky House (1958) and Marine City (1958) at the 1959 CIAM conference. Kikutake soon became the leading voice of Metabolism, the architectural movement formally launched at the 1960 World Design Conference in Tokyo and then featured at the New York Museum of Modern Art's 1960 "Visionary Architecture" exhibition. In 2011, Rem Koolhaas brought Metabolist history to contemporary discourse in his book, *Project Japan*, citing the movement's "radical makeover of the entire land."[1] For Kikutake, such dynamic, organically changing architecture drew on the centuries-old tradition of adaptable wooden structures in Japan to rebuild a nation ravaged by World War II and natural disasters; it then continuously evolved to address new societal and technological changes and challenges.

This book highlights Kikutake's lifelong exploration of a dynamic platform for living, floating above land and sea. This pursuit spans the scales of the individual dwelling unit, the public scale of landmark works such as the Administrative Building of Izumo Shrine (1963) and Hotel Tōkōen (1964), and the urban scale of his ongoing Marine/Ocean City project, continuing from the late 1950s to today. These works follow a dialectical process of *ka, kata, katachi,* inspired by Hegel's trilogy of essence, substance, phenomenon as well as by theoretical physicist Taketani Mitsuo's *Doctrine of the Three Stages of Scientific Development* (1936) that in architectural terms can be understood as the schematic, design development, and construction phases. Within this framework, Kikutake sought to maintain an ecological balance with the built environment and people's activities, rather than follow a positivist linear notion of modern progress.

As an outgrowth of the exhibition "Tectonic Visions between Land and Sea: Works of Kiyonori Kikutake" at the Harvard University Graduate School of Design, this volume presents work from the exhibition, analytical essays, Kikutake's writings, and additional contemporary photographs documenting the works' ongoing metabolic evolution. His own texts highlight his conceptual working method and bold, visionary personality.

Kikutake's connection with Harvard actually goes back to his lecture at the GSD in November 1982.[2] Three decades later, Itō Toyoo reflected on the life of Kikutake in asking, "What Was Metabolism?" for his lecture concluding the GSD exhibition, presented here as a permanent record of this event. Fred Thompson, who worked for Kikutake in the early 1960s, discusses his experiences in "Learning from Kikutake." Seng Kuan explores Kikutake's urban visions through his Tokyo Bay projects, in the context of "his broader poetic odyssey to build in the oceans" and Tange Kenzō's 1960 Tokyo Bay Plan, among others. Finally, Mark Mulligan investigates the tectonic implications and enduring lessons of Kikutake's imagination and dedication in his essay, "Structuring the Future." The essays in this book further illuminate this period through observations about his distinct personality and working

Chikugo River, Kurume, Fukuoka Prefecture.

View of Chikugo River from Suitengū shrine.

process, exploration of his urban projects for Tokyo, and further reading of the structures and material assembly in the built work. This volume reflects on the projects both as they were originally designed and as they have operated to the present in an ongoing test of Metabolism.

The year 2013 marked the completion of the cyclic rebuilding of two iconic structures in Japan: the Ise Shrine (following a 20-year cycle) and the Izumo Shrine (following a 60-year cycle). Izumo is not rebuilt in its entirety but rather embodies metabolic notions through the reuse of its constituent elements to create its current manifestation in parallel with Kikutake's own design to reimagine wood-frame construction in concrete for the Administrative Building. Moreover, both ritual shrine reconstructions undertaken in the years following Kikutake's passing could be seen as impetus to reify his vision through this publication, for future generations to extend.

METABOLIC ORIGINS

Kikutake's vision embraced the natural environment in sublime tension between its productive and destructive forces on both land and sea. Origins of this worldview can be traced to his formative years on Japan's southern island of Kyūshū. He was part of the 16th generation of a once large landowning family in Kurume, a former feudal city situated along Kyūshū's longest river, the Chikugo, that flows from the volcanic Mount Aso to the Ariake Sea. While the river irrigates some 400 square kilometers of rice fields on the Tsukushi Plain (where wet-rice cultivation was introduced to Japan during the Yayoi Period, 300 BC to AD 300), it has been prone to frequent flooding. The paddies themselves are filled with water in the spring, denoted by the characters 水田, which Kikutake considered to form his *genfūkei*—an indelible scene from his childhood.[3] Kikutake's family home was located close to the riverbanks and the Suitengū shrine. Here he witnessed how solid shrine structures made of stone could withstand floods, while temporal wooden elements could be easily replaced. Life entailed constantly adapting to the changing natural environment.

Yet it was post–World War II land reforms rather than natural disaster that led to the loss of the Kikutake family landholdings. Under the 1947 Land Reform Act, 38 percent of Japan's cultivated land was purchased from landlords by the government and resold at low prices to the farmers who worked on it.[4] The Kikutake household thereby lost their social position and historic role in the community. Kikutake noted in his 2005 interview with Rem Koolhaas, "My ancestors were landlords, and in Japan, the landlords were traditionally providers of infrastructure as well as the patrons of culture. They built schools, they build floodgates, they maintained and improved farmland, and they also supported Shinto shrines and Buddhist temples."[5]

HISTORIC PLANES

Kikutake's pursuit of architecture thus sought to create a platform for living, raised above the floodplain on land and over the sea, with

Eifukuji Kindergarten, Kurume, 1956.

infinite possibilities for expansion into new territories. As Kikutake wrote in his essay "The Order of Things One Can See: Floors and Columns," which appears in this volume:

> The first floor surface has a deeper significance than its plain, physical meaning as the base supporting human living. In our country, we have been trained to attach a definite psychological significance to the floor, which is relied on as a source of stability.

Such plateaus were often the result of great technological feats. Kikutake found particular resonance in the platforms and corridors of Itsukushima Shrine hovering above Hiroshima Bay, originating from the twelfth century; the great terrace of the Kiyomizu Temple in the eastern hills above Kyoto from 1633; or the sublime suspended structure of the Kasamori Temple from 1028 that rests on wooden stilts above a rock outcropping in Chiba Prefecture. Just as the Kasamori Temple has been destroyed by fire three times, the broader challenge for Kikutake was how to reincarnate the essence of such structures to accommodate contemporary needs of "man in the new democratic society (that) … should be neither for the gods nor for the powerful, but must be merely for man."[6] Along these lines, Kikutake believed that the Kiyomizu Temple could be rebuilt and reconceived as the Eiffel Tower of Kyoto. In fact, Kiyomizu Temple was published in 1956 in the contemporary architectural journal *Shinkenchiku*, underscoring its potential for reinterpretation and reincarnation.[7]

SHINCHINTAISHA—AN ARCHITECTURE OF CHANGE AND CONTINUITY

Kikutake's earliest independent design work set out to transform and reuse existing wood-frame structures. Such a practice followed the notion of *shinchintaisha* (新陳代謝), which literally translates as "renewal; replacement; metabolism." This practice replaces deteriorated wooden sections with new pieces to resuscitate remaining members. Upon graduating from Waseda University in Tokyo in 1950, Kikutake worked briefly for the Takenaka Construction Company and architect Murano Tōgo (1891–1984) before establishing his own office at the age of 25 in 1953. His first important client was Ishibashi Shōjirō (1889–1976), the founding president of the Bridgestone Corporation, to whom Kikutake's grandfather had lent funds to establish the corporation. Kikutake pursued his pivotal theory of a "system of replacement" for early projects including the Ishibashi Culture Center/Culture Hall (1956) and the Eifukuji Kindergarten (1956). For the former, Kikutake reused gable trusses by cutting them in half and reversing their direction to make a butterfly section. In the latter, he reused the wooden structures while creating a varied rhythm of door and window openings to enable a bright and airy new look.

Early work in wood-frame construction housing maintained traditional principles with double-aspect cross ventilation. Projects such as his Bridgestone Tonogaya Apartments (1956) and Bridgestone Mothers' and Children's Dormitory (1957) maintained *tatami*-based flexible living, with the former stacking units within a reinforced-concrete structure.

Itsukushima Shrine, Hiroshima Prefecture.

Kiyomizu Temple, Kyoto.

Kiyomizu Temple structure.

Kasamori Temple, Chōnan, Chiba Prefecture.

View from Kasamori Temple.

Sky House photo collage.

In his Inoue and Ijichi Houses (1954), Kikutake infused straightforward wood-frame residential construction with an operable window-wall using swinging rather than sliding openings. Kikutake further abstracted the traditional domestic principles within his square-plan Uryuu House (1958), which found its apotheosis in his own Sky House (1958).

Kikutake's Sky House, designed with his wife Norie, was their dynamic platform for the unfolding of family life. The Sky House, in considering the fundamental question of how to accommodate the changing needs of living, built on his previous Uryuu House in pushing the bathroom core from the center to the edge of the house to afford replacement flexibility and lessen the draw on the central living space. The main living space was suspended 6.6 meters above the sloped site from reinforced concrete piers on four sides, with a hyperbolic paraboloid (HP) shell roof above. The design afforded a 360-degree view akin to that from the ninth-century Kasamori Temple that Kikutake admired.

The Sky House design evolved from a pure modeled vision of the postwar single-family house to its built and lived-in reality. First published with the English title "A Plan for a Concrete House," the Kikutake home provided "protection from earthquakes, typhoons, and illness."[8] The Sky House model hovered above the low-rise tile roof houses of the Bunkyō District of Tokyo in the published collage of the unbuilt house. Upon the appearance of its built form, the Sky House instantly became a masterwork of modern architecture, published with Tange Kenzō's Kagawa Prefectural Building in the January 1959 issue of *Kenchiku bunka*. Kawazoe Noboru (1926–2015), journalist and soon to be mastermind of the Metabolist group, praised the two works for establishing a new realm of "humanist" architecture.

Through the design of his own house, Kikutake transformed the application of replaceable wood-frame construction to a reinforced concrete slab/pier structure. This afforded a new mode of flexible living that would serve the family's changing needs through many decades and come to epitomize the principles of Metabolism *avant la lettre*. The Sky House design followed the teachings of Kon Wajirō (1888–1973), ethnographic architect and one of Kikutake's professors at Waseda, whose theories of "Modernology" and "Living Science" advocated having few rooms with the sparest use possible of solid walls to divide space.[9] The open living space thus formed the heart of Kikutake's plan, served by his invention of a moveable kitchenette or bath unit that he termed "movenette" and that could be updated as technology advanced. In turn, the living space was modulated by the notion that "the most important feature in a Japanese home is the use of fittings that can be adjusted in highly complex manners according to the change of seasons."[10]

In counterpoint to the facilitation of constant change, the precise proportions of the Sky House provided the framework for lasting beauty. Its 10-square-meter plan, HP shell roof, and slight overhang to protect sliding screens below worked in perfect harmony. For Kikutake, the completed Sky House became a concrete conceptual structure, interchangeable system, and repeatable human-scale living unit to address burgeoning urban problems of inadequate quality and quantity of housing in postwar Japan.

Sado Grand Hotel, Niigata Prefecture, 1967.

In proposing the Tower-Shaped Community and Marine City in the journal *Kokusai kenchiku* (January, February 1959), Kikutake effectively extended his platform for living vertically and horizontally, from land to sea, rising to the sky. As he explained:

> I realized that [interchangeable architectural systems] would apply to urban environments as well. Would there be any way to add the dimension of replaceability to land, which forms the foundation of urban problems? Why not artificially produce an abundance of floating land, patches of which can be combined in a number of ways to prepare urban spaces.[11]

The movenettes of the Sky House could be scaled up to form telescoping living units attached to the structural core tower and open to views of the sea, sky, and Mt. Fuji. The idea of the Marine City would become a lifelong pursuit; Kikutake authored two full-length books on the subject.[12] For Kikutake, this was not science fiction but rather a vision based in everyday life in which he contemplated the "spectacular experience of the weather and horizon of the sea."[13] Such aspirations informed both unbuilt and built work, including the Hotel Tōkōen (1964–79), the Pacific Hotel (1966), and the Sado Grand Hotel (1967).

LAUNCH OF METABOLISM

The transformation of building technology at the multiple scales of the Sky House, Marine City, and the Izumo Administrative Building formed the ideological basis for Kikutake's pursuit of Metabolism as launched at the 1960 World Design Conference in Tokyo. Following the organic implications of the name Metabolism, Kikutake expanded on the Marine City to propose the Ocean City "*unabara* (ocean)" in which the metabolic city is formed by the process of continual organic cell division. Such a perspective brought together Kikutake's interests in architecture and biology; he had wanted to become a doctor before being encouraged to study architecture based on his drawing skills.[14] Kawazoe Noboru, in supporting Kikutake's organic stance, advocated designing projects to be like a "cell of bacteria which is constantly propagating itself."[15] Kawazoe believed the will of bacteria to live, like the will of man, would always remain. As he concluded, "the only difference will be men's capacity to dream a magnificent dream."[16] While such assessments may today seem naive or unscientific, they reflect sincere youthful aspirations and the worldview at the time.

With the official launch of the new movement with the presentation of the Metabolism book at the World Design Conference in Tokyo in May 1960, Kikutake led the group as its central architectural voice through his core principles articulated in Ocean/Marine City and the Sky House as the lead projects of the first 40 pages of the group's inaugural publication. Maki Fumihiko (1928–) would later describe the group much like a baseball team coming together for a common cause to address rapidly transforming postwar Japan through an organic architectural/urban strategy.[17] Maki described journalist Kawazoe Noboru as the coach, Kikutake as the ace pitcher, and Tange Kenzō (1913–2005) and Isozaki Arata

Izumo Shrine.

Administrative Building of Izumo Shrine.

(1931–) behind the backstop. Thus in center spotlight were Kikutake's Sky House together with his scheme for Marine Cities. For Kikutake, "Metabolism," meant the "introduction into architecture of such a method of replacing and changing the living equipment in accordance with living patterns. At the same time, this method helps us to delineate clearly the main portions of the building which will not change and which will continue to be the center and predominant part of the building. This also will help the architect to formulate his own goals clearly."[18]

The Sky House was also a platform for discussing ideas on architecture, including visits by a number of prominent architects from abroad, such as Louis Kahn, Peter Smithson, and James Stirling. In particular, the composition of space in the Sky House could be seen to align with Louis Kahn's notion of "served" and "servant" spaces, a topic of heated discussion upon Kahn's visit to the house during the 1960 World Design Conference.[19] The two discussed fundamental principles of design through elements such as the conception of "spoon" as "form made of inseparable parts of a container and an art." As Kahn explained, "If you take the container away you have a handle, if you take the arm away you have a cup. Together they are spoon."[20] This thinking tracked closely with Kikutake's own developing theory of *ka, kata, katachi.*

Moreover, Kikutake noted that Kahn took particular interest in his Tokuunji project and the Izumo Administrative Building. While Kahn could be seen to have informed Kikutake's design methodology, Kikutake's designs would find resonance with Kahn, especially in his design of the Salk Institute, in the relationship between concrete walls and wooden louvers. Kikutake and Peter Smithson could also be seen to share common concerns—toward "urban structuring" and in similar expressions of movenette bathroom units.[21] James Stirling's shared interests with Kikutake in prefabrication and housing could be noted in their respective designs for the PREVI experimental housing project in Lima, Peru (1969) and Stirling's attempt to crawl down through the Sky House floor opening to the children's movenette space below. Kikutake implied the difficulties in establishing universal standards and scale in noting, "the opening was just barely big enough for him to get through."[22]

TRANSFORMING HISTORY—IZUMO TO KYOTO

Following the completion of the Sky House and launch of Marine City in 1958, Kikutake extended his ideas of metabolically transforming wood-frame construction in his design of the Administrative Building for the Great Shrine of Izumo. For Kikutake, his encounter with Izumo Shrine had a profound impact, especially in imagining how the main sanctuary building had been rebuilt and restored repeatedly since the fourth century.[23]

The Izumo Shrine that so influenced Kikutake occupies a particular place in Japanese history in terms of both time and location. Situated on the Japan Sea with its cold northern currents, the Izumo Shrine undergoes a major restoration every 60 years. The equally revered Ise Shrine, championed by Tange Kenzō, lies on the Ise Peninsula on the Pacific Ocean and is rebuilt every 20 years. Ise Shrine finds its mythological origins in the formation of Japan as told in the *Kojiki* ("Record

Kyoto Community Bank, Kisshōin Branch, Kyoto, 1977.

of Ancient Matters"), as it enshrined the Sun Goddess of Amaterasu. Izumo Shrine is believed to originally have been a massive structure towering 48 meters above the ground, with a stair positioned for the divine Ōkuninushi (Great Land Master) to descend to earth.[24] For Kikutake, Ise Shrine was "delicate, elegant and feminine" in contrast to Izumo Shrine (along with the Itsukushima Shrine and the Kiyomizu Temple) in being "majestic, powerful and masculine."[25] The immense original Izumo Shrine was built more than 1,800 years ago using daring techniques by master carpenters also responsible for great Buddhist temples; the shrine incorporated the fundamental form of a raised-floor dwelling divided spatially by the central column.[26] Moreover, while the Inner (*Naikū*) Shrine at Ise is completely rebuilt on an alternate site every 20 years, the main shrine at Izumo is built on the same site as a reconstruction incorporating existing members—thereby underscoring the Metabolist ideology of sustaining the structure's life.

For Kikutake, the design of the Administrative Building of Izumo Shrine emerged from his metabolic three-step process of *ka, kata, katachi.* While he defines these terms as "image," "technology," and "function" for architecture, he added further definitions based on aesthetics, logic, and biology in his essay on "The Great Shrine of Izumo."[27] This theory as diagrammed was not a linear process but rather triangulated or even cyclical as seen through the organic notion of Metabolism. As he wrote, "In order to reflect dynamic reality, what is needed is not a fixed, static function, but rather one which is capable of undergoing metabolic change. Therefore, naturally, our ideas about architecture are also bound to change. We must stop thinking in terms of function and form, and think instead in terms of space and changeable function."[28] Kikutake's design of the Administrative Building at Izumo reinterprets the principles of timber-frame construction and the image of the traditional *inakake* wooden rack used to dry rice, using a post-tensioned concrete structure with a screen of precast concrete members.

Kikutake further extended his *ka, kata, katachi* process and use of long-span concrete beams in his competition plan for the Kyoto International Conference Hall (1963). If the concrete beams at Izumo were the reinterpretation of the Shrine's ridge beam, here they formed the *hijiki,* the wooden bracketry supports in traditional Japanese architecture. In a dramatic increase in scale from his Izumo scheme, Kikutake designed an inverted square pyramid complex that emerged from the central cloister-shaped lobby "space" rather than the "functional requirements" of the conference rooms. Following on many successes, Kikutake's failure to clinch the top prize in this major competition came as a great shock and was a turning point in his career—to no longer be the invincible architect.

Although Kikutake's scheme for the Kyoto International Conference Hall never came to fruition as a single complex, he would realize his broader social vision for providing space for Kyoto communities to gather. Working as part of the Communication Design Institute (which included Kawazoe, Kato Hidetoshi, and industrial designer Ekuan Kenji), Kikutake developed 30 branch designs for the Kyoto Community Bank in the 1970s. Each branch followed a common typology of

consistent scale and structure, featuring floating umbrella-shaped roofs adapted to particular neighborhood contexts. The interiors dedicated 20 percent of the total space for children's libraries, playgrounds, exhibition spaces, and community meeting and dining areas.

CREATING A FLOATING WORLD

Kikutake's embrace of function and current technology were concomitant tendencies to his "imaginative approach," creating amazing floating space both on land and sea. This could be seen as a "resistance unit" protecting human life from the ravages of flood or fire, as in the Sky House, or a jellyfish floating on the sea as a conceptual motif for his actual Floating City (1971), or Aquapolis for the 1975 Okinawa Ocean Expo. Kikutake translated the sacred floating planes of the Kasamori Temple and Itsukushima Shrine to secular contexts, from the elevated office slabs of the Tatebayashi City Hall to the Kyoto International Conference Hall. The Tatebayashi City Hall maintains the clear parti of four cores supporting the office slabs, akin to Louis Kahn's contemporaneous Richards Medical Center, yet at a larger public scale that affords expansive views of the city and surrounding landscape.

Kikutake's sketches typically depicted seascapes and landscapes with clouds floating above, modulating light and temperature. Such dynamic cumulus forms are symbols of the spirits at Izumo and are captured in the HP shell roof of the Hotel Tōkōen that similarly faces the forces of the Japan Sea. The motif of an umbrella—a floating, transportable structure—inspired the roofs of the Kyoto Community Banks. Kikutake also masterfully expressed a floating quality in the concrete columbarium at Tokuunji (1965), in which amazingly thin concrete walls hang from above to create a space for contemplating life and death. Within the domain of public space, Kikutake transformed steel to create floating enclosures for the civic hall and auditoriums at Hagi and Miyakonojō. At Hagi, steel spider web-like structures combine with a constellation of exposed lights to create the surreal space of a starlit evening. At Miyakonojō, Kikutake designed the hall enclosure with attention to the forces of air, light, and sound, hiding the exterior structural form to create a floating space.

The extension of Kikutake's living environment between land and sea converge in his design of Pasadena Heights terraced housing (1974), located near the base of Mt. Fuji at Mishima and adjacent to the tracks of the Tōkaidō Shinkansen high-speed train. The elevation above sea level is clearly marked on the building complex that faces the mountain. The 120 units cascade in a zigzag configuration to accommodate the sloping site and maximize expansive views, notwithstanding the identical minimal 68.3-square-meter units. Each unit is accessed from below via a hanging stair—just as the Sky House originally was—to afford a dynamic spatial experience daily. In fact, Kikutake retained a unit as his own family's second home. Also just as in the Sky House, the individual units maintain flexible living spaces with the movenette kitchen and bath units along the front edge for light, view, and ease of replacement. As a complement to the minimal interiors, the exterior private courts are rather expansive, offering a balanced house and garden. In occupying

Roof structure at Hagi Civic Hall, Yamaguchi Prefecture, 1968.

Pasadena Heights, Shizuoka Prefecture, 1974.

Sea-level marker at Pasacena Heights.

View from fourth-floor terrace at Hotel Tōkōen, Yonago, Tottori Prefecture, 1964.

Garden view Hotel Tōkōen.

Columbarium at Tokuunji.

Entry stairs at Pasadena Heights.

Loft, Shibuya, Tokyo, 1987.

these structures that are open to change and interpretation, the residents have transformed the units over time with a variety of add-ons and personal touches (that today can be seen in a time-lapse video).[29]

METABOLIC TRAJECTORIES

Despite Kikutake's crushing disappointment in not winning the Kyoto International Conference Hall competition and then facing increasing economic and ecological problems beginning in the 1970s, he continued to expand his work in scale and scope. Kikutake translated the conception of terraced slabs at Pasadena Heights to the commercial domain of the Seibu Ōtsu Shopping Center (1976) and other Seibu projects, including the Seibu Shibuya Branch "Loft" Building (1987). Kikutake's conception of the Tower-Shaped Community could be seen in part in the designs for the Osaka Expo Tower (1970) and Cosima (Sofitel) Hotel (1994)—or even in his schemes for the Fukuoka City Hall (1982) and Kurume City Hall (1994). The elevated planes of the Sky House and Kyoto International Conference Hall take form in the Edo Tokyo Museum (1992). Kikutake extended his floating roof to new extremes in the Shimane Art Museum (1998) and deployed dome roof structures in the 200-meter-long, 20,000-person Kita Kyūshū Media Dome (1998) and the undulating Kyūshū National Museum (2004). Moreover, Kikutake maintained his vision for building civic infrastructure between land and sea in his designs for rest-stop facilities at Mekari and Dannoura (1973) adjacent to the Kanmonkyo suspension bridge crossing the Kanmon Straits, between the islands of Honshū and Kyūshū. While Kikutake's dream of a Marine City continued throughout his life, works such as the Osaka Expo Tower, Aquapolis for the Japan Pavilion at the Okinawa Ocean Expo '75, and the Cosima Hotel would all fall prey to demolition.

Kikutake continued his pursuit of transforming wood-frame structures open to new uses, expressed most vividly in the design of his Kuroishi Holp Kodomokan (1975). Built in the northern Aomori Prefecture, this provincial library serves to bring together the rural community and inspires children to read books on an apple-patterned carpet and climb columns to the balconies.

Beyond the Metabolist movement and works themselves, the ongoing evolution of these ideas can be seen through the work of younger generations. The strength of Kikutake's work is in its tectonic construction, human-scaled spatial character, and capacity to embrace change over time. These key aspects have been highly influential for those who worked closely with him, including Itō Toyoo, Fred Thompson, Hasegawa Itsuko, Naitō Hiroshi, and a new generation of young architects. His vision lives on beyond his death in 2011, according to cycles of continued metabolic change. Learning about the Sky House as a young girl inspired Sejima Kazuyo's career in architecture, as she writes here in "Recalling Kikutake-*sensei*." Her SANAA partner Nishizawa Ryue has noted his own impression of the Sky House in terms of its efficiency, economy of materials, and almost microcosmic expression of the city.[30] In Toronto, Fred Thompson's scheme for Harbour City (1970) proposed a Marine City on old airport lands and adjacent fill; this project was actually built in part on the water as "Ontario Place."[31]

Kurume City Hall, Fukuoka Prefecture, 1994.

Mekari Rest Facility, Kita Kyūshū, Fukuoka Prefecture, 1973.

Hotel Cosima, Tokyo, 1994.

Thompson, Ontario Place, Toronto, 1970.

With the devastation of the Tōhoku earthquake and tsunami on March 11, 2011, Kikutake reaffirmed his belief in addressing both the devastating and benevolent forces of nature between land and sea through the creation of public infrastructure. He confirmed his confidence in the viability of the Marine City to withstand forces of such magnitude.[32] The vision of Kikutake's public architecture such as the Kuroishi Holp Kodomokan can be seen through Itō Toyoo's "Home-for-All" projects in tsunami-ravaged areas (2012–13). Itō's scheme for heavily damaged Kamaishi City in Iwate Prefecture incorporated both *minka* farmhouse-like housing and landscape elements of berms, greenbelts, and sloped building sites to mitigate future flooding and tidal waves. Moreover, the tsunami's great wake, affecting the entire Pacific Rim, underscored the necessity to look beyond national borders in designing for the constantly changing metabolic world.

While the Sky House has lived on, both physically and as an icon of postwar Japanese architecture, it has in fact proved to be a "resistance unit" to accommodate family changes through multiple generations and respond to an increasingly dense urban environment. In his twilight years, Kikutake asserted once again his vision of creating domestic and topographic structures between land and sea, which he noted is expressed vividly in the rice-paddy structures of terraced land such as those of his homeland. Such ecological megastructures that appear to transform from land to sea and back through the seasons thereby situate Kikutake's pursuit within a much longer historical trajectory and confirm his broader life-long aspiration to sustain human life.[33]

1 Rem Koolhaas and Hans Ulrich Obrist, *Project Japan: Metabolism Talks* (London: Taschen, 2011), back cover.
2 Kikutake lectured at the GSD on November 4, 1982.
3 Kikutake Kiyonori, "Kenchiku to mizu," *GA Japan*, no. 70, September 2004, 112–127.
4 Ibid.
5 Ibid.
6 Kikutake Kiyonori, "New Form and Old Tradition," *Arts & Architecture*, December 1964, 34.
7 Motoyoshi Isao, "Kiyomizu dera," *Shinkenchiku*, vol. 31, November 1956, 2–8.
8 Kikutake Kiyonori and Kikutake Norie, "Sky House," *Kenchiku bunka*, December 1957, 54–56.
9 Kikutake Kiyonori and Yukio Futagawa, "Sky House, Its Background and Significance: Interview with Kikutake Kiyonori," *GA Houses*, no. 100 (2007), 81.
10 Ibid.
11 Kikutake Kiyonori, *Metabolist Kiyonori Kikutake*, special issue, *Space Design*, no. 193 (October 1980), 31.
12 Kikutake Kiyonori, *Kaijō toshi* SD84 (Tokyo: Kajima Shuppankai, 1973), and *Kaijō toshi no hanashi* (Tokyo: NHK Books, 1975).
13 Kikutake, *Kaijō toshi no hanashi*, 154.
14 Iso Tatsuo, "Kikutake Yuki shi ni kiku [Interview with Kikutake Yuki]," in Iso Tatsuo, *Kikutake Kiyonori jun rei* (Tokyo: Nikkei BP, 2012), 201.
15 Kawazoe Noboru, "Material and Man," In *Metabolism/1960* (Tokyo: Bijutsu shuppansha, 1960), 51.
16 Ibid.
17 Maki Fumihiko remarks at Kikutake Kiyonori memorial service, April 13, 2012.
18 Kikutake, "New Form and Old Tradition," 16.
19 Fujisaki Keiichiro, "Kikutake sensei, ano yoru, kahn to nani ga attandesuka? [Kikutake-*sensei*, what happened on that night with Kahn?]," *Casa Brutus* (July 2004), 74–75.
20 Louis Kahn, "Law and Rule in Architecture," *Louis Kahn: Essential Texts*, ed. Robert Twombly (New York: W.W. Norton, 2003), 139.
21 "Bath Movenet," *Kenchiku*, April 1965, 86.
22 Kikutake Kiyonori in Koolhaas and Obrist, *Project Japan: Metabolism Talks*, 139.
23 Kikutake, "New Form and Old Tradition," 34.
24 The theories on the original form of Izumo Shrine are based on the research of Fukuyama Toshio, *Izumo taisha no honden* (Izumo: Izumo taisha shamusho, 1955).
25 Kikutake Kiyonori, "The Great Shrine of Izumo," *World Architecture*, no. 2 (1965), 11.
26 Kikutake Kiyonori, "Dentō ni tsuite; gijutsu no izumo [On tradition, Izumo's building technology]," *Taisha kenchikuron* (Tokyo: Shokokusha, 2008), 64–83.
27 Kikutake, "The Great Shrine of Izumo," 10–13.
28 Ibid.
29 http://tektworks.net/concept.html
30 Nishizawa Ryue, "Kikutake Kiyonori," *Shinkenchiku* special issue (May 2012), 94.
31 While Fred Thompson was the driving design force for Ontario Place, the design was further developed by Eberhard Zeidler.
32 Fukusawa Keita, "Hand Man: Kikutake Kiyonori," *Numéro* 53, no. 186 (January–February 2012), 185–186.
33 Ibid., 186.

Entry, Kuroishi Holp Kodomokan, Aomori Prefecture, 1975.

Interior, Kuroishi Holp Kodomokan, Aomori Prefecture, 1975.

Rice paddy at Akizuki, Fukuoka Prefecture.

VISIONS OF TOKYO BAY

Seng Kuan

There has been little if any perception of the ocean as an environment for man and his culture, his music, his art and his literature, as an environment conducive to urban living and the transportation of people as well as goods, an environment whose aesthetic and sociological potential is unlimited. The realization requires, as history has always required, an architect whose skills and vision are ahead of his time.
—John P. Craven[1]

Among architects identified with the Metabolist movement, Kikutake Kiyonori was curiously late in offering his version of the Tokyo Bay Plan—an exercise that was de rigueur among Japan's postwar avant-garde—preceded by Ōtaka Masato, Kurokawa Kishō, and Tange Kenzō. This delay, perhaps hesitation, is all the more perplexing considering Kikutake's pioneering efforts in proposing alternatives to the traditional terra firma as the site of architectural interventions, especially through the so-called Marine Cities (*kaijō toshi*) and artificial land (*jinkō tochi*) series begun in the late 1950s. Similarly, Kikutake's version of the Tokyo Bay Plan appears as an anomaly in his own oeuvre. Its acknowledgment of the city and urban context, along with aspects of industrialization grounded in functionalism, compared with the romantic visions of better-known and more widely publicized Marine Cities projects, allows us a glimpse into Kikutake's nuanced intellectual and emotional views on Japan's postwar urbanization and transformations of its landscape.

Kikutake's Tokyo Bay Project was originally planned for inclusion in the second installment of the Metabolism manifesto, which was never realized. Instead the study appears only in passing in a special feature on the architect's recent work in the November 1961 issue of the journal *Kenchiku*. This Tokyo Bay Plan's artistic and intellectual significance is further eclipsed by the instant and immense notoriety accorded Tange Kenzō's Tokyo Plan 1960, promoted through a media blitz in early 1961, just a few months before Kikutake's version emerged.[2] An even earlier proposal to territorialize Tokyo Bay was put forward by fellow Metabolist group member Ōtaka Masato in 1959.[3] It would be a mistake to dismiss Kikutake's version of the Tokyo Bay Plan as inferior in boldness and imagination to the seemingly more audacious series of mirage-like cities floating into the horizon, as he depicts in some of the most iconic drawings of utopian architecture. Similarly the scheme should not be seen as an afterthought or reactionary, or a concession to reality in giving the Marine Cities a sense of place, to anchor them to a site and contingencies for development.

This essay on Kikutake's Tokyo Bay Plan examines the reframing, by the postwar generation of Japanese architects, of the discourse of land and sea as criticisms of Japan's modernization process, projecting an environmental ideal that was profoundly romantic and rooted in a long tradition of landscape and riparian work central to the agrarian economy of early modern Japan. Kikutake famously describes his architectural process as consisting of a triad of order (*ka*), type (*kata*), and form (*katachi*).[4] (See his essay outlining this concept on p. 101 in

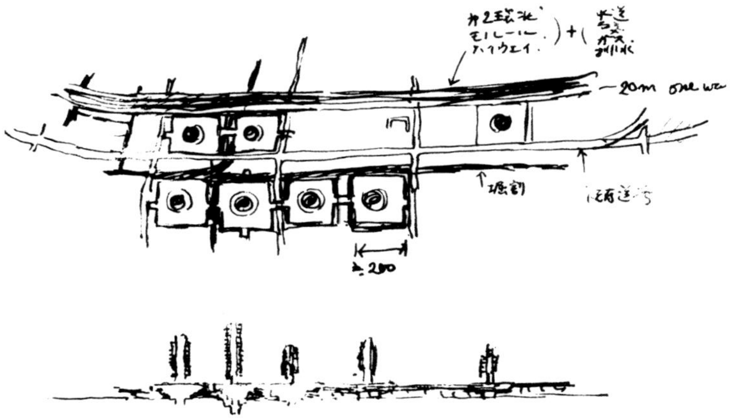

Kikutake Kiyonori, sketch, Tokyo Bay Plan, 1961.

Kikutake Kiyonori, photo collage, Kōtō Ward Plan, 1961.

this volume.) By examining Kikutake's approaches to urban-scale work in this critical phase of his intellectual development, it emerges that the struggle was also between functionalism and the exigencies of industrialization on the one hand and the natural environment on the other, reified through the design of housing and residential communities in a radically transformed context.

The Metabolist movement is often characterized by its embrace of modular construction and process-oriented building systems—fetishized by the postwar avant-garde in the West for its rhetoric of technological rationalization.[5] Another signal feature of Metabolist architecture is its penchant for megastructural, heroic scales, envisioning entire cities floating in the open sea or suspended over existing cities.[6] Proposals by Kikutake, Tange, and Ōtaka all territorialize the bay's vast expanse with floating islands of residential communities, office towers, and industrial districts. By looking beyond the formal, architectural qualities of these visionary schemes, this essay will also situate them in the broader construction industries of Japan during the high-growth period.

KIKUTAKE'S TOKYO BAY PLAN

From 1958, with the first Marine City project, to 1960 with the so-called Unabara study, Ocean City (*kaiyō toshi*) of 1968, and Aquapolis of 1975, Kikutake's reputation, especially abroad and among non-architects, was built on futuristic floating communities devoid of any self-conscious national and territorial context. It would be axiomatic to distinguish between two trajectories in Kikutake's urban-scale work: a deep-sea-based one that is radically decontextualized and a land/shallow-sea-based one rooted in his longing for the natural landscape. Jacques Cousteau's movie *Le Monde du silence*, dubbed into Japanese, was widely acclaimed when it opened in Japan in 1956. This vision of the brave new frontier, with freedom and vastness on an oceanic scale, comports with a set of universalist values of the postwar avant-garde and garnered sympathy for Kikutake's Marine Cities from an international audience. Yet the site of Tokyo Bay itself was never far from Kikutake's mind. In 1956 he was invited to join a competition for a new terminal at Tokyo's Haneda Airport, built entirely on reclaimed land from Tokyo Bay. At the 1959 meeting of the Congrès internationaux d'architecture moderne in Otterlo, Tange Kenzō presented the Sky House on behalf of Kikutake, who could not attend the event himself, as well as a preliminary view of the Marine City project, which was provocatively billed as "Ideas for the Reorganization of Tokyo."[7]

Kikutake's Tokyo Bay Plan (1961) consists of several rhetorically self-contained components, each deployable as a discrete urban and architectural strategy independent of the larger scheme. The various parts occupy an intermediary zone between the terra firma of historic Tokyo and variations to the Marine City proposals floating on deeper waters in the outer Tokyo Bay. The first part of Kikutake's Tokyo Bay Plan concerns the redevelopment of Kōtō Ward, a low-lying area to the northeast of Tokyo's center wedged between the Sumida and Arakawa Rivers and encompassing approximately 5,000 hectares of

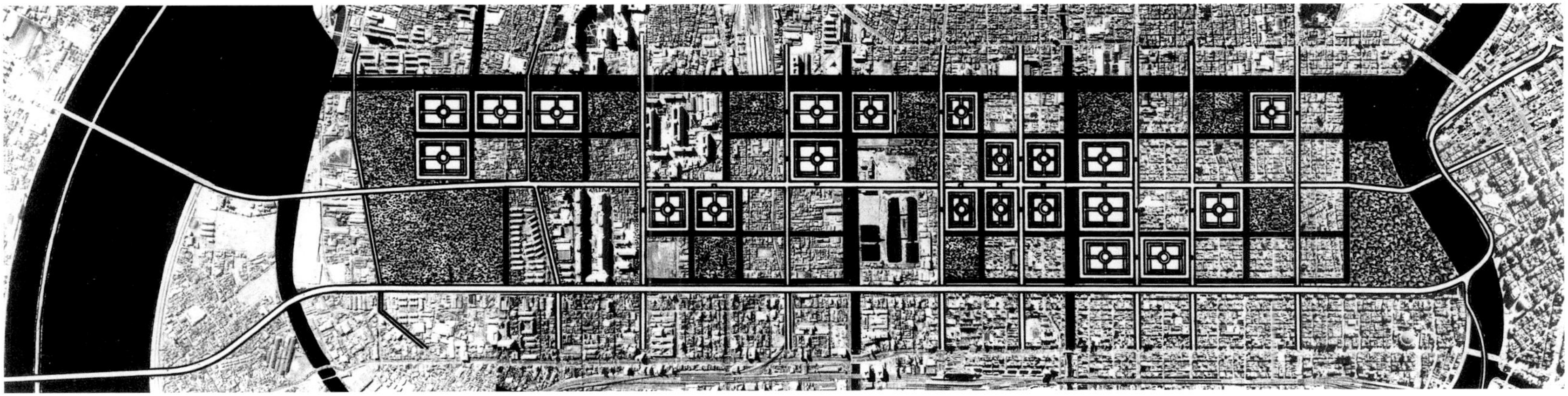

land and a half-million residents. With most of the land in Kōtō Ward hovering at sea level or even below, Kikutake identified five perennial threats to the region: earthquake, fire, flooding, tsunami, and land subsidence.[8] To counter these dangers, Kikutake proposes dredging the soil to a depth of 5–6 meters below sea level and using the excavated earth to construct artificial hills scattered about the area, forming a series of parks and green bulwarks. The inhabitable areas would be divided into a grid of 200 meter by 200 meter modular districts, floating platforms each anchored by a cylindrical tower set atop the gridiron base.

True to the spirit of Metabolism, at the heart of Kikutake's Kōtō Ward Plan is an infrastructural project, both as a coastal and riparian management strategy and a transportation system. While the individual floating platforms constitute the basic unit of neighborhood organization and incremental urban growth, the broader territorialization of the region is premised on an orthogonal system of bridges, roads, bulwarks, and canals. As Kikutake makes clear in an aerial photo collage, the primary ordering strategy of the Kōtō Ward Plan is composed of these bridges and canals. The main axis, running east-west through the district between the Sumida and Arakawa Rivers, consists of a pairing of an elevated highway and a canal. The elevated highway itself is a bundled infrastructural spine that also includes a monorail, water, sewage and gas mains, and electric power lines. Equally important as this modern trope of functionalist planning is the system of canals, which harks back to the historic geography of Tokyo.[9] In addition to the main canal corridor between the Sumida and Arakawa is a series of lesser waterways that define the boundaries of each floating platform. In much the same manner as the roads and bridges, the canals in Kikutake's plan are meant to be read as positive spaces that play an active part in both in the functional and imaginary geography of the region.

The second in Kikutake's trilogy for Tokyo Bay, the South Tokyo Plan (*minani Tōkyō keikaku*) can be understood as an extension of the Kōtō Ward Plan, but located in the deeper waters of Tokyo Bay proper. Unlike the Kōtō Ward Plan, which sits on an already developed and inhabited area of the city, the South Tokyo Plan is located almost entirely on the sea, albeit in shallow waters. Hovering off the coast of the Kasai, Shibaura, and Shinagawa areas, all of them reclaimed land on which modern industries are largely concentrated, the new floating city would provide living space for 1 million inhabitants.

Kikutake's tower-shaped type is predicated on the idea of artificial land, first advocated in Japan by the architect Yoshizaka Takamasa (1917–80).[10] The tower is designed to form a community of 1,250 households, or 5,000 residents. In contrast to the structural frame of Le Corbusier's Obus or Unité models, which are three-dimensional megastructural systems, the so-called artificial land in Kikutake's tower type is the vertical walls of the cylindrical shafts, providing the structure and the infrastructure that in turn support the individual dwelling units grafted onto it.[11] The contents of the platforms that hover closer to ground are not defined in the Kōtō Ward Plan, though we

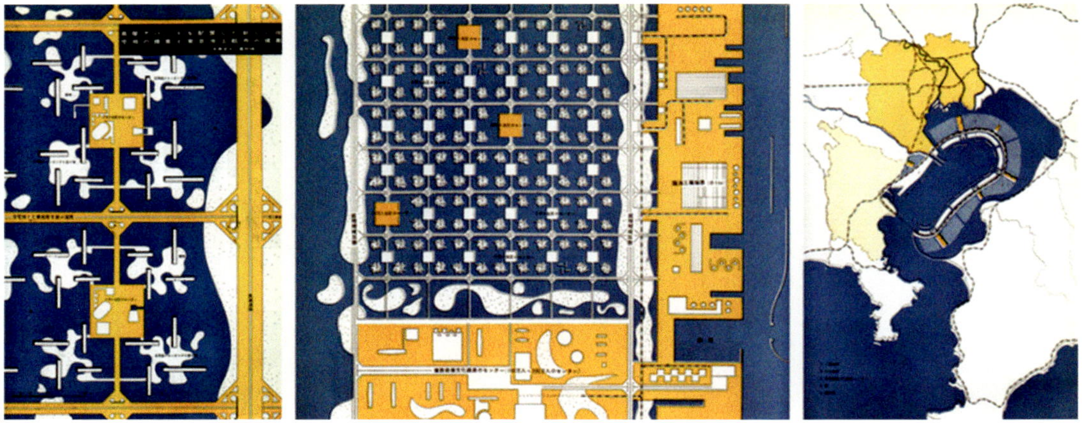

Ōtaka Masato and Okumura Keiichi, Tokyo Bay Plan, 1959.

are able to sense Kikutake's vision of this component in the Ikebukuro Redevelopment Project (1962), produced soon thereafter as a case study of the tower type.[12] Intended for one of Tokyo's most important subcenters, alongside Shinjuku and Shibuya, Ikebukuro is a major commuter hub to the northwest of the city center. The sizable blocks to either side of the main railway station are covered with large oval decks, each six to seven stories high and containing parking, utilities, and shopping. These decks range 300–500 meters on each side and may support several cylindrical towers on top.

Yet a third part of Kikutake's Tokyo Bay Plan would be located in the center of the bay, yielding more than 230 square kilometers of new area for industrial use. This industrial component of the overall vision is pushed further into the deeper waters of Tokyo Bay. An enlarged grid structure of superblocks is suspended in the bay's center, connected to the mainland in all directions by a series of highways and rail lines. This transportation grid is circumscribed by a ring highway that hovers along the shoreline. Along the periphery of this floating industrial city are crenellated edges, depicting piers for tankers and cargo ships whose rapidly expanding size in the postwar period required deeper waters further from the shoreline.

Kikutake's Tokyo Bay Plan is situated in a broader regional system, as implied in the title of the preliminary study presented at CIAM Otterlo, "Ideas for the Reorganization of Tokyo." From a narrowly defined functionalist perspective, Kikutake's proposal suggests little overt attempt to weave the different parts of his urban-scale interventions into a cohesive, hierarchically arranged whole, on a metropolitan or regional scale as Tange Kenzō's and Ōtaka Masato's respective versions clearly endeavor to achieve. Nor is there the same degree of saliency of major transportation infrastructure. The highways, railways, seaport, and airport in Kikutake's Tokyo Bay Plan appear more as responses to the land or land-like parcels created in the middle of the bay, rather than the primary drivers of urban development.

Kikutake's Kōtō Ward Plan and South Tokyo Project are both situated in the inner bay, closest to Tokyo's urban shoreline, stretching from the Kasai area to the northeast and continuing all the way to the Shibaura and Shinagawa areas to the southwest. Both the Kōtō Ward and South Tokyo studies are primarily residential in program, contrasting sharply with the industrial character of the shoreline strip as developed since the second half of the nineteenth century.

Historically Kōtō Ward was part of the broader landscape of the so-called Low City of Edo (*shitamachi*), describing not only the low-lying terrain on the banks of the Sumida River and crisscrossed by a dense network of canals but also the urban culture of tradesmen, merchants, and laborers.[13] While the east bank of the river was not developed as part of an urban area until the second half of the Edo Period, by the modern period the area had become fully entrenched in the urban imagination of the *shitamachi*, with some of the densest agglomeration of housing stock and population in the city. Kikutake further notes that the urban economic fabric of Kōtō Ward historically consisted of small-scale industries and independent, family-based workshops. The Kiba area, literally "timber field," is representative of the often trade- or guild-based neighborhoods that prospered in *shitamachi*. Located on the east bank of the Sumida, it began as the warehousing area for timber that came down the network of waterways in the broader Tone River Basin, and this led to the congregation of carpenters in the area.

This type of economy lacks the large pools of capital required for ambitious infrastructural investments. This density also made the *shitamachi* the most vulnerable to disasters, natural or man-made, and indeed Kōtō Ward was entirely obliterated in the Great Kantō Earthquake of 1923, especially by the conflagration that came after the seismic shock.[14] This also left Kōtō Ward as essentially a blank slate. Indeed, the area was perhaps the only part of Gotō Shimpei's grandiose post-earthquake reconstruction plan that was actually implemented.[15] In other words, unlike many parts of Tokyo, Kōtō Ward has an essentially orthogonal road network, hierarchically organized with broad trunk routes like Eidai-dōri, and a series of neighborhood parks.

ŌTAKA MASATO'S TOKYO BAY PLAN

While Kikutake's proposal for Tokyo Bay was conceived as an infrastructural and regional land use strategy, in which housing plays a merely perfunctory role, he was also responding to the earlier scheme by Ōtaka Masato that was fundamentally the regional-scale extrapolation of a high-rise housing project. Born in 1923 and the oldest member of the Metabolist group, Ōtaka was also the first major architect to produce a comprehensive vision for Tokyo Bay. Against the background of Japan's rapid and haphazard urban recovery, particularly during the Korean War, Ōtaka lamented, "Only 14 percent of Japan's land is flat. Agricultural land is constantly eroded by the plan-less spreading of urban buildings all two stories or less."[16] He looked toward the bay to relieve Tokyo of its mounting population and industrialization pressures. Ōtaka's Tokyo Bay study grew out of a design commission from the Japan Housing Corporation in 1955 to explore the potential of high-rise living.[17] Completed in 1958, Harumi Apartments was heralded as Japan's answer to Le Corbusier's Unité d'habitations. Ōtaka acted as project architect for the office of Maekawa Kunio, who was the first among Le Corbusier's three Japanese protégés. In contrast to the European Unités, which are located in the outskirts of established urban centers, Maekawa/Ōtaka's Japanese iteration was built on reclaimed land in Tokyo Bay.[18]

A linear block more than 100 meters in length, Harumi Apartments is megastructural in its proportions and concept.[19] The site of Harumi itself is an artificial island reclaimed from the Sumida estuary beginning in the late nineteenth century, hence it was necessary to bury the new building's foundation pylons deep in the loose landfill below. When Harumi Apartments was being designed, the structural engineers had to reckon with a bedrock depth of 30 meters below ground. With building height capped by an outdated national building code to 31 meters, Harumi Apartments' structural frame was almost equally divided between the aboveground and below-ground portions.[20] In

other words, the lesson from Harumi is that the act of land reclamation as the creation of large, generic parcels is rendered superfluous by megastructural techniques. Buildings can rest directly on submerged pylons without any alterations to the landscape.

As a prototype experiment for a national housing strategy, Harumi Apartments was subject to the relentless economizing of Japan's early postwar construction industry.[21] The project was also emblematic of a new approach to territorialization in the postwar era. In February 1959 Ōtaka Masato in collaboration with colleague Okumura Keiichi expanded the housing at Harumi into a comprehensive study of an entirely new city located in the middle of Tokyo Bay.[22] The basic module is a housing slab like that of Harumi Apartments. Every four slabs, placed in a pinwheel pattern and rotated around the center, constitute a community of 20,000 people.[23] At the center of this community would be an artificial island that provides communal amenities. This larger agglomeration could be conjoined with other units and extended virtually ad infinitum, circumscribing the shoreline of Tokyo Bay. Ōtaka and Okumura's design is sympathetic to the pure linear city model proposed by Nikolai Miliutin in 1930, which was well known in Japan, but extends the belt almost around the full circumference of Tokyo Bay.[24] The urban belt consists of five layers: a ring highway, residential communities, another ring highway, a railway, and a 1-kilometer-wide strip for industrial use. Using a multi-tiered system first developed by the Rationalist urban plans of the prewar period, Ōtaka's plan for Tokyo Bay structures the spaces for labor and leisure in clusters of ascending order: the pinwheel block, community centers, and metropolitan subcenters designed for 1–2 million people each.

TANGE KENZŌ'S A PLAN FOR TOKYO, 1960

Kikutake and Ōtaka's respective schemes for Tokyo Bay have been invariably overshadowed by Tange Kenzō's breathtaking image of a megastructure over Tokyo Bay. When it was published in early 1961, A Plan for Tokyo garnered the instant attention of colleagues around the world, as seen in critical commentaries by Reyner Banham, Robin Middleton, Peter Smithson, and other members of Team 10.[25] Tange's scheme, in contrast to Ōtaka's and Kikutake's, was less driven by the particular contingencies of Tokyo Bay as a geographic location than the pursuit of a generic, universal response to the socioeconomic demands of a very large metropolitan region. It was an entirely forward-looking, unsentimental call for the complete spatial reorganization of capital, labor, and land for the post-industrial city. Critical components of the study were produced while Tange was abroad, teaching a studio at MIT in fall 1959 on a housing prototype to be placed in Boston Harbor. The most salient part of Tange's vision for Tokyo Bay is a vast megastructure that straddles the full width of the bay—a distance of nearly 30 kilometers—as the civic axis. As Banham noted, the scale of this megastructure is so unprecedented that each of its constituent parts can be rightly considered a megastructure on its own terms.[26] Giving primacy to transportation and communication, the most prominent feature of the civic axis is an elevated highway and

Maekawa Kunio with Ōtaka Masato as project architect, Harumi Apartment Building, 1958.

Kikutake Kiyonori, Tonogaya Daiichi Apartment Building, Kanagawa Prefecture, 1956.

Tange Kenzō, Plan for Tokyo 1960.

rail infrastructure, lifted 40 meters above land and 50 meters above water, suspended from piers spaced at 1-kilometer intervals.

Starting at Harumi, the outermost of central Tokyo's existing major man-made islands, the axis would be divided into eight so-called cycles, or internally coherent units, each with a discrete identity and function and forming a link in the overall axis. In a fishbone-like structure, a series of residential sub-spines run perpendicular to the civic axis. Appended to them can be any number of floating residential islands, each taking the form of an A-frame megastructure, developed through the MIT studio.[27] The civic axis is also conceived in terms of a transportation plan, with airports and intercity rail that situate the new Tokyo into a rationalized system on national and global scales.

Beyond a formal proposal of a megastructural system, as Tange's Tokyo Plan is often represented, the lavish study consisted of seven major parts: 1) The Nature of the City of 10,000,000; 2) The Physical Structure of Tokyo; 3) A Plan for Tokyo, 1960; 4) From a Radial Structure to a Linear Structure; 5) Organic Unification of the City, the Transportation System, and Architecture; 6) The Restoration of Spatial Order to the City; and 7) Program for Construction.[28] Some of the considerations are particular to the history and geography of Tokyo, but the basic concern of this study is handling growth in very large metropolitan areas, a universal problem. The project is built on Tange's belief in the irreversible progress that industrial societies experience as they transition from emphasis on the secondary sector to the tertiary. In contrast to the agrarian overtures of urban plans prior to 1945, particularly those by Tange's mentors in continental Asia, the tenor of Tange's report in 1961 is fundamentally marked by optimism and faith in the city as the source of capital and cultural production: "We recognize the necessity of Tokyo's growth, the importance of its existence, and the validity of the functions that it performs .... The city of 10,000,000 is an organism which has appeared only in the latter half of the twentieth century. It is a historical novelty. In order to remain alive and to grow, it must have a structure befitting the twentieth century."[29]

A MICRO HISTORY OF TOKYO BAY

The most important catalyst for this series of Tokyo Bay studies by Japan's architect-urbanists were the two so-called Kanō Plans, put forth in 1958 and 1959 by Kanō Hisaakira (1886–1963) under the auspices of the Council for Industrial Planning (*sangyō keikaku kaigi*), an influential think tank.[30] Kanō was at the time serving as the first president of the Japan Housing Corporation and worked closely with Ōtaka Masato and others in Maekawa's office on the high-rise residential prototype at Harumi.[31] The most astounding aspect of Kanō's plans for Tokyo Bay is that they were premised on the use of nuclear bombs to level the Nokogiriyama mountain range on Chiba Prefecture's Bōsō Peninsula, on the southeastern edge of Tokyo Bay.[32] Not only would the rubble provide landfill material, but also allow wind from the Pacific to blow more easily into Tokyo and cleanse the city of the dense smog from its industries.

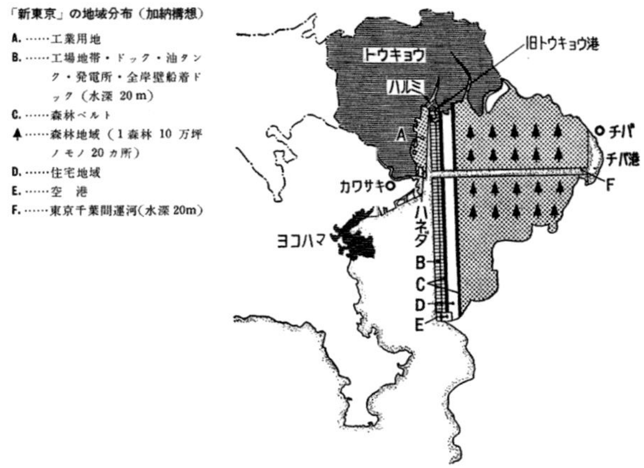

Kanō Hisaakira, New Tokyo Plan, 1959.

The first Kanō scheme, published in April 1958, further proposes a merger of the Sumida and Arakawa Rivers, Tokyo's two main waterways in this eastern side of the city, rechanneling them through a common man-made channel.[33] A narrow band of land on the west bank of the channel was designated for industrial use and port facilities. The more expansive east bank would be turned into a nature reserve. The 1958 Kanō scheme's bundling of the canal and the industrial strip is clearly reminiscent of Nikolai Miliutin's linear city concept, transmitted to Japan via Le Corbusier and the London-based MARS Group among others.[34] The second Kanō scheme, published in July 1959, fills Tokyo Bay with a radiating series of reclaimed land parcels.

The photographer Ishimoto Yasuhiro recalls Tange gasping in shock when he first heard the idea from Kanō at a monthly dinner of the Japan Design Community, occurring sometime in early 1958.[35] As architectural historian Fujimori Terunobu has traced, Tange's plan to territorialize Tokyo Bay has its origins in several related efforts starting in the late 1950s to reimagine Tokyo's landscape.[36] As early as 1955, Tange began criticizing the lack of urban contours, or order, in Tokyo. Viewed from an airplane, Tokyo was nothing but "a sprawling rural village (*ōki na inaka*)."[37] There was no discernable shape to the city, no highlights. Bustling central districts such as Marunouchi and Ginza could scarcely be made out, not to mention satellite nodes such as Shinjuku and Shibuya. Tange went on to say that living in Tokyo, one would have no idea that a sea engages the city: "A fatal flaw of living in Tokyo is the inability to enjoy the pleasure of the sea."[38]

In 1957, artist Okamoto Tarō (1911–96), who was working on a series of ceramic murals for Tange's Tokyo Metropolitan Government Building, invited the architect to collaborate on a man-made island project—a folly, or a provocation—located in the middle of Tokyo Bay.[39] Illustrated with broad stroked lines, vivid colors, and animistic forms typical of Okamoto's work at the time, the Okamoto/Tange proposal was published in June in the journal *Sōgō*.[40] The centerpiece of this plan is Relaxation Island (*ikoi jima*), floating in the middle of Tokyo Bay close to the present-day Ōdaiba area and connected on either end by tunnels to the mainland.

The Relaxation Island project reflected a widespread awareness that Japan was suffering from a severe shortage of leisure and recreational facilities, or public space in general, a crisis that was increasingly incongruent with the postwar ethos of democracy pursued in Tange's civic architecture and Okamoto's art. The large island, appearing to be at least 2 kilometers deep by 4 kilometers wide, is programmed exclusively with cultural and leisure facilities: aquarium, stadium, zoo, music hall, baseball field, art museum, horse-race track, and "Coney Island."[41] Tange's hand as architect and planner is unequivocal in how Relaxation Island is connected to the mainland and even more saliently in its reinvention of Tokyo's inner core. By relocating the imperial residence to the countryside, Tange's plan is to build a cultural center on the vacated land—the largest and most centrally located expanse of open space in Tokyo.[42] The idea of opening up the Imperial Palace grounds was discussed enthusiastically by Tange and Kanō Hisaakira

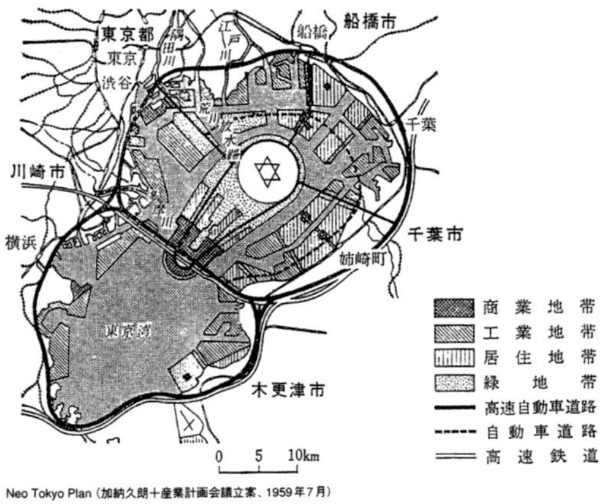

Kanō Hisaakira, Neo Tokyo Plan, 1959.

at a separate forum. To have the emperor continue to reside in Tokyo's city center would be tantamount to *lèse-majesté*: "The pines [on palace grounds] are withering, and the cranes in the [palace] moat are blackened by smoke and soot."[43] To have such a large, protected swath of land in the center of the city was also obstructive to traffic.

Tange's earlier proposal for the rebuilding of Hiroshima called for a similar set of facilities in Central Park, to be located in the heart of the city and anchored by the Edo-period castle keep.[44] In this expanded vision of the Relaxation Island project, the center of Tokyo is anchored by a low-density inner core, and the palace ground would be programmed with parks, art museums, and libraries, as well as cafés and restaurants. This would be circumscribed by a boulevard, which Tange remarked as having the same length as the Champs Élysées in Paris, ideal for leisurely strolls.[45] In other words, Tange and Okamoto's *esquisse* in 1957 essentially harked back to Ebenezer Howard's Garden City that had been deeply influential in modern Japanese planning thought, but the vision of an island in the middle of Tokyo Bay and the transformation of the palace grounds into open space sowed the seeds for a radically different idea that would come to define Tange's Tokyo Plan three years later.[46]

"*ŌKI NA INAKA*," OR TOKYO AS A SPRAWLING RURAL VILLAGE

Returning to Kikutake Kiyonori's Tokyo Bay Plan, on the regional scale beyond the floating cities, we find the curious placement of two recreational zones, together forming a north-south macro axis to the entire bay region. The southern recreational zone is sited on Miura Peninsula, a hilly promontory in Kanagawa Prefecture that serves as the gateway between Tokyo Bay and the deep seas beyond. Miura Peninsula also encompasses the Shōnan coast, home to some of the most popular beaches in the greater Tokyo metropolitan region as well as the historic temples of Kamakura, many dating to the thirteenth century. The Miura/Shōnan area was among to the first to be connected to central Tokyo via railway and developed into a popular weekend leisure destination at the turn of the twentieth century for Tokyo's modern bourgeois constituency, becoming in effect Tokyo's Riviera or what the Hamptons on Long Island are to New York City. Hayama, one of the towns in the area, is also home to the imperial family's seaside villa retreat and indeed was proposed as the permanent replacement to the palace in the 1950s by Kanō and Tange.[47]

The northern recreation zone in Kikutake's Tokyo Bay Plan has a dramatically different geography and landscape. Without the culture of leisure and cosmopolitan glamour associated with the Miura Peninsula, the Tone River Basin to the north of Tokyo Bay historically was plagued by the capricious waterways that carve through the region. The Tone River, the second largest in Japan and the main riverway in the Kantō Plains, changed course frequently. It was not until 1594 when Tokugawa Ieyasu, the newly appointed lord (*daimyō*) of Edo and ruler of the Kantō region, inaugurated the ambitious Tone River Eastern Diversion Project (*Tonegawa tōsen jigyō*), completed 60 years later.[48] The main course of Tone River was rechanneled away from Tokyo Bay and eastward, draining into the Pacific instead. Also involved

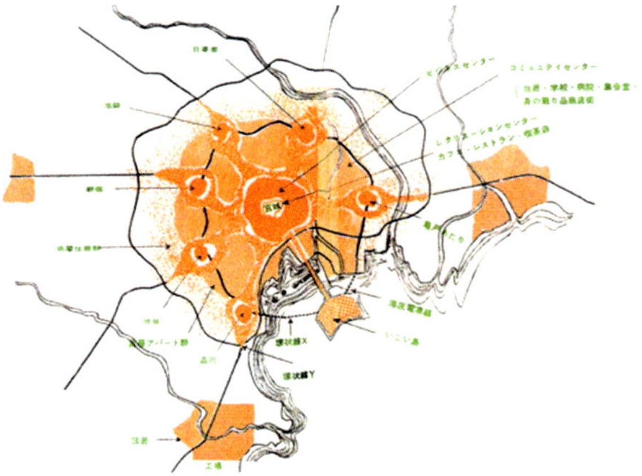

Okamoto Tarō and Tange Kenzō, Relaxation Island, urban plan, 1957.

was the engineering of a complex web of lesser waterways and tributaries into a navigable network of trade routes, establishing the Kantō Plains as a prosperous agricultural and commercial region. Kasumigaura Lake, now the second largest in Japan, was desalinated through this monumental riparian and hydraulics project and transformed into a center of aquaculture in the Edo period. In the modern era, the Tone River Basin has also been the site of one of the earliest and most devastating environmental disasters, the Ashio Copper Mine Incident, which launched a highly charged and well-mobilized environmental protection movement. A booming economy of copper smelting beginning in the second half of the nineteenth century in the upstream region quickly exerted a heavy toll on the Tone Basin's environment and economy.[49] Toxic emissions of sulfur dioxide from the smelting process generated chronic acid rain, causing widespread deforestation and landslides in the short term, which quickly evolved into pervasive loss of farmland and flooding in the broader region. This environmental damage persisted well into the middle of the twentieth century.

While Kanō Hisaakira's two plans for Tokyo Bay are mainly remembered for their mind-boggling premise of blasting away a mountain range with atomic bombs to reclaim land, Kanō's vision for the new capital was linked to a regional water and energy program for the Tone Basin—in effect a late-twentieth-century continuation of the 400-year endeavor to redefine Tokyo's relationship with the Tone River. Until then Tokyo's water needs were mostly fulfilled, inadequately, by the Tama River, which flows eastward along the southern edge of Tokyo. As noted, Kanō's studies were conducted under the auspices of the Council for Industrial Planning, led by the industrialist Matsunaga Yasuzaemon. The think tank counted among its members virtually the Who's Who of Japan's high-growth era: politicians, captains of industry, and leading academics.[50] Matsunaga himself founded nine of the largest power companies in Japan. Between 1956, when the think tank was established, and 1965, the year of Matsunaga's death, the Council for Industrial Planning issued fourteen official recommendations of national policy, ranging from the development of Hokkaidō to a national highway system, a new airport for Tokyo at Narita, a national energy policy, the reclamation of Tokyo Bay, and the Tone River Basin project. An astounding number of these ambitious proposals were actually implemented, though not all. One of the hallmarks of the initiative, to reconnect the Tone River with the Tokyo metropolitan region, would have entailed the construction of an enormous dam at Numata, Gunma Prefecture, measuring 125 meters high and having a capacity of 800 million tons.[51] The reservoir would have been the largest man-made lake in Japan had it been realized, and the hydropower produced also would have helped to relieve Tokyo's explosive growth in electricity consumption.

Kikutake Kiyonori's proposal to turn the Tone River Basin into a recreation zone serving the entire Tokyo metropolitan region must be seen as a response to this broader environmental aspect of the Council for Industrial Planning's ambitious, arguably callous remaking of Japan's landscape.[52] Kikutake's drawings of the Tokyo Bay Plans, across

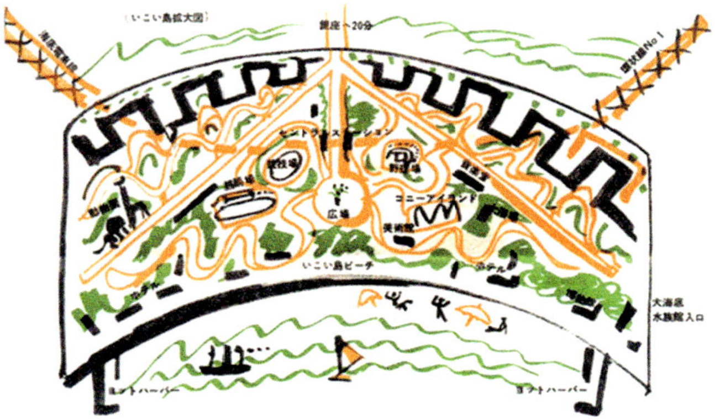

Relaxation Island conceptual plan.

scales, convey a dramatically different aesthetic sensibility from either Tange's or Ōtaka's versions, the latter two with far more hierarchical, differentiated structuring of the myriad functions of the floating city. Whereas Ōtaka's and Tange's studies for Tokyo Bay took Kanō's vision as a cue and developed it into visually and technologically compelling design schemes, Kikutake's proposal for Tokyo Bay was in fact a critique, if not an act of protest. At first glance, Kikutake's Tokyo Bay Plan looks as if he is proposing to cover the bay with rice paddies. There is no doubt that this was a conscious gesture by Kikutake, who was highly skilled and nuanced at his drawings, to evoke an agrarian ethos through these vignettes. In the same vein, the 2-by-2 gridiron form of the floating platform, in the Kōtō Ward Plan and the South Tokyo Plan, is clearly the idiogrammatic representation of the kanji character *ta* (田), literally field, or rice paddy in its most common connotation. The geometric precision with which Kikutake's Tokyo Bay Plan is laid out, in contrast to the amoeba-shaped Marine Cities schemes, for example, suggests that the orthogonal design was driven less by the goal of efficiency than by the allegorical significance of a pastoral ideal.[53]

It is now well established that Japan's rapid modernization in the nineteenth and twentieth centuries was predicated on a robust agrarian economy that had developed gradually during the Edo period, from the seventeenth to the nineteenth centuries.[54] During the Edo period Japan experienced dramatic economic expansion, much of this from domestic commerce, but even more significant was growth in the agricultural sector through a series of technological breakthroughs and structural changes. New engineering techniques, such as irrigation devices and even larger-scale riparian work, permitted the development of new productive rice fields. Marshlands were filled in as polders (*kantaku*) and protected with dykes, and hillsides were terraced into multi-tiered paddies, or *tanada*. Development of new rice fields, or *shinden kaihatsu*, almost doubled the amount of productive agricultural land in Japan in the seventeenth and eighteenth centuries.[55] The Kyōhō Reforms of the first half of the eighteenth century, promulgated under shōgun Tokugawa Yoshimune to address rice production and trade, further incentivized the creation of new arable land through *shinden kaihatsu* by the private sector of landlords and merchants, moving away from traditional reliance on feudal lords. Starting in this period, the landlord class (*gōnō*)—literally farming elite, to which the Kikutake clan belonged—emerged as a formidable force in Japanese society. In the aftermath of the Kyōhō Reforms, starting in the mid-eighteenth century, this non-samurai class of landlords began to play a central role in local economies as moneylenders, entrepreneurs, and eventually public administrators.[56]

Kikutake's hometown of Kurume, in today's Fukuoka Prefecture, Kyūshū, is located on the banks of the Chikugo River, the largest in Kyūshū and historically noted as one of the three most violent waterways in Japan, a distinction it shares with the Tone in the Kantō region. Like the Tone Basin, the Chiguko Basin was also a site of robust riparian engineering and land reclamation during the Edo period. Raised to become the 15th- generation patriarch of the Kikutake clan, Kiyonori

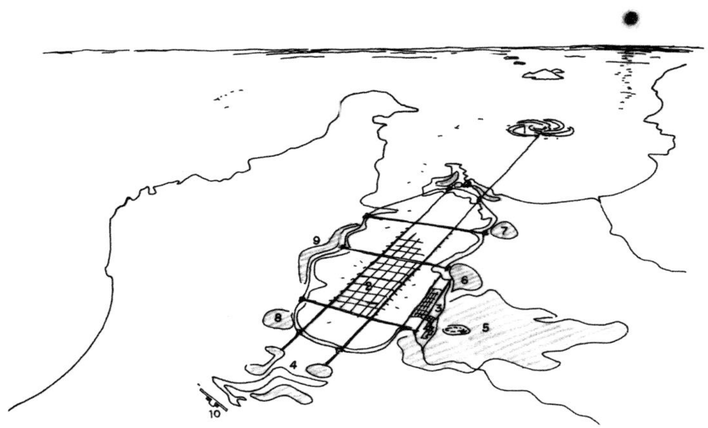

Kikutake Kiyonori, drawing, Tokyo Bay Plan, 1961.

was made aware very early of a strong sense of duty in the family's traditional connections to Kurume's land and people.[57] Even late in life he recalled his childhood home in vivid detail, particularly the shrine room (*butsuma*) where ancestral offerings and various rites were carried out almost daily. Suiten-gū, a national network of shrines devoted to the water god, is headquartered here, very close to the Kikutake homestead, and indeed the Kikutake family customarily served as civilian leaders (*sōdai*) in its annual festivals. "My ancestors were landlords, and in Japan, the landlords were traditionally the providers of infrastructure as well as the patrons of culture. They built schools, they built floodgates, they maintained and improved farmland .... My architecture was my protest, as a former landlord, against the dismantling of the entire landowning system."[58] Kikutake revealed this emotional, private context of his early work at an interview in his later years. Land reform, along with the dismantling of the patriarchal *ie* family system and the *zaibatsu* industrial conglomerates, was one of the first and most profound initiatives imposed by the American-led occupation.[59] Ownership of some 70 percent of Japan's farmland changed hands as a result, from large landowners to former tenant farmers. The low prices at which land was purchased by the national government, to be resold to tenants, amounted to virtual confiscation of the most valuable repository of wealth and capital.

With his family's wealth disappearing overnight, Kikutake came to see this rural transformation as the loss of a way of life.[60] The land reforms fundamentally altered the landscape of Japanese rural society. What separates Kikutake's Tokyo Bay Plan from Ōtaka's and Tange's versions is in the former's attempt to preserve and even revive a certain way of living through the creation of new spatial platforms. In the same manner as how the Sky House (1958) engages an imaginary landscape of the historical Musashi Plains, Kikutake's Tokyo Bay Plan must be seen from the vantage point of the Tone Basin, the Chikugo Basin, and Kikutake's childhood home in Kurume where the young Kiyonori watched his family's retainers (*bantō*) deal with the affairs of their land.

A GENEALOGY OF THE METABOLISTS

The differences between Kikutake's Tokyo Bay Plan and Tange's and Ōtaka's respective versions betray an ideological as well as methodological rift in Japan's architectural academe. Both Tange and Ōtaka were graduates of Tokyo Imperial University and their architectural *Bildung* evolved within the so-called Rationalist School, which was established in the 1910s by faculty members such as Sano Toshikata and Uchida Yoshizō and reinforced by their protégés such as Mutō Kiyoshi (1903–89) and Takayama Eika (1910–99), founders of modern structural design and urban planning respectively as disciplines in Japan.[61] Tange enrolled in graduate school in 1942 and was appointed to the faculty after the end of World War II, and it was from this platform that some of most important research initiatives in architecture and city planning were launched in postwar Japan.[62] Tange's laboratory at Tokyo Imperial University nurtured such prodigies as

Aerial view of Miura Peninsula and Shōnan Coast, Kanagawa Prefecture.

Fumihiko Maki (b. 1928), Isozaki Arata (b. 1931), and Kurokawa Kishō (1934–2007), who would achieve international notoriety.

Ōtaka Masato was closer in age if not also in sentiment to Tange than he was to younger members of the Metabolist group such as Kurokawa. Ōtaka also attended Tokyo Imperial University—its satellite campus in Chiba Prefecture, formed at the height of World War II as an even stronger bastion of the Rationalist School than the Hongō main campus—graduating in 1947 and attending graduate school until 1949.[63] He joined the office of Maekawa Kunio soon thereafter and quickly rose to become one of Maekawa's trusted lieutenants, responsible for some of the most important projects in the office in the 1950s, such as Kanagawa Prefectural Library and Music Hall (1954), Fukushima Education Center (1956), and Tokyo Metropolitan Festival Hall (1961), in addition to Harumi Apartments. In the same vein, on the Council for Industrial Planning's subcommittee on the Tokyo Bay study, Kanō Hisaaskira was assisted by a coterie of young cadres associated with the Rationalist School at Tokyo University, many of whom would soon emerge as leading urban planners of the postwar era. Particularly notable were Honjō Kazuhiko (1913–2002), Higasa Tadashi (1920–1997), and Shimokōbe Jun (b. 1923).[64] These genealogical affinities therefore suggest that Kanō, Ōtaka, and Tange's respective interventions in Tokyo Bay in the late 1950s should be seen more as a contiguous conversation, sharing a functionalist, developmentalist ideology and pursuing key intellectual threads as part of a single project.

Kikutake Kiyonori's architectural education at Waseda University—a rival, private institution that he attended in 1947–50—could not have been more different from that of Tokyo Imperial University. Even in the 1930s, Japanese architecture students were already fond of the adage, "To learn design, one has to go to Waseda."[65] This sentiment was especially popular at Tokyo Imperial University, where hardly anyone on the faculty was interested in architectural design in the narrower sense. Waseda's architecture faculty during the same period was led by Imai Kenji (1895–1987) and Satō Takeo (1899–1972), who represented an alternate strain of modernism in Japan that embraced a much higher degree of formal expression, welcoming surface decorations and ornaments with regional and period styles such as medieval, art nouveau, and Nordic.

Kikutake graduated first in his class from Waseda in 1950, and as a second-year student he garnered national fame by winning a third prize in the prestigious competition for the Hiroshima Peace Cathedral project.[66] After working briefly first at Takenaka Construction Company and then at the office of Murano Tōgo, Kikutake opened his own office in 1953. Among his first clients was the Bridgestone Tire Company, which commissioned him to design a series of housing facilities. The most elaborate among them is the Tonogaya Daiichi Apartments (1956), which can be interpreted as a direct critique of the Unité model advanced by Ōtaka at Harumi or the other prototypes by Honjō Kazuhiko at the Japan Housing Corporation. Kikutake's long slab at Tonogaya is broken into a series of entryway cores. Rather than celebrating the communality of long interior corridors, Kikutake accentuates the discreteness of each unit by offsetting adjacent units on the same core by half a floor. The roofline undulates with the same rhythm, a feature Kikutake likens to a mountain ridge in a photo collage.[67]

CODA: LAND VERSUS SEA

The frontier in Kikutake's radical recalibration of human habitat was the Pacific. He began his long personal association with Hawaii in 1964, through an exhibition of his work there. In 1971, a teaching appointment at the University of Hawaii allowed him to develop the proposal *Marine City 1971: Project in Hawai'i*, which eventuated in the Marine City prototype Aquapolis, realized for the Okinawa Ocean Expo in 1975.[68] Aquapolis was a 100 meter by 100 meter semi-submersible floating structure, built with technology developed by the American Navy and offshore oil operations. His collaborator, John P. Craven (1924–2015), quoted at the start of this essay, was previously chief scientist at the U.S. Navy Special Projects Office, where he directed such experiments as underwater habitats. As a synecdoche for this aspiration toward oceanic voyages, the Aquapolis structure itself was manufactured in shipyards in Hiroshima and towed for 1,000 kilometers to the exhibition site in Okinawa.

This turn toward Oceania as "Our Sea of Islands,"[69] away from the continental ambitions of Japanese imperialism, which ended in trauma, toward the healing powers of the Pacific's vast emptiness, can be easily projected onto Kikutake's Marine Cities series. As historian Matt Matsuda has shown, the reorientation of thinking about the Pacific not as the ring of land-based cultures on its periphery but as archipelago-based network of historical kinships and cultural ties "restores movements and autonomies—migrations and navigation of island peoples engaged in cross-cultural contacts, shifting social organizations, and ethnic diasporas."[70] Japan's empire in fact expanded as aggressively southward as north, first toward the Ryūkyū Islands and later Taiwan. Japan was the beneficiary of the South Pacific Mandate at the end of World War I, taking over from Germany the administration of a chain of islands and atolls, including the Marianas and Carolines that encompassed Saipan and Palau. Commensurate with this geographic expansion of Japan was the proliferation of ethnographic research linking the peoples of ancient Japan and the Pacific islands racially and culturally, especially through the study of linguistics and religion.

Recent scholarship has confirmed historical continuities between the megastructural, technocratic, and territorial instincts of the postwar Metabolists with Japan's prewar and wartime efforts on continental Asia.[71] Building on the vast, empty, and fertile expanse of Manchuria conditioned an abstract and superlatively scaled thinking about land and buildings that deeply influenced Japan's modern architects and urbanists, but the war's end brought them suddenly back to the restrictive confines of their homeland. Sea and sky were the obvious new frontiers, enabled by new technologies, many of which were developed through the war effort itself.[72] But the mode of thinking of the

Kikutake Kiyonori, model, Kōtō Ward Plan, 1961.

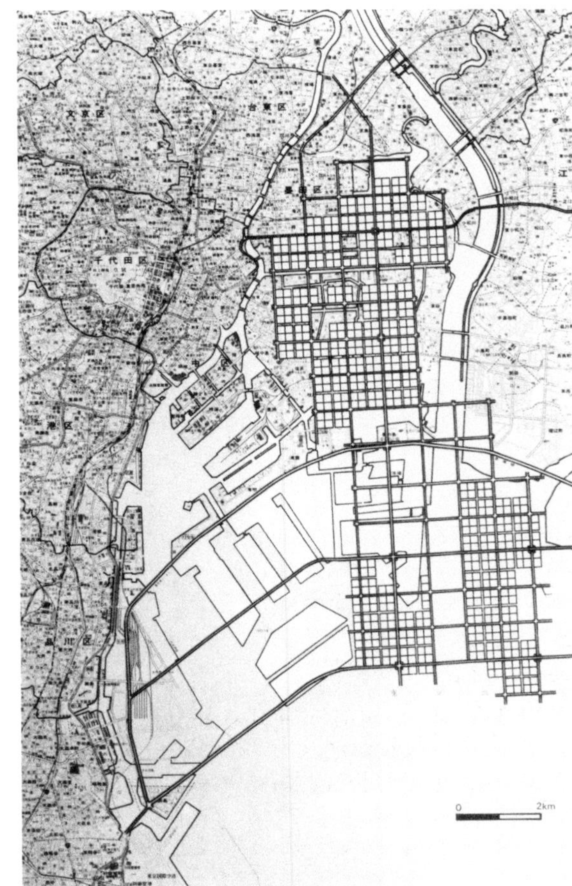

Kikutake Kiyonori, Tokyo Bay Plan, 1961.

vast majority of the postwar avant-garde remained terracentric. In their projects, epoch-making as Tange's Tokyo Plan might have been, the civic axis does little to engage with the sea and does not have to be placed on water at all. In later variants of this proposal, such as his plans for Kyoto (1964) and Bologna (1971), we find the axis placed comfortably in these two ancient cities on land. More than anyone else in the Metabolist cohort, Kikutake designed with the deepest sympathy for Japan's pre-industrial landscape. This passion also drove him resolutely away from land itself on a poetic, if unfulfilled, odyssey to build in the oceans.

1 John P. Craven, "For Kiyonori Kikutake Concepts and Planning," in Kikutake Kiyonori, *Kikutake Kiyonori: kōsō to keikaku* (Tokyo: Bijutsu shuppansha, 1978), 11.

2 Tange presented a preliminary version of the Tokyo Plan in the popular magazine *Asahi Weekly* in October 1960: "Umi no ue ni gohyukuman: shin Tōkyō ga jiken sureba," *Shūkan Asahi* 65, no. 44 (Oct. 16, 1960): 32–33. Although the year 1960 is included in the title of Tange's study, it in fact debuted on an hour-long television special on NHK, Japan's national broadcasting company, in January 1961. The proposal appeared in print in the March 1961 issue of *Shinkenchiku*, followed by an English translation in the April 1961 issue of *The Japan Architect*.

3 Ōtaka Masato included an updated version of the Tokyo Bay Plan, now located on terra firma, in this second installment of the Metabolist pamphlet, alongside Kikutake's version.

4 Kikutake Kiyonori, "Sekkei kasetsu," *Kenchiku* (Nov. 1961): 72–79. An English translation of a version of this theory is "The Great Shrine of Izumo" published in this volume.

5 Notable studies of Metabolism include Günter Nitschke, "Tokyo 1964: Olympic Planning/Dream Planning," *Architectural Design* (Oct. 1964): 485–524; Cherie Wendelken, "Putting Metabolism Back in Place: The Making of a Radically Decontextualized Architecture in Japan," in *Anxious Modernisms: Experimentation in Postwar Architectural Culture*, eds. Sarah Williams Goldhagen and Réjean Legault (Cambridge, MA: MIT Press, 2000), 279–323; Zhongjie Lin, *Kenzō Tange and the Metabolist Movement: Urban Utopias of Modern Japan* (London: Routledge, 2009); and Rem Koolhaas and Hans Ulrich Obrist, *Project Japan: Metabolism Talks*, eds. Kayoko Ōta with James Westcott (Cologne: Taschen, 2011). In fall 2011 the Mori Art Museum organized the exhibition *Metabolism: The City of the Future*. The catalogue is published as Maeda Naotake et al., eds., *Metaborizumu no mirai toshi ten: sengo Nihon ima yomegaeru fukkō no yume to bizyon* (Tokyo: Mori bijutsukan and Shinkenchikusha, 2011). Also to be noted here is Mark Wigley, "Network Fever," *Grey Room*, no. 4 (Summer 2001): 84–122.

6 Reyner Banham, *Megastructure: Urban Futures of the Recent Past* (New York: Harper and Row, 1976), esp. 45–57.

7 Oscar Newman, *CIAM '59 in Otterlo, Group for the Research of Social and Visual Inter-relationships* (London: Alec Tiranti, 1961), 185. Tange presented his own Tokyo Metropolitan Government Building and the Kagawa Prefectural Government Building, both completed in the previous year.

8 Kikutake Kiyonori, *Kikutake Kiyonori: kōsō to keikaku* (Tokyo: Bijutsu shuppansha, 1978), 60.

9 Suzuki Masao, *Edo no kawa, Tōkyō no kawa* (Tokyo: Nippon hōsō shuppan kyōkai, 1978); and Henry D. Smith II, "Sky and Water: The Deep Structures of Tokyo," in *Tokyo: Form and Spirit*, ed. Mildred Friedman (New York: Harry N. Abrams, 1986), 21–35.

10 For a synopsis of artificial land projects by Japan's postwar avant-garde, see Koolhaas and Obrist, *Project Japan*, esp. 341–345. Ideological

aspects of artificial land are discussed in Seng Kuan, "Land as an Architectural Idea in Modern Japan," in *Architecturalized Asia: Mapping the Continent through History*, eds. Vimalin Rujivacharakul, Hazel Hahn, Ken Tadashi Oshima, and Peter Christensen (Hong Kong: University of Hong Kong Press; Honolulu: University of Hawaii Press, 2013), 189–203.

11 Kikutake Kiyonori, "Jinkō tochi wa 'kabe,'" in *Kikutake Kiyonori: kōsō to keikaku* (1978), 100–101. An earlier version of this is published in Kawazoe Noboru, *Metabolism 1960* (Tokyo: Bijitsu shuppansha, 1960), 16–17.

12 Kikutake, *Kikutake Kiyonori: kōsō to keikaku* (1978), 104–105.

13 Two classic studies in English are R. P. Dore, *City Life in Japan: A Study of a Tokyo Ward* (Berkeley: University of California Press, 1958); and Edward Seidensticker, *Low City, High City: Tokyo from Edo to the Earthquake* (New York: Knopf, 1983).

14 Kikutake, "Sekkei kasetsu," 72–79.

15 See Koshizawa Akira, *Fukkō keikaku: bakumatsu, Meiji no taika kara Hanshin Awaji daishinsai made* (Tokyo: Chūkō shinsho, 2005), especially chapter 2, "Kantō daishinsai to teito fukkō," and Ishida Yorifusa, *Nihon kingendai toshi keikaku no tenkai, 1868–2003* (Tokyo: Jichitai kenkyūsha, 2004), especially chapter 6, "Kantō daishinsai to fukkō toshi keikaku. It is also summarized in English in André Sorensen, *The Making of Urban Japan: Cities and Planning from Edo to the Twenty-First Century* (London: Routledge, 2002), 125–133.

16 Ōtaka Masato and Okumura Keiichi, "Kōsō apaato wo haichi shita atarashii jūtakuchi no teian wo Tōkyō wanjō toshi no teian," *Kenchiku bunka* 14, no. 2 (Feb. 1959): 42.

17 The Japan Housing Corporation sponsored two prototypes for high-rise apartments in 1955, one for Tokyo and the other for Osaka. The building in Osaka was Nishi Nagahori Apartments.

18 In addition to the original iteration of the Unité in Marseilles, additional sites include Rezé (1952–55), Briey-en-Forêt (1957–63), Firminy (1956–63), and Berlin (1958).

19 According to Reyner Banham, the term "megastructure" was invented by Maki Fumihiko, one of the original members of the Metabolist group, in his 1964 essay "Investigations in Collective Form." Reyner Banham, *Megastructure* (New York: Harper and Row, 1976), 8. The building slab extends 116.54 meters in length and asserts a monumental presence along the edge of Tokyo Bay. Every six units, grouped two across and three on top of each other, are plugged into each bay in the building's structural frame. Elevators stop at every third floor, repeating the system of Le Corbusier's Unité.

20 Whereas the European iterations of the Unité were all in excess of 50 meters in height, at the time Japanese building code still maintained a nationwide cap of 31 meters, or 100 feet, a rule that was repealed in 1963.

21 The structural engineer in charge of the Harumi Apartment project was Kimura Toshihiko, one of the foremost figures in structural engineering among the postwar generation. His summary of the project is in Kimura Toshihiko, *Kenchiku zasshi*, no. 1289 (Sept. 1989): 8; and Kimura Toshihiko, "Kanshin wo atsumeru 'jinkō tochi ron no shozō: 2, sono kōzō,'" *Kokusai kenchiku* 26, no. 2 (Feb. 1959): 53–54.

22 Ōtaka Masato and Okumura Keiichi, "Kōsō apaato wo haichi shita atarashii jūtakuchi no teian wo tōkyō wanjō toshi no teian," *Kenchiku bunka* 14, no. 2 (Feb. 1959): 39–42.

23 Perhaps not so coincidentally, Tange Kenzō's studio problem at MIT in the fall semester of 1959 was a residential community of 25,000 to be located in Boston Harbor.

24 Kishida Hideto and Takayama Eika, *Gaikoku ni ogeru jūtaku shikichikatsu ruireishū* (Tokyo: Zaidan hōjin dōjunkai, 1936).

25 Peter Smithson, "Reflections on Kenzo Tange's Tokyo Bay Plan," *Architectural Design* 34 (Oct. 1964): 479–480; Robin Middleton, "The Lumbered Image," *Architectural Design* 38 (Dec. 1968), 565; Reyner Banham, *Megastructure: Urban Futures of the Recent Past* (London: Thames and Hudson, 1976), 51–57.

26 Banham, *Megastructure*, 51–57.

27 The Tokyo Plan is in response to a city with 10 million residents. Tange's intervention would increase its capacity by another 5 million by building across the bay and rationalizing transportation and the distribution of urban functions.

28 The summary of the project provided here is based on an in-house offprint from Tange Kenzō's Laboratory that had expanded slightly upon the earlier publications from *Shinkenchiku* and *Japan Architecture*: Tange Kenzō Team, *A Plan for Tokyo: Toward a Structural Reorganization*, 1961.

29 Tange Kenzō Team, *A Plan for Tokyo*, 10.

30 In English the Kanō plans were discussed in "Tokyo Bay: A Planning Frenzy," Koolhaas and Obrist, *Project Japan*, 266–293. Kanō's full-length treatise is published as Kanō Hisaaskira, *Atarashii shuto kensetsu* (Tokyo: Jiji Tsushinsha, 1959).

31 The Japan Housing Corporation was founded in 1955 as the successor entity to the prewar Dōjunkai, which began experimenting with reinforced concrete residential buildings in the late 1920s under the guidance of the architecture faculty of Tokyo Imperial University. See *Nihon jūtaku kōdan 10 nen shi* (Tokyo: Nihon jūtaku kōdan, 1965). An in-depth study of Kanō postwar activities, especially his tenure as president of the Japan Housing Corporation, remains a lacuna. For a broader biographical sketch of Kanō, see Takasaki Tetsurō, *Kokusai jin: Kanō Hisaakira no shōgai* (Tokyo: Kajima shuppankai, 2014). The Kanō family historically served as lords of the Ichinomiya domain, now in Chiba Prefecture. Hisaaskira's father, Viscount Hisayoshi, was notably the first president of the Imperial Agricultural Cooperative (*Teikoku nōkai*). Hisaakira studied law at Tokyo Imperial University and his professional career until the end of World War II was at Yokohama Specie Bank, an institution closely associated with Japan's colonial program.

32 Kanō Hisaakira was elected governor of Chiba Prefecture for a brief period before his death in 1959. The pamphlet published by the Council for Industrial Planning includes the full Japanese translation of the article: Gerald W. Johnson and Harold Brown, "Non-Military Uses of Nuclear Explosives," from *Scientific American* 199 (December 1958): 29–36.

33 For detailed proposal of the canal project, see Nonomura Sōitsu and Tsubata Shūichi, "Tōkyō wan unga no teian," *Kokusai kenchiku* 26, no. 4 (Apr. 1959): 12–13.
34 Seng Kuan, "A Short Genealogy of Tange Kenzō's Modernist City," in Maeda Naotake et al., eds., *Metaborizumu no mirai toshi ten: sengo Nihon ima yomegaeru fukkō no yume to bizyon* (Tokyo: Mori bijutsukan and Shinkenchikusha, 2011), 226–233. Kanō served as head of the London branch of Yokohama Specie Bank from 1934 to 1942. It is reasonable to speculate that he was exposed to some of the debates on London's planning such as those by Patrick Abercrombie or even the MARS Group.
35 Ishimoto Yasuhiro, interview by Fujimori Terunobu, *Shinkenchiku* 83 no. 5 (May 1999).
36 Tange Kenzō and Fujimori Terunobu, *Tange Kenzō* (Tōkyō : Shinkenchikusha, 2002); extensive historical data were collected by the Yatsuka Hajime Laboratory at Shibaura Institute of Technology: Yatsuka Hajime et al., eds., "Tōkyō daigaku Tange Kenzō kenkyūshitu ni yoru 'Tōkyō keikaku 1960' to koreni kanren suru sakuyō no kyōteki kenshō," unpublished manuscript, 2008. An English-language summary can be found in Lin, *Kenzō Tange and the Metabolist Movement*, 133–171.
37 Tange Kenzo, "Tōkyō no toshi keikaku," *Yomiuri Shinbun* (Dec. 18, 1955); quoted in Tange and Fujimori, *Tange Kenzō*, 342.
38 Ibid.
39 Isozaki Arata, still a young staff member in Tange's laboratory, was assigned to this project and spent two months in Okamoto's atelier.
40 Okamoto Tarō, Tange Kenzō, Teshigahara Sōfū, Abe Kōbō, Itokawa Hideo, Ishikawa Satoshi, "Bokura no toshi keikaku," *Sōgō*, no. 2 (June 1957): 165–171.
41 Later in the 1970s, Tokyo Disneyland and the broader Maihama and Kasai Relaxation area, which includes a large aquarium, were built on reclaimed land not far from the location originally proposed by Okamoto Tarō. Okamoto, Tange, et al., "Bokura no toshi keikaku."
42 It appears to be Kanō Hisaakira who first proposed to relocate the emperor's residence to the imperial villa in Hayama. See Tange Kenzō, Kanō Hisaakira, and Kawaguchi Takeyoshi, "Sankai ni sumai ari," *Chūō kōron* 73, no. 3 (Mar. 1958): 234–243. A more extensive argument is made in Kanō, *Atarashii shuto kensetsu*, 89–96.
43 Tange, Kanō, Kawaguchi, "Sankai ni sumai ari," 239.
44 Tange's 1950 proposal for a Central Park in Hiroshima is sited on the north shore of the Ōta River, directly extending from the main axis of the Hiroshima Peace Memorial complex. The program encompasses a children's library, boathouse, children's art museum, children's science museum, art and science museum, and auditorium. Only the children's library was realized. See "Hiroshima keikaku: heiwa toshi no kesetsu," *Kokusai kenchiku* 17, no. 10 (Oct. 1950): 27–39. Original master plan and a small number of architectural drawings of the park facilities are maintained at the Hiroshima Municipal Archives.
45 The circumference around the Imperial Palace (excluding the Kitanomaru) in Tokyo is approximately 5 kilometers, roughly matching the distance from the Place de la Concorde to the edge of the Seine in Neuilly.
46 For an English-language account of an early case study of the Garden City movement in Japan, see Ken Tadashi Oshima, "Denenchōfu: Building the Garden City in Japan," *Journal of the Society of Architectural Historians* 55, no. 2 (June 1996): 140–151.
47 The imperial villa at Hayama was established in 1894 for Crown Prince Yoshihito, the future Taishō Emperor. Also given the strategic location of Miura Peninsula in relation to Tokyo Bay, it should not be surprising to find the tip of the peninsula occupied as Japan's largest naval base, which has been home to the U.S. Seventh Fleet since the end of World War II. Kikutake's plan for a recreation zone on Miura Peninsula can well be interpreted as his protest against continued American military presence in Japan.
48 The most authoritative and comprehensive history of Tone River's hydraulic interventions is Ōkuma Takashi, *Tonegawa chisui no hensen to suigai* (Tokyo: Tokyo daigaku shuppanbu, 1981). For a socioeconomic view of the Tone River region, see Suzuki Kuninao, *Tone no hensen to suigō no hitobito* (Chiba: Ronshobō, 1985).
49 F. G. Notehelfer, "Japan's First Pollution Incident," *Journal of Japanese Studies* 1, no. 2 (spring 1975): 351–383; and Gaven McCormack, "Modernity, Water, and the Environment in Japan," in *A Companion to Japanese History*, ed. William M. Tsutsui, (Chichester: Wiley-Blackwell, 2009), 443–459.
50 A sampling of its membership roster includes Aikawa Yoshisuke, head of the Nissan *zaibatsu* and Chief Economic Advisor to the Kishi Cabinet, Kaya Seiji, President of Tokyo University, Kobayashi Ataru, Founding President of the Development Bank of Japan, and Mizuta Mikio, Minister of Finance in the Ikeda and Satō Cabinets.
51 Kanō, *Atarashii shuto kensetsu*, 119–130. The series of recommendations were published as serialized pamphlets by the Council for Industrial Planning by Keizai zasshi daiyamon-do-sha. Kanō would continue his advocacy for the water management project and in 1962 published *Mizu shigen* [Water resource], co-authored with Sugaya Jūji (Tokyo: Jiji tsū shinsha).
52 Among the members of the Metabolist movement, Kurokawa Kishō participated the most directly in the conservation project of the Kasumigaura region. Kurokawa's Floating City, Kasumigaura, was produced in the same year as Kikutake's Tokyo Bay Plan, modifying the helix structure he first designed for the center of Tokyo to be harmonized with the pastoral and marshland landscape and recreational scale.
53 In an interview given just two months before his death, Kikutake made a direct connection between rice paddies and Metabolism: "People in the modern world know nothing about the rice paddies that have nurtured Japan's way of living. In fact rice paddies are extremely precise, enormous systems. When we speak of Metabolism we often refer to megastructures, but our ancestors were building them hundreds and thousands of years ago." Interview by Fukasawa Keita, "Otoko no kikite: Kikutake Kiyonori," *Numéro Tokyo*, no. 53 (Feb. 2012): 186.
54 Thomas C. Smith, *The Agrarian Origins of Modern Japan* (Stanford University Press, 1959).
55 Ōishi Shinsaburō, *Kyōhō kaikaku no keizai*

seisaku, vol. 1 *Kyōhō kaikaku no nōson seisaku* (Tokyo: Ochanomizu shobo, 1961).

56 The idea of the *gōnō* class as the Japanese analogue to the European bourgeoisie is fundamental to the theory of Edo period as proto-modern and proto-capitalist that was absorbed into Thomas C. Smith's work. In Japan, the so-called *gōnō* theory was formulated by the Marxist historian Fujita Gorō in *Hōken shakai no teikai katei* (Tokyo: Yuhihaku, 1952).

57 "Kikutake Kiyonori," in Senda Mitsuru, ed., *Kodomo to sumai: 50 nin no kenchikuka no genfūkei*, vol. 1 (Tokyo: Sumai no toshokan shuppankyoku, 1990), 84–95.

58 "Kiyonori Kikutake," interview by Rem Koolhaas and Hans Ulrich Obrist, in *Project Japan*, 133.

59 R. P. Dore, *Land Reform in Japan* (London: Athlone, 1959), 139. Purchase prices of farmland were set at values that predated postwar hyperinflation, thus virtually wiping out the wealth of the landowning class. Whereas a *tan* of rice field, equivalent to just under 1,000 square meters, could buy 3,000 packets of cigarettes before the postwar hyperinflation, by 1948 the same amount in yen could buy only 13 packets.

60 Kikutake's position on the *gōnō* class's leadership roles, especially in riparian infrastructure, appears rather romanticized in the view of empirical studies. The anthropologist William W. Kelly, in his seminal work on Edo-period irrigation work in the Shōnai region northern Japan, discovered that "There was never effective elite control nor strong local autonomy in Aka River irrigation. Domain officials tried to avoid exercising authority in irrigation matters, peasant cultivators remained rather unorganized as water users, and large landholders showed remarkable non-intervention." See William W. Kelly, *Water Control in Tokugawa Japan: Irrigation Organization in a Japanese River Basin, 1600–1870*, Cornell East Asia Papers, no. 32 (Ithaca: Cornell University Press, 1982), 2.

61 Seng Kuan, "Tange Kenzō's Architecture in Three Keys: As Building, as Art, and as the City," PhD diss. (Harvard University, 2011), especially chapter 3 "Rationalist Urbanism."

62 Toyokawa Saikaku, *Gunzō toshite no Tange kenkyūshitu: sengo Nihon kenchiku, toshi shi no meinsutoriimu* (Tokyo: Ohm-sha, 2013).

63 The architectural faculty at the Chiba campus represented a highly energized, intellectual cohesive group of young designers that would come to define the creative framework of the postwar era. They included structural designers Ono Kaoru and Tsuboi Yoshikazu, urban planner and designer Uchida Yoshifumi, and architect Ikebe Kiyoshi. See Minohara Kei, Matsukuma Hiroshi, and Nakajima Naoto, *Kenchikuka Ōtaka Masato no shigoto* (Tokyo: X-Knowledge, 2014), especially chapters 0 and 1.

64 Honjō graduated from Tokyo University in 1938, the same year as Tange. Honjō entered government architectural service and worked directly under Kanō in the Japan Housing Corporation as the head of the design department. Higasa graduated in 1942, and Shimokōbe in 1947. Higasa likewise joined the Ministry of Construction after the war and headed the bureau of planning research. In the early 1960s, both Honjō and Higasa became professors in the newly founded Department of Urban Engineering at Tokyo Imperial University, established by Takayama Eika and Tange Kenzō in 1962. Among the youngest member of Kanō's Tokyo Bay team, Shimokōbe was also one of the first members in Tange's laboratory as a graduate student. Shimokōbe entered government service after the war, and in 1957 as a technocrat in the Ministry of Construction was charged specifically to study Japan's rivers and ports, including Tokyo Bay. Throughout a long career in civil service, he remained a powerful functionary in construction and planning.

65 Tange Kenzō, *Ippon no enpitsu kara* (Tokyo: Nihon tosho sentaa, 1997), 34–35.

66 Tange Kenzō was awarded second prize, while first prize was not given out in the Hiroshima Peace Cathedral competition. Also in 1948, Kikutake placed first in a competition for a shopping center.

67 "Burijizuton taiya, Tonogaya daiichi apaato," *Kenchiku* (Nov. 1961): 102–103.

68 Maeda, *Metaborizumu no mirai toshi ten*, 216–219; Koolhaas and Obrist, *Project Japan*, 152–155.

69 The term comes from Epeli Hau'ofa, "Our Sea of Islands," *The Contemporary Pacific* 6, no. 1 (1994): 148–161.

70 Matt K. Matsuda, "The Pacific," *The American Historical Review* 111, no. 3 (June 2006): 758–780.

71 Yatsuka, *Metaborizumu nekusaus*; Koolhaas and Obrist, *Project Japan*; Kuan, "Tange Kenzō's Architecture in Three Keys."

72 Jean-Louis Cohen, *Architecture in Uniform* (Paris: Editions Hazan, 2011); Aaron Moore, *Constructing East Asia: Technology, Ideology, and Empire in Japan's Wartime Era, 1931–1945* (Redwood City, CA: Stanford University Press, 2013).

Kikutake with Fred and Barbro Thompson at the Administrative Building of Izumo Shrine, 1963.

LEARNING FROM KIKUTAKE

Fred Thompson

The enigma that was Kikutake Kiyonori is aptly suggested by his contemporary, the architectural critic Kawazoe Noboru, in an interview describing preparations for the 1960 World Design Conference (WoDeCo) in Tokyo:

> Everyone was working very hard, going in and out of the space, as if it was a combat zone. There was a person sitting in the middle of the room doing nothing. He was Mr. Kikutake. Mr. Kikutake had heard the news of the conference preparation and thought he had better be there, but did not know what to do so he sat waiting.[1]

Nothing better reflects the character of Kikutake Kiyonori. He was a man of solitude, determination, and boundless creative energy and patience; his often seemingly passive appearance was misleading.

At his core was an awareness of "tradition," which he so often referenced in his work. It was more precisely the "spirit of tradition" typical of a tea master, who has enough experience and confidence in his art to enable him to listen twice as much as he needs to speak.

I was among the group of architects working for Kikutake in the early years, when his office was quite small and producing some of its greatest work. The period between the WoDeCo in 1960 and the Olympics in 1964 was pivotal both for Kikutake and for Japan as it emerged from the postwar era. I arrived in 1960, when one of his signature buildings, the Administrative Building for the Izumo Shrine, was under construction:I remained until after the Kyoto International Conference Hall competition in 1963. Kikutake, along with architectural historian Itō Teiji, was my greatest mentor in Japan. A lifetime later, I wish to offer both a tribute to Kikutake and my interpretation of the architect and his approach and impact.

AT WORK IN THE KIKUTAKE OFFICE

I arrived in Japan with my wife and had the privilege of studying the roots of Japanese architecture with Itō Teiji. His doctoral dissertation had been on rural Japanese houses (*minka*). I asked Itō-*sensei* for his advice about finding work with an architect who was not yet too much in the spotlight, leading an office with challenging working hours. He sent me to Kikutake; I got what I asked for and, as with Itō-*sensei*'s generosity, I was guided in learning much about Japan and its architecture.

My time with Kikutake was superb. I came to his office at a prime moment, when some of his most interesting projects were being built, such as the Administrative Building of Izumo Shrine, the Tatebayashi City Hall, the Asakawa Apartment Building, the Marine City exhibition in the Seibu Department Store in Ikebukuro, and other smaller works, such as my first attempt at designing a Japanese temple, Chōryū-ji. The office was small and struggling; we worked in a corridor-like space under the Sky House, Kikutake's innovative design for his own home. There were no holidays, though once a year the office arranged a group outing to a hot spring. Two oil burners kept the office warm in the winter. The practice was so poor that we had to extract leads

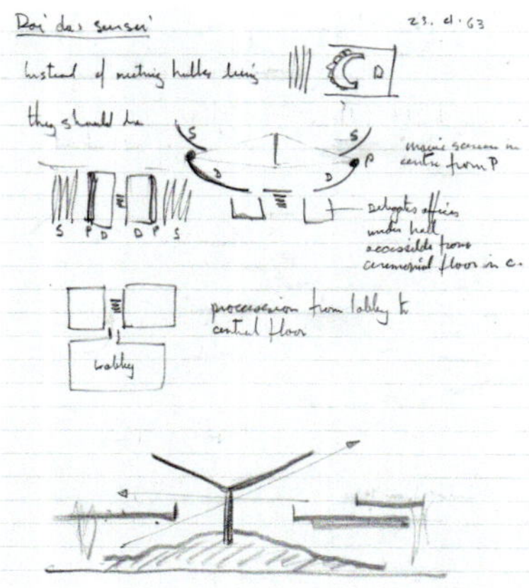

Preliminary sketch of Kyoto International Conference Hall competition.

Chōryū-ji, Taitō-ku, Tokyo.

from wooden pencils with a razor blade to use them in our mechanical drafting pencils.

My income was $100 per month, and the rent for my family's 9-by-12-foot, 6-mat room without restroom was $60 per month. This space welcomed the addition of a son in 1961. I taught English six nights a week, and Kikutake granted me time off to study with Itō-*sensei* once a week. Kikutake did not speak English well, but was so fluent with sketching that the poetry of his thoughts reached me with ease. With Kikutake, I was given the opportunity to work with someone who had come from a rural background and respected "roots" in both theory and practice; for he was a discoverer, someone deeply interested in his antecedents and in those of Japanese architecture, which were a manifestation of the rural lifestyle.

Possibly due to my lack of ability to do working drawings in Japanese, I was given the task of imagining solutions for the expansion of the Hotel Tōkōen. This experience and the Kyoto International Conference Hall competition had a great effect on my subsequent development as an architect, teacher, and thinker-researcher. I remained with the office when it moved to a larger office space, during which the Tatebayashi City Hall, the Asakawa Apartment Building, and other projects were under way. I left the office at the end of 1963, having worked on the design of the restaurant at the 1964 Tokyo Olympic site.

The Kyoto International Conference Hall competition was a turning point, the first big competition after the WoDeCo of 1960. Four architectural journals were lined up to publish the results—in particular Kikutake's contribution was anticipated, as the leader of the new Metabolism movement. The widespread expectation that Kikutake's Metabolist design would win was thwarted for a variety of reasons; the journals wondered in shock where to look next. This loss and other events led to big changes for Kikutake's office: the office expanded, all but one of the office members moved on and newcomers came on board, and bigger corporate projects included department stores and large commercial buildings. From what I understand, the tenor and atmosphere of the office changed as well. Good people continued to work there of course, such as Itō Toyoo, who to this day acknowledges Kikutake's influence.

THE METABOLISTS AND MODERNISM

Modernism had played a large role in the development of Japanese architecture from 1920 onward. Central to this was the influence of European architects such as Le Corbusier, Mies van der Rohe, and Alvar Aalto. Le Corbusier had been a founding member of the Congrès Internationaux d'Architecture Moderne (CIAM), which became the meeting point for many of the European and eventually international architects of the time.[2]

It was probably only natural that Maekawa Kunio, who had worked in the Le Corbusier atelier from 1928 to 1930, and Tange Kenzō, who had worked in Maekawa's office from 1938 to 1942, should be invited to represent Japan at CIAM. After the 1951 CIAM conference

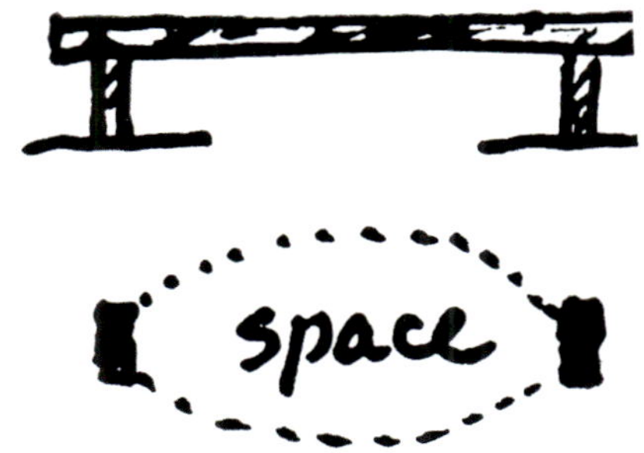

出雲のスケッチ

Wall pillar of Sky House model.

Diagram of "space" for Izumo.

at Hoddesdon, England, which Tange attended, a younger generation emerged from CIAM called "Team X." This new group of international architects met at Otterlo, the Netherlands, in 1959 and began changing their focus from the "city core" to "growth and metamorphosis." Tange, who had been a member of this group, in turn introduced Kikutake Kiyonori.

The WoDeCo in 1960 brought together 150 delegates from 24 countries. The outcome was a newfound confidence in the Japanese attitude to architecture and tradition. The adoption and adaptation of Western modernism had all but run its course and it was the time to introduce, in Kikutake's words,

> The Japanese idea of *jizatei* is that in which architecture confronts itself not only with space but also with time. Architecture was no longer satisfied with the transformation of geometric space into historical space or a replacement of memory but in a superior form of balance, where the present vitality is rooted in the past.[3]

Together with other members of the Metabolist group, Kikutake published a manifesto at the WoDeCo that would be a guide for his generation and those to come. The *Manifesto* stated that Metabolism was the name of a group that sought to present a concrete version of the coming society:

> We [the Metabolists] regard human society as a process—a continuous development from atom to nebula. The reason why we use such a biological term "metabolism" is that we believe design and technology should be a denotation of human vitality. We are not going to accept metabolism as a natural historical process, but … encourage active metabolic development of our society through our proposals.[4]

In postwar modernism, the wall tended to take the place of the pillar as a structural member, with the result that space and function were defined by its structure. With Kikutake, we have a break from the modernism of the 1950s, and the pillar resumes its role in the structure. In the case of the Sky House, we have what Kawazoe called the "wall pillar." The "wall pillars" of the Sky House appear in another form as the wall pillars of the Administrative Building of Izumo Shrine, holding up two large beams.

The "wall pillar" raises the question of our word "space" in the Japanese context. As I have discussed in depth elsewhere, "space" in Japanese is not a noun; rather, the word *ma* as space-time refers to an action, and to an intersection of events:

> *Ma* is constantly awaiting or undergoing transformation by the availability of physical components and potential uses.[5]

With *ma*, a space is not enclosed as an object but rather open to development. The essence of the Japanese notion of space is that it is not perceived as the package within the walls, but by the structuring of space so that it can move on the platform under the roof. Louis Kahn once made a diagram showing four pillars that enclosed a dotted circle, and in the circle was the word "space." In Japanese, *ma* refers to an interval, or the space between things.[6] In Kikutake's sketch of the Administrative Building of Izumo Shrine, the "space" is between two posts or wall pillars. Unlike Kahn's sketch where space is enclosed by the pillars, however, Kikutake's does not contain the space but offers interpretations for the space between the pillars.[7] The Metabolist idea of mutability was not limited to the Western notion of what could happen within the idea of space as a package, but rather space as an opening for change.

Metabolism is thus the introduction into architecture of a method of changing living equipment in accordance with living patterns. Probably the best example of this was in the Sky House, where Kikutake added modular "movenettes" to the sides of the living space and a movenette to the underside of the house for their first daughter, Yuki-chan, that later was changed into a tea room. Change is part of the Japanese culture; however, it needs to be qualified by the idea of beauty. Itō-*sensei* once said that beauty is evident by the way something is taken care of. In *Nature and Thought in Japanese Design*, Itō-*sensei* states that "traditional Japanese design does not intend to bring the materials at one's disposal; instead, it endows them an expression and a position which fits their respective value and cosmos."[8]

WESTERN AND JAPANESE ARCHITECTURAL CRITICISM

Relatively little is known of Kikutake outside of Japan, partly because he did not speak or write well in English, and partly because the spotlights were elsewhere. Kikutake's first big break with his designs for the future had come with the WoDeCo in 1960; I believe that the importance of his initiative was underrated by Western participants due to difficulty in translating his visionary ideas.

Western criticism of Kikutake's work often showed no understanding of the "essence" of form or what Kikutake was to call *ka* in his theory of the cognition of design. Western media and journals wanted to see the form, while Kikutake wanted to concentrate on the forming.

Isozaki Arata, the youngest member of the Metabolists by the time of the 1960 WoDeCo, later commented:

> In architecture, the genealogy of Japan-ness was problematic, and had long been associated with the external gaze, which reflected at each stage such issues as were then current in the West. The enthusiasm for the Beaux-Arts and modernist composition (implying art) as well as function and technology from Weiner Werkbund to the Bauhaus (enjoying life) were invariably applied to Japanese beauty.[9]

The new order of Japanese architectural critics included people such as Kawazoe Noboru, Itō Teiji, and Kōjiro Yūichirō, in what Maekawa Kunio called "the Atomic Age."[10] The critic Kawazoe was removed from his editorial position at the architectural magazine *Shinkenchiku* for his criticism of Murano Tōgo. Murano's analysis of modernist architecture in the 1950s had included the idea of enclosing the pillar in the wall, a revolutionary idea to the "tradition" of Japanese architecture. The pillar, the platform, and the wall all have their respective places in the development of this tradition.[11]

In 1955, Konrad Wachsmann visited Japan to give lectures at the International House of Japan and Tokyo University; it was one of the first postwar exchanges with the West. Kawazoe edited a special 1956 issue of these Wachsmann lectures and subsequent discussions in *Shinkenchiku*. Wachsmann's theory of architecture as being made up of skin, bones, and joints was analogous to the later ideas of Metabolism to the extent that it acknowledged the industrialization of architectural components and in many cases led to the idea of spatial enclosures as architecture in and of itself. For Kikutake and his generation, this would mean that the process of building had not only become industrialized but allowed for new ways of structuring and servicing space.

KIKUTAKE'S THEORY OF DESIGN

Kikutake was born and brought up in a remote setting on the southern island of Kyūshū. He was well aware of tradition and of his position within a family of landowners, along with his role in the community at large. He was also acutely conscious of the requirements of architecture within that framework, and how the form of the house supported specific rituals under its roof.

Itō Teiji would greatly influence Kikutake's generation. Itō-*sensei*'s statement that there were two categories of architectural history—one concerning the rulers and the other the ruled—was important to Kikutake, who was also said to have been influenced by the writings of Kon Wajirō, a philosopher engaged with "the ruled." Kawazoe writes extensively about the prewar Sōusha group and its theme of "architecture of the people for the people," which also had a great effect on Kikutake's generation.

The second parallel between Itō Teiji and Kikutake lies in their shared concern for the architecture of the common people and the essence of the Japanese farmhouse: the structure (*jikugumi*) and the fittings (*zōsaku*). I once made the embarrassing mistake of asking Itō-*sensei* how I could tell the difference between *jikugumi* and *zōsaku*. He looked at me in utter amazement and said, "If you take away something and the house starts to fall down, you will soon know that what you took away was *jikugumi!*"

Kikutake's philosophy is based on this idea of structure—be it physical or metaphysical—complemented by fittings that are movable, removable, disposable, and in many places recyclable; it is a metabolic form of existence embracing the "spirit" of tradition. After graduating from Waseda University, Kikutake's first job involved rebuilding and relocating many postwar wooden structures in Kyūshū.[12] Here he would work with old school buildings, disassembling and then reassembling them and fitting the space for its new functions. This is a good example of the reuse of structural systems with the necessary addition of modern fittings in the spirit of good design. The idea of

recyclable parts can also be seen in Kikutake's Marine City projects, in which the factories in the center of the complex were the places where the recycling would happen.

His dissection of the Japanese word for "form," *katachi,* into *ka, kata,* and *katachi* became a principal thesis for his theory of design. *Ka* refers to "image," as in the image of the Itsukushima Shrine entrance gate, or *torii,* which drove the idea for the Hotel Tōkōen. *Kata* means the technological possibilities, such as the use of steel rods to hang two slabs from the major beams. The hotel rooms could then be reassembled on the two slabs, virtually floating in the space under the beams. (In the end, it proved more efficient to build new rooms rather than to reassemble old rooms.) And finally, *katachi* is the resulting form.[13]

At the same time, Kikutake was pushing the boundaries of what we might call both geopolitical and phenomenological space. Geopolitically his designs reached for the sky and explored the sea; his plans went far beyond the bounds of Japan. By the time Kikutake left work in the office of Murano Tōgo and other architectural offices, he was ready to start on his own with a dream, a place above the earth, in the Sky House, and over the sea, with his design of Marine Cities. In the case of the Marine Cities, Kikutake elaborated on the need to free the land for the living by reminding us that mountains cover 80 percent of the landmass of Japan. In addition, most of the raw materials for production of goods come from abroad, and after goods are produced in Japanese factories, they are exported. So why use up 20 percent of the Japanese landmass for industrial production? Why is the sea, which covers 70 percent of the world, not considered a potential industrial space? There is nothing to prevent floating industry from moving about international waters to more effective locations—with lower transport costs for raw materials and finished goods—except our lack of imagination.

Phenomenologically, he searched for new connections between inside and outside; we see it in the Japanese tradition of the *engawa*, that space under the eaves that belongs to the architect and the landscape architect alike, where the building and the landscape are sewn together. It is a kind of space that the Metabolists would consider gray rather than black or white, inside or outside.

Examples of *ma* "space" abound. In the Sky House, fittings can be added, removed, or replaced in both plan and section. In the Hotel Tōkōen, the distinctions between structure and fittings are obvious, and the relationships to the garden and the lobby are of equal interest. The Asakawa Apartment Building, with its variable forms, defies the concept of a structured space. It is not a building merely bounded by its walls; instead, the spaces are set around the wall pillars and the form is determined by the functions applied to the spaces, rather than by the look of the building. In Tatebayashi the service cores push the building's protrusion into its surroundings. A less obvious example are the doors in the concrete core shaft of the Tatebayashi City Hall, which would allow the building to expand outward from the service stairs. In the Kyoto International Conference Hall competition, the platform

Marine City, 1963.

Detail of rain screen panels.

Wall pillar of Administrative Building of Izumo Shrine with herringbone pattern circa 2012.

Sketch of extension slot at Kyoto International Conference Hall.

Izumo Administrative Building grillwork pattern by Awazu.

Tatebayashi City Hall circa 2014.

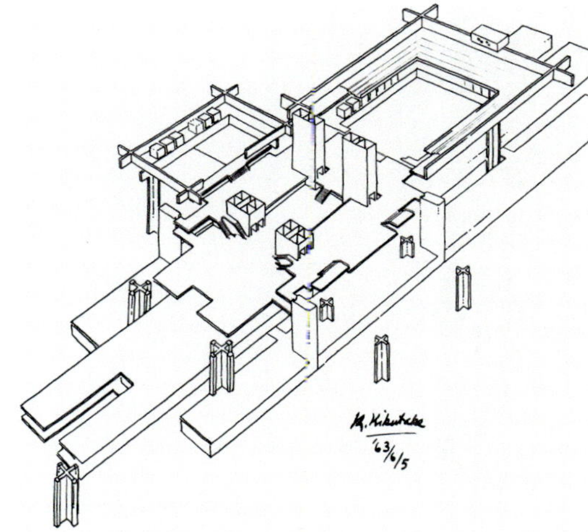

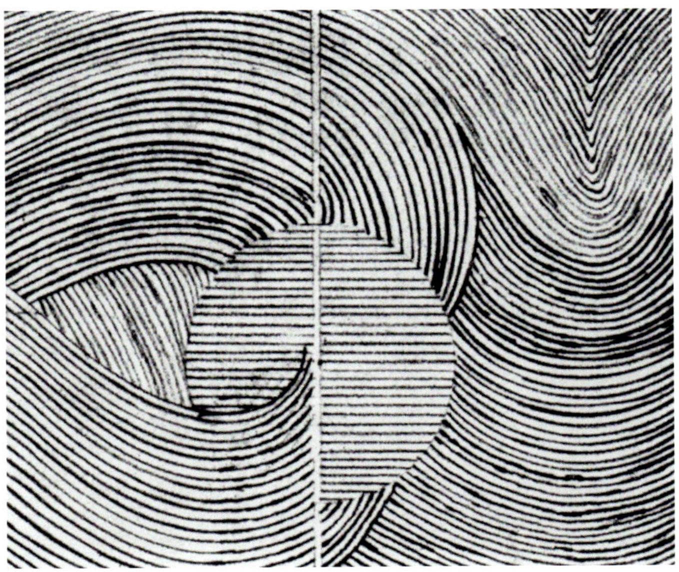

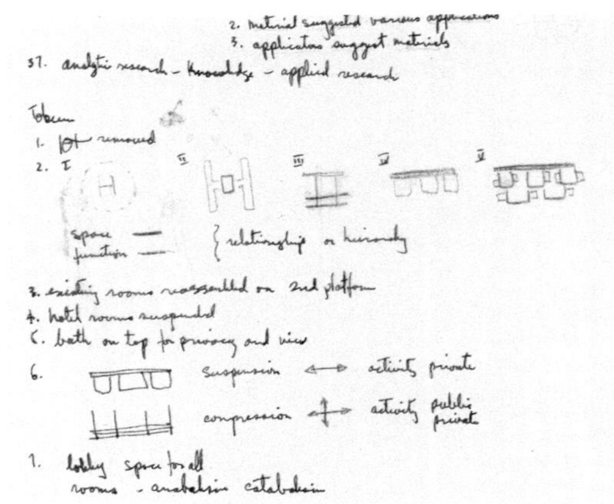

"H" of Hotel Tōkōen.

"H" of Lily pads.

on which the building was mounted has a negative slot at the end, so that future expansion could be keyed into the existing platform.

A further example of the phenomenological nature of Kikutake's work can be seen in the details of the Administrative Building of Izumo Shrine. The forces of wind and rain in that region cause the concrete to be constantly washed by rain. To take advantage of this natural environment, the forms for the concrete wall pillars at each end were given a herringbone pattern, and pieces of metal inserted into the concrete form. When the rain sweeps over the surface, it falls in rivulets on the pattern, causing rust from the metal fragments to stain the concrete. Another example of the phenomenological quality exists in the rain-screen panels along the sides of the building. As can be seen in the detailed section of these panels, the spacing between the louvers is larger at the top than at the bottom, so that the rain falls at different rates as it nears the bottom of the panel.

I remember well the day Awazu Kiyoshi, a graphic artist connected with the Metabolists, came to the office and was asked by Kikutake to design the doors to the main entrance to the Administrative Building. Awazu-san stuck his thumb in a pad of red ink and made a fingerprint on a piece of paper, and the idea for the grillwork was born.

The overall structure of the Izumo Administrative Building acknowledges the differentiation between structure and fittings (in this case, the rain-screen walls), which aligned with Kikutake's urge to leave something unfinished. This design is "unfinished" in the sense that that rain-screen walls could be replaced or reconfigured independently of the structure, an opportunity for functions to be installed and later changed. In Japan, perfection is frowned upon because it leaves little else to be done. There is a sense of humility in allowing someone else to complete a thought, a vision, or a piece of art.

THE IMPORTANCE OF TEAMWORK

Although his outward appearance was typically calm and collected, Kikutake had an electronic-like mind, an almost childlike amazement at other people's ideas, and a genuine concern for the betterment of human living conditions. His creativity jumped from idea to idea with such speed that at times his staff was unsure whether he was still talking about the same project. This did not slow him down. Kikutake would often refer to a new form of architecture that would support both the individual and the community. It was up to the staff to catch up with him, but since the discussion was often conducted in the form of an image and was presented by a member of the group, it was easy to follow the path of creativity. This is a creativity that reinforces the value of the individual as part of a group. Kikutake marveled at the human endeavor that had sent a satellite (*Sputnik*) into outer space. He said, "You can't just gather materials piece by piece ... we will have to work the same way."[14] By this he meant teamwork.

In the office, the structure of the group was built on role-playing. Sometimes Kikutake was almost like a client looking for ideas; sometimes he was like a wild child at play with the members of the office; and sometimes he was like a facilitator who led the discussion but

Itsukushima Shrine, Hiroshima Prefecture.

Model of Tōkōen with bath on roof.

always with the tradition of respect, and always so that everybody's role could change with the understanding of the group.

A good example of the way Kikutake's office functioned when I was employed there is the process of the design of the Hotel Tōkō en. The original form of the hotel was that of an "H". The garden, located on the northern side of the horizontal bar of the "H", was flanked by hotel rooms and baths. The entrance to the hotel was on the southern side of the horizontal bar of the "H". The hotel wanted to increase the number of rooms and enlarge the lobby and administrative areas while maintaining the garden. In effect, this could be accomplished by removing the horizontal bar of the "H" and replacing it with an upgraded series of amenities. Technically, this could be done by dismantling the wooden structure and building a new structure of slabs, like lily pads in the air, and reassembling the dismantled rooms of the original horizontal bar of the "H" onto the newly constructed slabs. All was possible, but there was the lack of a clear image or *ka*.

Then came the critical meeting with the structural engineer Matsui Gengo, during which the innovative power of teamwork and respect for ideas would result in an inspirational piece of architecture. The meeting centered around the structure, the *jikugumi*, and its insertion into the cross bar of the "H". The critical question was one of earthquake resistance; central to that discussion was how to accommodate the lateral forces on posts so high in the air. Then came the image of the Itsukushima Shrine, supporting long posts with the help of cross-braces (*nuki*) holding up a large beam in the gateway (*torii*). From that image on, it was a matter of "What if . . . ?"

"What if" we could suspend two floors on steel rods from the oversized horizontal beams up in the air? "What if" we could reassemble the old rooms on the horizontal slabs hanging from those beams? "What if" we could build a lobby and reception area two floors up from the ground level, leaving a gap between the lower two floors in compression and the upper two floors hanging from the beams in suspension? "What if" rooms could face the lobby with views of the inside of the hotel? The most controversial "what if" was a model of a hyperbolic paraboloid roof built as a separate study, to be put on top of the beams as a bath house. (This was much to the consternation of Matsui-*sensei*, who found out about this latest innovation—a structural nightmare—later in the process.)

Another example of the spirit of the tradition of working together as a team while respecting each person's responsibilities came up with the design of the Asakawa Apartment Building. This scheme, in its simplicity, is one of the clearest examples of structure and fittings. The building was a generic structure in which the addition of movenettes defined the use. Although it was designed as an apartment building, by means of adding, removing, or altering the staircases, kitchenettes, and bathenettes, it could easily become a school or a medical clinic or whatever was desired. It was in the tradition in which function gives space its form. *Jikugumi* was made up of wall pillars and platforms, *zōsaku* of staircases, kitchenettes, and bathenettes.

Asakawa apartments, Kanagawa Prefecture, 1964.

The individual working on the project at the time was having difficulties developing the program. Kikutake announced that everyone in the office was to take a day off from their projects to work on the Asakawa project. From early morning until evening, all eight members of the office were to focus on Asakawa, in effect holding an in-house competition. Yet it was not a competition in which one person wins and the rest lose. At the end of the day all schemes were pinned up and the leading ideas agreed upon, so that work could resume as usual. On that scheme, and all work done in the office, the names of all participants appeared on the final outcome, including the name of the secretary.

Probably one of the greatest examples of teamwork was with the design competition for the Kyoto International Conference Hall. For a period of a month or more, the office was secluded in a Quonset hut, in which work as a team was a cultural experience hard to forget. Leading up to this was a period in which each individual was assigned a role as an expert in some facet of the work. One person was to look into structural implications for conference halls, another into acoustics, another into supporting amenities, another into where the most significant exchange of ideas usually took place, and so on. Thus each member of the team could be called upon to address specific concerns as the project developed. The process of design was electric—full of images, discussions, radical changes, and constant progress.

THE SPIRIT OF TRADITION AND THE EVOLUTION OF JAPANESE ARCHITECTURE

By 1964, Kikutake was moving into the next stage of his development after the Kyoto International Conference Hall competition. He was positioning himself more firmly with the idea that tradition is something to be respected—not so much in the formal sense as in the "spirit" of tradition. This means that while the form of a space might change, the spirit of tradition in the use of that form can remain by means of borrowing or reviving past norms.

The Sky House is probably the preeminent example of Kikutake's evolution of Japanese architecture. In a videotape of the Sky House, Mrs. Kikutake offers a cup of tea by rotating the cup the prescribed number of turns before setting it in front of her guest. This is tradition in a very modern setting. The Kikutakes were not bound by traditional formalism but rather by the "spirit of tradition."

Kikutake insisted that Japan had not copied Europe; rather, it tried to assimilate European style in a free-style manner. In fact, the spirit of a Japanese gardener's *zukuri* (mode of creation) is not merely to take all of the standard pieces of a Japanese garden to a foreign site, but rather to use the soil, sand, rocks, and natural growth of the new site as his raw materials. In Metabolist terms, *jizai* (unrestricted) meant making the living environment more adaptable to change by making structures extendable, alterable, and removable.

Kikutake would propose that function determines form, rather than "form follows function," an idea that led to things looking like they were functional. However, there are cases in which a space lacks a purpose, and hence there are spaces without function until something is added that gives them form. The Sky House is an example of space waiting for functional units, such as a bathroom and a kitchen, to be attached to the infrastructure of plumbing to determine the use to be played out in a particular place: sleeping next to the bathroom, and eating next to the kitchen. But the bathroom and the kitchen could be moved to different locations in the space, thereby changing the form. The Sky House had a specific form, to house a "conjugal family," in Wajiro's terminology. This means that by applying furnishings to the space, the form for the family was realized. As the functions changed by moving fittings, so did the form of the house.[15]

Kikutake encouraged systems to allow for additions, renovations, transportability, and recycling in an effort to maximize the efficient use of natural resources while honoring the individual's right to develop his or her own lifestyle. In Kikutake's case, the family as a unit was paramount, and he often used the English phrase "just size" in that context. He said, "The living unit of tomorrow should be studied as a unit of life instead of a unit of housing."[16]

1 Noboru Kawazoe, interview by Reiji Nakaya and Meruro Washida, April 3, 2009, Oral History Archives of Japanese Art (http://www.oralarthistory.org/archives/kawazoe_noboru/interview_02.php), 7.
2 Mamoru Yamada at CIAM acknowledged that "international movements encompassed universal culture, gradually eroding the particular characteristics of tradition." Ken Tadashi Oshima, *International Architecture in Interwar Japan* (Seattle: University of Washington Press, 2009), 63.
3 Kikutake Kiyonori, *Kikutake Kiyonori: From Tradition to Utopia,* Introduction by Maurizio Vitta (Milan: L'Arca Edizioni, 1997), 19.
4 Kawazoe Noboru, ed., *Metabolism 1960* (Tokyo: Bijutsu shuppansha, 1960), 5.
5 Fred Thompson, "A Comparison between Japanese Exterior Space and Western Common Place," *Nordisk Arkitektforskningen* 11 (1998), 121.
6 Fred and Barbro Thompson, "Unity of Time and Space," *Arkkitehti* 2, 1981, 68–70.
7 In writing about the rebuilding of the Ise Shrine every twenty years, Günter Nitschke says: "Thus the continuity of the eternal in the transient is guaranteed. The same awareness is expressed in *kanji*, Japan's adopted Chinese script, the ideographic roots of which are not pictures of abstract things, *i.e.*, of nouns, but of actions. The majority of original Chinese ideograms are shorthand images of natural processes and operations. There is no such thing in nature as an isolated abstract thing, corresponding to a noun. Things are always only endpoints, or rather, the intersecting points of events, the intermediate stages of process, comparable to a snapshot. An abstract movement, corresponding to a verb in grammar, is impossible in nature." Günter Nitschke, "Metabolists of Japan," *Architectural Design,* 1964 (originally published in BAUWELT, 1961).
8 Itō Teiji, *Nature and Thought in Japanese Design* (Tokyo: Toppan Printing, 1960).
9 Isozaki Arata, *Japan-Ness in Architecture* (Cambridge, MA: MIT Press, 2006), 56.
10 *World Design Conference 1960 in Tokyo* (Tokyo: Bijutsu shuppansha, 1961), 14.
11 Isozaki, *Japan-Ness,* 62.
12 Kikutake, *From Tradition to Utopia*, 10.
13 See Kikutake Kiyonori, "The Great Shrine of Izumo," this volume.
14 "Architects of the Month," *Japan Architect* 34 (January 1959), 124.
15 The bold attachment of these theories to Kikutake's work reflects my opinion.
16 Kawazoe, *Metabolism 1960,* 101.

Itō in front of the Yoyogi National Gymnasium circa 1963.

Itō at the Tama Garden City site.

WHAT WAS METABOLISM? REFLECTIONS ON THE LIFE OF KIKUTAKE KIYONORI

Itō Toyoo

Kikutake on the cover of *Shūkan Asahi* (April 10, 1964).

It is a great honor to have the opportunity to reflect on my mentor, Kikutake Kiyonori. In 2010, about a year before Kikutake-san passed away, Mohsen Mostafavi and I went together to his office with the hope that there would be an exhibition of his work at the Harvard University Graduate School of Design while he was alive. It is such a tragedy that he is not with us today.

I will begin by discussing a kind of a strange photo of me in front of Tange Kenzō's Yoyogi National Gymnasium from 1963. I was in my fourth year at university and I spent a month in the Kikutake office as an intern in the "open desk" (internship) system. This photograph shows the Gymnasium for the Tokyo Olympics just about to be completed, when I went with my friends at the time. The Tokyo Olympics were held the following year. This was a really fantastic era; I was in university and then worked with Kikutake-san during this period of dramatic transformation.

The photo of me wearing a straw hat shows me during my first year working in the Kikutake office. I was the slimmest ever in my life—15 kilograms less than I am now. At the time, I was working on the Tama Garden City plan and visiting the site as pictured.

In introducing the legacy of modern architecture in Japan, we can see the tremendous influence of Le Corbusier on a whole group of architects. Maekawa Kunio worked directly under Le Corbusier in the atelier in Paris. And then Tange worked for Maekawa in his office for a short period. Maki Fumihiko, Isozaki Arata, and Kurokawa Kisho were all in either Tange's office or in the university laboratory with him. Kikutake was born in the same year as Maki. I worked in the Kikutake office between 1965 and 1969. Then Sejima Kazuyo worked in my office from the late 1970s to the late 1980s.

When I was at the University of Tokyo, Tange was the esteemed professor, and Kurokawa and Isozaki were there as doctoral students. However, Tange was so busy at that time with the Yoyogi National Gymnasium that I heard him lecture only twice at the university. My impression of Tange was of a dapper man wearing pantaloons and bow tie. When I was in the third year, the popular weekly magazine *Shukan Asahi* featured Kikutake at the age of 35 or 36, a real inspiration for me.

I believe it is enlightening to highlight Kikutake's work in comparison to Tange. Tange's house was in the outlying area of Seijō in Tokyo, and I had the opportunity to see it once from the outside. There is a strong influence from the Katsura Imperial Villa in Kyoto. In comparison, Kikutake's house is simple but very dynamic and bold. Tange's house can be associated with Katsura Villa in the use of piloti, or piers, and the white wall planes.

By contrast, the main living space of Kikutake's Sky House is suspended on only four piloti. And the characteristic of Kikutake's work is that it is very high up on these piloti, raised and floating. When we think about the Japanese culture, we have two types. One is very sophisticated, as in the city of Kyoto, and another is based on land or an agricultural community. Japanese architects tend to prefer the sophisticated style, and today we can see this legacy in the highly sophisticated minimalist work.

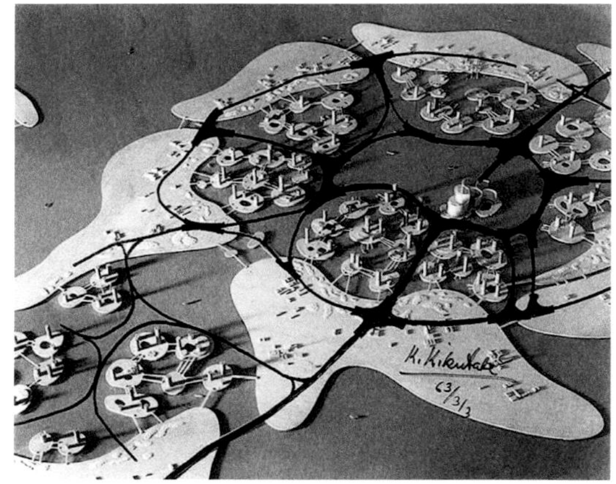

Tange Kenzō, Tokyo Bay Plan 1960.

Marine City 1963.

However, the influence of Kikutake makes me think of sophistication as the devil. As Japanese culture reflects the tremendous influence of China and Korea, it is excellent at being sophisticated in refinement of these sources. By refining something, something very beautiful can be made. However, I find that there will be nothing beyond the sophistication. Though the Katsura Imperial Villa is quite photogenic, we can create something better from something dynamic, raw, and primitive—like earlier farmhouses. One might think that the farmhouse, as an example of Kikutake's early influences, is quite humble, but it reflects the position of his family as a large landowner overseeing such farmers' domains.

We can also consider the dialogue between Tange and Kikutake through their urban plans—A Plan for Tokyo by Tange and Marine City by Kikutake—express a remarkable difference. Tange's is a really urban scheme with a focus on the city of Tokyo. By contrast, Kikutake's Marine City is a city, but is closely related to the water, almost like a field akin to the Garden City ideal.

Tange's Kagawa Prefectural Government building from 1958, which I admire most as one of his masterworks, stands in contrast to Kikutake's plan for the Kyoto International Conference Hall, reminding us of the path to a shrine with the gates. This comparison also expresses the contrast of the refined aesthetic by Tange and the dynamic in its overall impact by Kikutake.

For me, Kikutake's notion that "columns set off space, floor defines space" is profoundly important. This implies that spatial force can emerge by only setting one column. In Kikutake's work, the floor platform is often elevated and defines that space in a very particular lofty way, separated from the ground.

I would like to discuss the Suwa Shrine in my hometown, with the sacred "Onbashira" column rising up to explain Kikutake's spatial notion more specifically. This is in an older drawing, but you can note the four pillars that rise up. This is a unique example of a shrine. Though we see lots of buildings here, they are not the space for the gods. These buildings are for praying, and the sacred space is defined by those four columns where those gods live. This illustrates the notion of how that force emerges from those columns and is defined by the ground plane here. The column is rebuilt or replaced every seven years. The local people treasure these columns so much that we can say that they almost live for this festival. This is a ceremony where they cut the log, bring it from the mountain, and then hoist it up.

Kiyomizu Temple in Kyoto is also a prime example of the floor plane defining the space. Both Kikutake and I really admired this work.

One can perhaps understand Kikutake's notion of the column and floor in his masterful own home, the Sky House. This design is the most simple and clear example of those four columns and piers raising up the space. In contrast to the prevalent high modernism of the time, with flat roofs, the Sky House's almost pitched roof could even be seen to recall a farmhouse. Sky House's square plan features the half-inside, half-outside interstitial verandah space known in Japanese as the *engawa.* Here is an expression of Metabolist thinking with the

Sky House model.

Administrative Building of Izumo Shrine.

primary living space unchanging, while the surrounding space, including the kitchen and the bathroom, actually changing quite a lot over time.

I visited this space about three times, and once just before Kikutake-san passed away after many decades. I felt that the proportions are really incredible, especially when sitting on the floor. During this period, Marcel Breuer's horizontal louvers were very influential. But in contrast, the vertical louvers of the Sky House are much more reminiscent of farmhouses.

When we really think about that period when the Sky House was designed, it is quite remarkable—especially in the interstitial spaces, the kitchen and the bath units, and the hanging children's room. However, Kikutake himself considered this very tiny space a failure and the children never quite felt settled within it.

As an expression of Metabolist ideals of growth and replacement, the creation of the "movenette" idea clearly exemplifies Kikutake building on industrialized technology. I myself studied how the company had started to manufacture these bath and kitchen units. What I find profoundly interesting is that during this period of developing mass industrialization, Kikutake looks to the rural, agrarian ideal as seen in the farmhouse in contrast to other Metabolists. Rather than just pure theory, the overwhelming power of this space is really a tremendous legacy.

The next important design of Kikutake's trajectory is the Administrative Building of Izumo Shrine. Kikutake-san appeared on the cover of the magazine *Shukan Asahi* when this building was just completed. It was truly a shock that it was built during his mid-30s—to create something of such power at that age. A few years ago I was able to visit this building again. I thought at that time that a building constructed half a century ago can still be seen as newly built architecture. We can see the power of clarity in the overall composition as well as how all details of the elements are extremely finely crafted and designed. These pre-cast panels express paddy rice before being polished. The overall symbolization is of a rack where rice sheaves are cut and dried.

The 40-meter span is hand-built and rustic, which was truly impressive. The clarity of that overall composition has tremendous refinement in the individual pieces. It is unbelievable that such architecture was designed at that time. In the shadow-space in this structure is actually glass imported from France. Dripping water was a motif of this louvered wall.

Kikutake would always talk about "systems" such as the stone masonry wall of a castle in that arrangement of the stones. This is more than a systematic mechanical composition; it was a much more human one inherited by physicalized memory. Today the interior has been changed quite a bit, but at that time you could see the light softly emitted into the space. The iron gate by graphic designer Awazu Kiyoshi (1929–2009) was inspired by clouds emerging in the cumulus pattern. What might be considered ornament is expressed in a particular character.

Next I would like to discuss the competition proposal for the Kyoto International Conference Hall. It is almost like an upscaled Sky House. This scheme was designed during my third year at university, and I was impressed by the design. Yet Kikutake was quite shocked in losing this competition and not being able to realize this scheme. Though one of the disciples of Maekawa Kunio (1905–1986), Otani Sachio (1924–2013), actually won the competition, Kikutake's scheme was far superior in my opinion. Within the conference meeting spaces, the seating for the two sides was lifted up just like the Sky House. But the lifted-up design was probably one of the reasons for not winning the competition. Nevertheless, when you look at those drawings, especially the detail section, it is truly remarkable. You can see Kikutake's passion in the drawings for the Kyoto Hall that are almost like working drawings, despite it being just for a competition. The structure recalls traditional wooden bracketry.

As I wrote in *Harvard Design Magazine* 35 [reprinted in this volume], it is through Hotel Tōkōen that I am still an architect insomuch as I admire this architecture. This is in a small-scale hot-springs area on the Japan Sea. This is a seemingly simple yet actually complex composition of the hotel that faces the ocean. When the hotel is viewed from the garden, one see the composition of the columns that form the Shinto gatelike structure such as at Itsukushima Shrine, with the impressive gate supported by sub-columns on the side. Floors above define the space almost as at Sky House, with hanging spaces below and the elevator and stair shafts on the side. In particular, the hotel's spectacular structural model expresses the principle of the columns activating the space, and then the floors defining the space. I was able to see the hotel just at the time of the Tokyo Olympics. So I really experienced the difference between the space suspended with five-centimeter steel members and the space supported by columns.

While I was in the office, the Pacific Hotel Chigasaki was completed. This fairly small hotel resort faces the Pacific Ocean with a pool and a bowling alley. The bath units are on the exterior. It goes without saying that this is something of a realization of the idea of Marine City. Metabolist thinking can be seen in the sloping corridor with surrounding rooms and in the changeable bathroom units on the exterior.

Miyakonojō Civic Center made a strong impression on me, as I was in my fourth year at university doing the open-desk internship. This was the time when the project was just starting up and Kikutake asked me to research the area. After having done the research, I presented the results for the whole team on the final day. I asked him if I could work for the Kikutake office, and he replied "yes." When I eventually went to the office to work, I was quite shocked in seeing the actual design. It is very difficult to explain what this design is all about. This theater has the idea of its closing-up with this almost light accordion-like roof. Kikutake probably envisioned that the condition without roof is of the theater. In looking at the vents, we can understand that the roof is molded by the form of the airflow. At this time we were told to follow the invisible elements, such as lights and air. I can now at this late

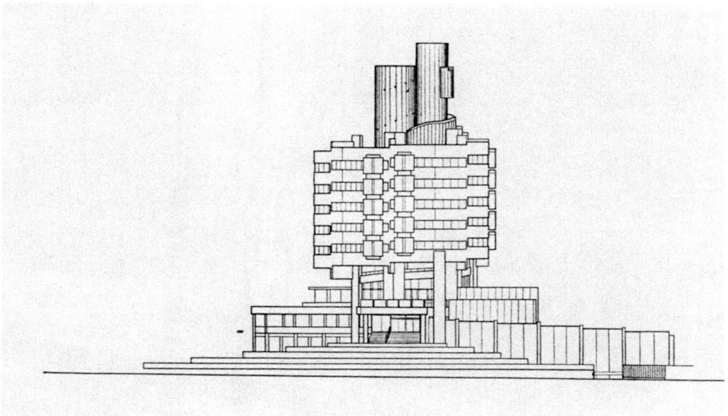

Hotel Tōkōen at night.

Hotel Tōkōen lobby.

Pacific Hotel Chigasaki.

Miyakonojō Civic Center.

date finally understand that idea, which I continue to pursue. I think Kikutake was a genius in understanding design with reference to bodily experiences.

The three key ideas from Kikutake would be "agricultural landscape," "primitiveness," and "symbolism." Through these terms we can perhaps see his particular sensitivities in going counter to pure, orthodox tenets of modernism.

Though I myself am not so aware of Kikutake's influence on me, I will try to discuss this further. My design of Sendai Mediatheque perhaps expresses those principles, with the tube-like columns forming space for people to gather and the platforms of the raised floors defining the space in this section-like design. In the library floor at the College of Social Sciences in National Taiwan University, one can see a plant-like, organically inspired design and the space that emerges from those columns akin to Kikutake's notion. I have replaced columns with a multiple center defined by floating domes in the two-level mediatheque, "Minna-no-Mori" Gifu Media Cosmos, opened July 2015. In the floating domes called "Globe," air circulates while light is reflected to create a relaxing space. National Taichung Theater, which Dean Mostafavi was a juror for, might be seen to be the most un-Kikutake scheme thus far. Yet here the column, floor, and wall have been all melted into one.

So to end I would like to briefly discuss "Home-for-All" in Rikuzentakata. This "Home-for-All" project emerges from "KISYN-no-Kai," a group of five architects coming together to work for the relief of the Tōhoku disaster. And separate from that group, I worked with three young architects for the one in Rikuzentakata. The site is at the foot of the mountain. This is a small house for people who lost their houses to come, gather, eat, and talk. The three 40-something architects—Fujimoto Sou, Inui Kumiko, and Hirata Akihisa—gathered to create something and had discussions every week. It was a real struggle to figure out in which direction to go, but we explored the possibilities through various schemes and process models. One was by Sugawara Mikiko, who was really a catalyst in bringing everyone together. She herself lost her home, but put that energy into bringing people together. Through communication with her, we really started to see the direction of what that "Home-for-All" would be. In the "Kenka-Tanabata" festival at Rikuzentakata, splendid colorful floats emerge in this completely lost gray land to enliven the space, which gave us a strong impression about community building.

For this vertical architecture that could be seen to continue the spirit of Kikutake, we decided to reuse Japanese cedar columns that were damaged from the disaster, based on the advice of Sugawara. The seawater basically killed those trees. These 19 columns, brought back to life from the dead, have a symbolic meaning. In April, the construction began. During the Tanabata festival this year, this column-raising ceremony took place. In the 2012 Japanese Pavilion at the Venice Biennale, we displayed the whole process of asking the question "Architecture. Possible here?" to consider the essential character of the architecture under that condition and in this place. The exhibition space displayed

about 130 of the models by three architects. The photos surrounding the space were by Hatakeyama Naoya, who is from that area and lost his home.

Finally, I would like to reconsider the symbolic nature of the agricultural landscape in terms of Kikutake's work. In Kikutake's later years, he spoke about how Japanese culture was formed through the development of agrarian culture. Some examples are the system of setting water on paddy fields, farmhouses between them, and farmhouses with close relationships to the outside. Kikutake would mourn the loss of tools and furniture from this farm culture in the postwar period.

However, we can reexamine the importance of this landscape in light of the disaster on March 11, 2011. Sugawara had a very normal life in her tranquil town before losing her town and becoming an activist. Through this disaster, a primal motherly force emerged to transfix the area. These three architects could create what we call "primal" architecture by the encouragement of her force. I see the need to rethink the fundamentals of architecture now solely oriented toward the paradigm of the city. The future may reside in the village or even in the model of Japan's agriculture. At this point, I see Kikutake's Metabolism not as a vision of the industrial future. Rather, I believe the paradigm is situated in this natural context shaped by organic forces and is constantly changing metabolically.

Based on a lecture given at the Harvard University Graduate School of Design on October 16, 2012, at the close of the exhibition "Tectonic Visions between Land & Sea: Works of Kiyonori Kikutake."

Sendai Mediatheque.

"Minna-no-Mori" Gifu Media Cosmos.

Home-for-All in Rikuzentakata detail.

Home-for-All in Rikuzentakata.

Home-for-All model.

Sejima Kazuyo at the Sky House during Kikutake's 80th birthday celebration.

RECALLING KIKUTAKE-*SENSEI*

Sejima Kazuyo

After seeing the Sky House as designed by Kikutake Kiyonori, published in the journal *Shufunotomo* that my mother had purchased, I proceeded along an architectural path. I saw the structure raised up on pilotis on the sloping site and thought that this could be a house coming from someone who had grown up in the countryside. It had a powerful impact on me, and based on that experience I decided to apply to study architecture upon taking university exams.

After I opened my own office and started to create architecture, Kikutake-*sensei* would sometimes visit. When he was solicited to make a nomination for some kind of prize, he would request that architectural materials be sent to the Kikutake office. Upon one such request, I showed him the House in a Plum Grove that I had designed. That was the first occasion that I was able to really spend time with him. I was extremely nervous, but upon seeing the house he said, "It's a very transparent house, isn't it?" I was flabbergasted, since there are many walls in this house, but then he explained: "There are many understandings of transparency in Japan. That is because buildings in Japan from ancient times on are for some reason transparent."

Then upon Kikutake-*sensei*'s 80th birthday, I looked forward to the opportunity to visit the Sky House. Having stood for 50 years, it was a very beautiful building. In spite of being an unbelievably challenging building, it was very natural and comfortable, and upon returning to my office I pulled out plans and photos and felt I now understood the design. This inspired me to think about the many aspects of the possibilities and joys of architecture, and it made me want to look to architecture afresh once again.

I offer my prayers as last respects.

"Memorial to Kikutake Kiyonori," *Kenchiku chishiki*, March 2012.

Hotel Tōkōen, 1964,
structural model.

NON-INTEGRATED INTEGRATION: KIKUTAKE KIYONORI'S 1964 HOTEL TŌKŌEN

Itō Toyoo

Kikutake Kiyonori's Hotel Tōkōen, which I love for expressing the joy of living, was completed in the spring of 1964. It is from roughly the same period as Tange Kenzō's Yoyogi National Gymnasium for the Tokyo 1964 Summer Olympics. Why do I choose the hotel over the gymnasium, which is known as Tange's great masterpiece? Because of my personal feelings and experiences of this work.

I began working at Kikutake Kiyonori's atelier in April 1965. The preceding year, however, I spent one summer month during my fourth year in Tokyo University's Architecture Department as a student intern in his office. Shortly thereafter, I had the opportunity to visit the construction site of the hotel, which was in its final phase. I had just started studying architecture, and this experience left such an intense impression that it motivated me to immerse myself in architectural design.

During my student years, I could not fully appreciate and participate in design, perhaps because I had assumed that in architecture, one must first set up a logic and then design according to that logic. My encounters with Kikutake and with the Hotel Tōkōen blew away such conceptions. I learned that the logic was not established before the design, but was born out of the process of the struggle with the object. From the moment that I came to know this truth, architecture seemed worth a lifetime of energy.

The first distinctive characteristic of the Hotel Tōkōen is its structural system: six columns and two girders, evoking the large *torii* gate of a Japanese shrine. Each column is reinforced by four auxiliary struts and horizontal bracing, its figure suggesting the silhouette of the gate of the Itsukushima Shrine in the Seto Inland Sea. Two tiers of guest room clusters hang from the girders; the floating sensation one experiences in these rooms uniquely stems from such suspended structures. On top of the girders sits the observatory restaurant, where a light hyperbolic paraboloid (HP) shell crowns the steel columns and beams. While the HP roof is not very large, it has great symbolic weight on the exterior of the building. The HP shell is one of the elements seen in Kikutake's early works, including his personal residence, Sky House, and the Administrative Building of the Izumo Shrine, but it has a large effect here as well.

The 1960s, the decade when this architecture was built, was the first peak in Japan's Modernist architecture. It was an age when Japan was looking toward the outside: The economy was suddenly growing, and all attention was focused on catching up to and overtaking the West. At a time like this, it is surprising that the Hotel Tōkōen could be realized in a way that, while employing concrete and steel structural components, directly draws on Japanese tradition. Kikutake, son of a wealthy farmer, was born and raised in Fukuoka Prefecture and spent his early childhood in an environment with strong ties to traditional Japanese culture. These experiences must have deeply influenced him.

In addition, the allure of this architecture is not only that it retains the independent character of its multiple elements but also that they are unified while *confronting* each other. The lower floors stand up from the earth, the upper floors hang from above, and the sky room sits atop the large girders; the stairwell and elevator shaft line up and jut out perpendicularly from these three spaces on the garden side. The large structural components tie everything together. Force vectors heading in different directions compete within a unity. Perhaps we might call this *non-integrated integration.*

Contemporary Japanese architecture has for the most part become sophisticated, displaying a beautiful abstraction achieved by paring off various elements. But what awaits us at the end of this kind of sophistication? Perhaps only lifelessness. Surrounded by such architecture, Kikutake's Hotel Tōkōen, however rough and naive, vigorously embodies the joy of living.

First published in *Harvard Design Magazine* 35, 2012.
Translation by Miura Yuhka.

STRUCTURING THE FUTURE

Mark Mulligan

METABOLISM: THEORY AND PRACTICE

More than half a century has passed since the publication of *Metabolism* and its distribution to attendees of the 1960 World Design Conference in Tokyo.[1] Though frequently referred to as a manifesto, the pamphlet was in fact a collection of essays and urban design projects by architectural critic Kawazoe Noboru and four young architects launching their practices at the time: Kikutake Kiyonori, Kurokawa Kishō, Maki Fumihiko, and Ōtaka Masato. Their combined texts and design proposals revolved around a core idea: that the increasingly disparate rates of change in cities and their constituent parts required new paradigms for architectural and infrastructural design. The pamphlet's modest production values did nothing to detract from the potency of this core message in the context of the mid-twentieth century's rapid urbanization and embrace of mass production. The document soon found its way into academic and professional discussions in far corners of the globe. In postwar Europe, avant-garde groups such as Archigram had already theorized the plug-in, or replaceable-part, consumerist city; however, no attempts had yet been made to implement realizable architectural projects to test these ideas. By contrast Japan, with its tabula rasa, top-down planning methods and fearless embrace of innovative construction techniques, appeared a fertile testing ground for the Metabolist philosophy. Indeed, the 1960s—and to a lesser degree the ensuing decades— saw a profusion of built and unbuilt architectural works that, one way or another, grappled with the implications of metabolic change.

This body of built and unbuilt work has lately become the subject of renewed critical interest among contemporary architects, urban designers, and theorists—coinciding with a decade in which most of the group's founding members and associated figures have passed away (Metabolist mentor Tange Kenzō, 1913–2005; Kurokawa, 1934–2007; Ōtaka, 1923–2010; and Kikutake, 1928–2011).[2] Late in life, many of these architects agreed to be interviewed about their early works, enabling numerous critical studies, retrospective exhibitions, and monographs to take shape.[3] Thanks to this scholarship—and supported by evidence from its protagonists' long and diverse design careers—Metabolism no longer appears to us as a uniform ideology but as a series of thought and design experiments by authors espousing very different sensibilities, philosophies, and even political affinities. Among them, none has attracted more intense critical focus today than the group's intellectual leader and core instigator, Kikutake Kiyonori. Though arguably the media-savvy Kurokawa scored the movement's "greatest hit" with the construction of his 1972 Nakagin Capsule Tower,[4] it was Kikutake whose more than 50-year design career most profoundly and persistently explored Metabolism's core polemic on the lifespan of buildings and their systems.[5] His writings and works invite further attention today precisely because they are not glib or simplistic but rather fully articulated statements of a particular worldview—in which politics and economics, land use planning, technology, human psychology, and aesthetics all play important roles.

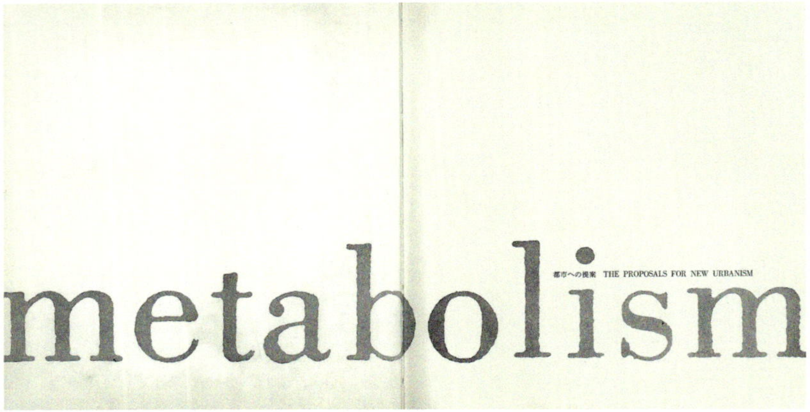

Metabolism 1960, title page.

One of Kikutake's great gifts as an architect was the ability to synthesize these diverse aspects into intellectually charged essays introducing each of his works in publication, such that no design decision seems arbitrary or unrelated to his stance on a spectrum of contemporary concerns. This was as true for the publication of his first small-scale built works as for the large-scale futuristic urban visions he published simultaneously. In the context of Japanese architectural publishing in the late 1950s—when established architects such as Tange, Maekawa Kunio, Sakakura Junzō, Yoshizaka Takamasa, Taniguchi Yoshirō, and Seike Kiyoshi were at the height of their creative powers, publishing a string of photogenic masterworks—it might strike us as odd that a prestigious journal such as *Kenchiku bunka* would invite a relatively unknown 30-year-old architect to publish a full-page essay and two pages of model photos to publicize his small unbuilt house (an image of the Sky House as first published appears on p. 16 of this volume)[6]. Yet Kikutake was given this opportunity in recognition of the seriousness and eloquence of his message, which raised the stakes for contemporary architectural discourse among his elders.

Architects, Kikutake argued, needed to better understand their role in society; their responsibility was to address the underlying sociological and psychological unease of contemporary citizens before determining how, where, and what to build. He advocated beginning a design not with a list of preconceived rooms but with questions about how one relates to, and lives among, one's surroundings. Unfettered horizontal view and independence from the ground plane defined for him an ideal condition for the urban dweller; all else in the Sky House's design, including the impeccably considered construction detailing, followed from these conditions. The compositional and technological strategies employed in the Sky House—the exteriorized concrete pier structure with column-free corners, the long-spanning waffle slab, the thin HP (hyperbolic paraboloid) shell roof, the provision of prefabricated modules for kitchen and bath—had all been seen before in earlier projects less remembered in history. Our understanding of the Sky House as technologically innovative relies largely on Kikutake's transcendent narrative on architecture and the urban dweller, which in turn makes these techniques necessary components of his architecture.

Given the continuing strength of Kikutake's reputation as urban visionary, it is possible today to underestimate the relative importance that his early built works—the Sky House and those that followed—played in the development of his architecture, particularly in terms of structural design research and innovation. With the passage of time, it has proven easier to problematize and celebrate political and social dimensions of his more daring unbuilt work and to assign a supporting role to technological investigations.[7] This interpretation is partly due to the architect's own broad framing of design problems as noted, and partly due to the fact that the construction techniques that he employed on built works, though innovative by mid-twentieth-century standards, have become either commonplace or obsolete today, while the technologies required to build entire cities floating on the ocean seem almost as futuristic today as they did 50 years ago.

Nevertheless, it is useful to remember that over his career, the architect devoted far more energy to resolving technical problems at a building scale than he did at a city scale; and it is this activity that I would like to explore more deeply in this essay.

In his project work, Kikutake was deeply engaged in collaborations with engineers, manufacturers, and builders who were pushing the forefront of their respective disciplines; he saw technological experimentation as both instrumental to individual projects and as a continuous thread of research whose value transcended isolated instances of its application. It was not unusual, for example, for the first effort to incorporate a new technique into his architecture to start at a small scale, as a test, only to be used more daringly at larger scale in subsequent designs. The notion that structural geometries and configurations could be tested at room and building scale, then translated to city scale, is a continuous thread running through Kikutake's work. At the same time, built works were never mere prototypes or representations of grander ambitions; they elicited from Kikutake a unique set of poetically conceived details in response to the particular place and use. Structural gestures, often sited to spectacular effect, were woven into specific project narratives so inextricably as to resist the idea of originating in an independent line of research.

TECHNOLOGY IN MID-TWENTIETH-CENTURY JAPAN

Before exploring in detail two early works that clearly illustrate the virtues and challenges inherent in Kikutake's approach to construction, it is useful to consider the general state of construction technology in 1960s Japan. At this time, reinforced concrete had already been established for more than 40 years as the structural material of choice for Japanese architects, particularly those working on public and institutional commissions.[8] Concrete moment frame construction was by far the most common structural paradigm, but folded plate and shell structures were also in wide use, enabling large, column-free interiors for auditoriums, factories, transit hubs, and other places of gathering. Structural steel was also used, though in the aftermath of the Japanese steel industry's wartime devastation, steel frame construction was considered relatively expensive. More frequently, steel was assigned a specific role (e.g., as lightweight, long-spanning roof structure) within an otherwise concrete structure. Reinforced concrete therefore was the default choice and the central focus of technological experimentation.

While concrete structures in the prewar period were typically clad in stone, brick, tile, and a variety of plaster- or cement-based finishes, the postwar period increasingly saw the architectural qualities of exposed concrete as aesthetically acceptable, even desirable.[9] Inspired by Le Corbusier's expressively formed *béton brut* work in France and India, Japanese architects began experimenting not only with concrete's remarkable sculptural and structural capabilities (including excellent seismic resistance) but also its surface qualities, which could take on a handcrafted appearance. Although Japan already had by the 1960s a sizable stock of aging concrete buildings, the vulnerability of exposed concrete to the long-term effects of weathering was perhaps not fully

Kagawa Prefectural Government Offices, Tange Kenzō, 1958.

recognized by architects at this time; still in the future was the development of durable, transparent coatings and chemical sealants that help maintain new Japanese concrete structures in pristine condition today. Precast concrete technology represented a significant advancement for Japanese construction in the postwar years. Slender linear elements, delicate screens, and intricately patterned cladding panels could be produced off-site in idealized factory conditions, then shipped to the construction site for easy assembly by means of welding, bolting, or additional casting.

Among all nations, Japan is famously vulnerable to strong earthquakes. Throughout its architectural history, and particularly over the last century, this condition has acted both as constraint on the design of building structures and as inspiration for innovative research on seismic resistance. Modern construction techniques developed in Europe and America for resisting gravity and wind loads must, when translated to a Japanese context, take into consideration the possibility of far more extreme lateral loads due to earthquakes. In the context of the mid-twentieth century, the forms of concrete construction being advanced by architects and engineers in the West—moment frames, folded plates, thin shells, waffle slabs, and so on—needed to be tested against a more rigorous and diverse set of loading conditions in Japan, frequently with the result that members (columns, beams, slabs) needed to be thicker and more densely reinforced. Due to the self-weight of such robust horizontal spanning members, maximum spans tended to top out at 10–12 meters in ordinary concrete construction during this time; this was significantly smaller than what was possible in steel construction. Only with the introduction, during the 1960s, of techniques for pre- and post-stressing concrete beams using high-strength steel cables (which reduce the amount of concrete needed in cross-section) did Japanese concrete construction begin achieving significantly longer spans in concrete. Though pre- and post-stressing techniques were originally developed for bridge building on a larger scale, their ability to reduce the number and frequency of columns within otherwise conventional building structures in Japan soon made them popular among architects of the Metabolist generation. The act of translating such construction techniques from an infrastructural scale to an architectural (or human-centered) scale elicited from these architects some of the most distinctive and thought-provoking design expressions of the day.

THE IZUMO GREAT SHRINE'S ADMINISTRATIVE BUILDING

If not for its relative disengagement from problems of urbanism, Kikutake's design for the Izumo Great Shrine's Administrative Building (designed and constructed 1961–63) might be considered a kind of quintessential thesis work. Certainly it is a great work of architecture: nowhere are Kikutake's powers of imagination more evident than here in synthesizing symbolic, technological, and spatial-experiential facets into a unique work. To fully comprehend the architect's achievement here, it is important to acknowledge the challenges he faced. The Izumo Great Shrine is one of Japan's two most important centers for

Main compound of the Izumo Shrine.

its indigenous Shinto religion, along with the more famous Ise Shrine. Located on the Japan Sea coast of Shimane Prefecture, in a remote corner of western Honshū, it is closely associated with Shinto's folk traditions, inherently inward-looking and conservative. The Great Shrine is located at the northern edge of Izumo City and abuts hundreds of acres of protected forests and mountain preserves.

Within the context of this remote site and tradition-bound clientele, it would be difficult to imagine an architect today proposing to introduce reinforced concrete as a recommended construction method for extending the shrine's campus of traditional wooden structures—indeed, Kikutake's example has found no concrete successors at Izumo. But even here, the special conditions of Japan's postwar mood must have been palpable in the early 1960s. Good-quality wood for construction, depleted during wartime, was still in short supply two decades years later. Architects across Japan were embracing reinforced concrete as a material that not only would prove more durable over time but also, in the right hands, could replicate many of wood's structural, figural, and textural qualities. Of course, a great many temple and shrine structures were built in reinforced concrete during the 1950s and 1960s literally following the forms and iconography of wooden architecture (and resulting in a predictably ersatz feeling when closely inspected). On the other hand, leading architects of the day—Tange, Maekawa, Taniguchi, and others—were using wood assembly techniques as inspiration for expressing delicacy and lightness analogously in concrete, while simultaneously investigating the dimensional limits specific to engineered concrete itself, both poured-in-place and precast (and frequently interweaving the two systems). During these decades, an entire genre of governmental and institutional "Japan Style" buildings emerged in parallel to a "tradition debate" (*dentō ronsō*), in which the familiar elements of International Style Modernism (slabs, shear walls, columns, beams, balcony rails, fenestration, and screens) were tweaked and shaped to emphasize visual analogies between Japanese timber frame and concrete moment frame structures. At Izumo, Kikutake neither invented the idea of figurally substituting concrete for wood nor was he the first to weave together in situ and precast elements into a single structure; but certainly his design took both these ideas to new lengths, and to an extremely successful resolution.

The Administrative Building is sited just to the west of the Great Shrine's ceremonial north-south approach road, one of a series of support structures visitors encounter on their path to the main shrine. It features a modest interior program of offices, meeting rooms, and a double-height space originally used for displaying shrine treasures that required weather enclosure (currently serving as a reception area). Kikutake's response to these conditions was to propose a simple, elongated structure—10.5 by 42 meters in plan—parallel to the approach road. Seen as a continuous backdrop across a forecourt by visitors to the shrine, the broad east facade (and the parallel west facade) would, though built of concrete, achieve a lightness and porosity more typically associated with the frames and screens of traditional wooden shrine architecture. Site and space planning gestures were thus simple

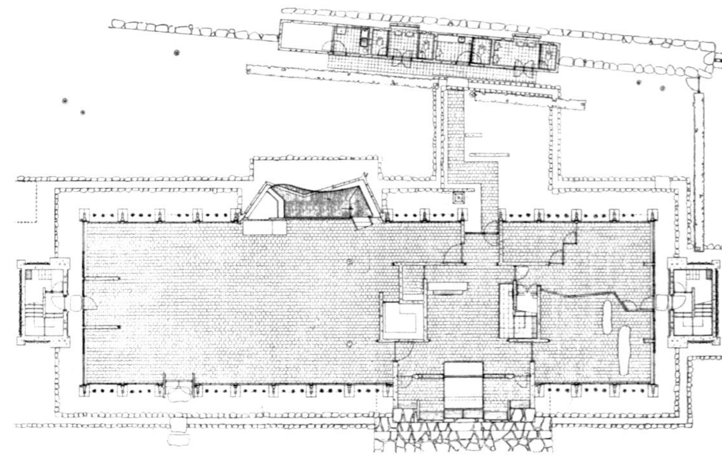

and assured, creating a framework in which porosity and lightness in concrete could be explored with singular focus.

Another young architect might have been content at this stage to follow the example of Tange's earlier "Japan Style" work in rationalizing the structural spans into a system of optimally slender, stylized columns and beams, infilling the rest with a free design of precast screening elements—indeed, many such imitative examples exist at this scale of building. But Kikutake had other concerns to bring into play on this project: principal among these was the problem of connecting contemporary construction to traditional shrine culture in a meaningful way. Shinto has long been associated with acts of building in Japan; Shinto priests perform rituals and ceremonies to mark the completion of certain stages of construction, even on today's contemporary high-rise structures. In this most traditional of building contexts, the sequential pouring of a conventional concrete moment frame, followed by nonstructural cladding layers, would seem utterly alien to Izumo's traditions. Kikutake's challenge—and ultimate source of inspiration—was not only to produce a handsome building as final product but to design a construction process that resonated with his clients' familiarity with wood construction at every stage. To a great extent, this meant adopting a strategy of dry-assembling the majority of construction elements rather than casting or otherwise forming them on site.

Principal among the architect's resources for designing this new approach to concrete construction was the collaboration of Matsui Gengo (1920–1996), professor of civil engineering at Waseda University and a key motivator of structural innovation among three generations of Japanese architects.[10] Matsui had collaborated with Kikutake on several projects in the past and found in the Izumo project an ideal opportunity to experiment with new structural techniques for concrete. Early on, the architect identified the ridge beam, supported on two end posts, as the key symbolic element of Shinto architecture; this diagram exists in its simplest form in the familiar *torii* gates that mark the approach to any shrine and is also seen in more elaborated forms in the construction of shrine roofs.[11] The abstract figure of an elongated ridge beam and its end-supports would be the basis of Kikutake's new construction system—elaborated, with Matsui's support, as follows.

The roof of the Administrative Building consists of a pair of parallel concrete ridge beams supporting a series of precast roof slabs between them. Though spanning nearly 40 meters without intermediate support, the concrete beams are only 2 meters deep—a remarkable 1:20 depth-to-span ratio not ordinarily achievable in conventional concrete. Matsui's key innovation in achieving this astonishing slenderness was to pre-stress the concrete beams using a technique relatively new in Japan at this time: embedding pre-tensioned reinforcing cables into the formwork prior to the concrete pour, then releasing this tension once the concrete has cured. The result of pre-stressing is to produce an upward camber in the beam that reduces tension forces in its lower portion. Though less discernable on the building interior, the ridge beams are an iconic feature of the exterior, due to careful

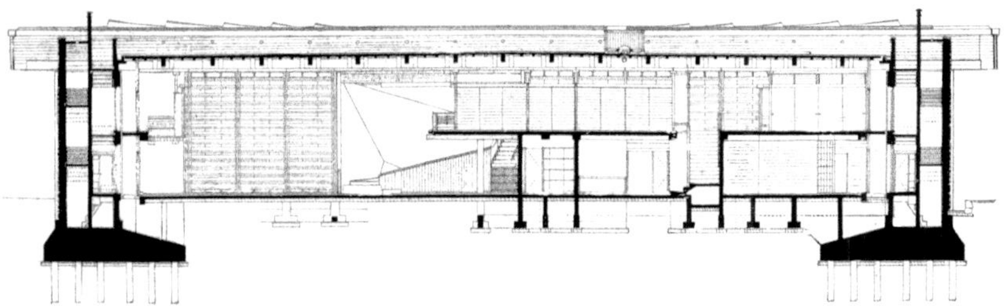

Administrative Building of Izumo Shrine, Kikutake Kiyonori, 1963.

Administrative Building, ground-floor plan.

Administrative Building, longitudinal section.

articulation of beam support and end conditions (including plugs denoting the location of stressing jacks on beam ends).

Two stair towers placed at either end of the building's elongated north-south axis are the sole supports for the roof structure and are responsible as well for half the load of the east and west facade assemblies and the entirety of longitudinal lateral loads. Though windowless and structurally reliant on the continuity of their shear walls, the towers are articulated not as monolithic volumes but as column-and-beam moment frames with decorative precast panel infill. Because of the concentration of heavy structural loads on only two relatively distant points, Matsui needed to specify massive footings below each stair tower; in turn, due to poor soil conditions, each footing required deep caisson foundations to resist uneven settlement. This part of the construction, though invisible once the site was backfilled, added significantly to construction time and cost.

Independent of the preceding structural frame, shallow foundations and ground slabs for the main floor were constructed of conventional in situ concrete. Similarly, the second-floor slab and its supporting columns, beams, and shear walls were conventionally poured, with great attention to articulating their slenderness, hence their autonomy from the great roof structure.

A series of precast concrete ribs, spaced approximately 2.5 meters apart, are installed diagonally along east and west facades (with some interruptions where entrances are needed); each rib leans inward from its ground-beam base against the more closely spaced ridge beams, to create a modified "A-frame" interior space. Unlike a typical A-frame structure, however, the ridge beams remain primary structure—they support the diagonal ribs, rather than being supported by the ribs. This is a critical distinction to make in understanding how Kikutake managed to create such a diaphanous wall of concrete louvers. The precast concrete ribs have been custom-designed and shaped for attachment via welding to plates embedded at regular intervals along the ridge beams, as well as for the attachment of subsequent layers of concrete louvers. All such welded attachments are then sealed with mortar and silicon sealant to prevent exposure of joints to water and humidity. At the point of the ribs' attachment to the ridge beams, a secondary set of precast slab and cantilever beam elements are joined to the assembly, creating a delicate outrigger beam to cap the east and west facades.

The Izumo Great Shrine Administrative Building's slender horizontal precast concrete louvers—with the delicate glazing strips inserted between them—represent the aspect of the construction that is perhaps most impressive on close inspection. The louvers are continuously gradated in size from bottom to top, so that more light pours in above and construction is more opaque below. Despite minimal structural depths, no louver appears to sag over its span due to precisely calibrated pre-cambering. Each member is precisely shaped and finished in a way that recalls the wood joinery of traditional carpenters. Lastly, the gap between stair tower end walls and the east and west facades is glazed, completing the building enclosure while maintaining the articulation of autonomous structural parts.

Administrative Building, detail of precast concrete lattice members.

Administrative Building interior (2013, after alterations).

The Administrative Building's design stands out as exceptionally elegant and cohesive among Kikutake's many works, despite its apparent detachment from his core concern with anticipating metabolic change. Yet even in a nominally timeless site such as Izumo, no work of architecture can stop the clock or escape taking on new readings over time. I visited the Izumo Great Shrine in April 2013—50 years after Kikutake's concrete structure was completed, and little more than a year after the architect's death. By chance, my visit also coincided with the completion of a multiyear restoration project for the main shrine's wooden roof structures, whose freshly shingled surfaces looked resplendent in the late spring sunlight. Delegations of officials and photographers had assembled in various locations around the shrine grounds, observed by crowds of religious tourists. Located somewhat off to the side, away from the excitement immediately attending the monumentally scaled Great Shrine itself, Kikutake's Administrative Building appeared at first glance more diminutive and restrained than the "megastructure" I had imagined it to be—it felt modest and very much part of the background. Surprisingly, the familiar view of the 62-meter-long east facade had been cut off by the recent addition of a new (and ironically, much larger) wooden structure nearly abutting the northern third. This new building undoubtedly added to the overall impression of diminution —not only of the Administrative Building but also of its forecourt.

Though the Administrative Building seemed generally well maintained, a patina of soot and mold absorbed into the folds of the concrete work attested to the building's age and made it feel part of the shrine's natural site. As frequently is the case with buildings of this era in Japan, the interior had been significantly altered from its original condition. The insertion of new opaque walls and built-in furniture on both ends of the main double-height space had compromised the sense of transparency Kikutake achieved in the original design, not to mention the legibility of his remarkable long-span structure. But the delicate lighting effect introduced by the precast concrete louvers along east and west facades has been beautifully maintained, as have a number of handcrafted details (stair treads, door handles), producing still a refined interior atmosphere.

THE HOTEL TŌKŌEN

Kikutake's creative collaboration with Matsui produced a second great masterpiece of integrated process design in the Hotel Tōkōen of 1964. Initiated around the same time as the Izumo project, the hotel features an even more imaginative and complex structural diagram, while its larger scale and more diverse programs create more ambiguous readings than seen in previous work. While Kikutake may have seen the challenges of building at Izumo (particularly site and program) as exceptional, he was eager to understand Tōkōen as an architectural prototype whose principles could be extracted and replicated elsewhere. In his view, resort hotels and leisure facilities were not frivolous projects; they had an important role to play in reconnecting urban dwellers to the natural environment. As such, they needed to be considered as an integral part of his larger schemes for Japan's urbanization.

Hotel Tōkōen, Kikutake Kiyonori, Yanago, 1964.

Tōkōen is situated on the Japan Sea coast of Tottori Prefecture, approximately 75 kilometers east of Izumo, in the hot-springs resort town of Yonago. Close to, though not immediately bordering, the seacoast, it enjoys excellent views and fresh sea air. The Hotel Tōkōen first opened in 1952, and by the time Kikutake was commissioned to design what would become its new main wing a decade later, replacing the hotel's original entrance, the site already housed a number of guest room structures and communal baths designed by Shibaoka Isao and a Japanese-style strolling garden designed by Nagare Masayuki. From the outset, Kikutake understood his building as part of a larger ensemble, and he reasoned that the overall composition of the hotel would continue to change over time to meet the demands of future owners and their clientele.[12] Following a narrative that closely paralleled his theory of metabolic urban growth, the architect set out to design a robust eight-story structure that could flexibly accommodate future additions and renovations.

The architect sited the new main wing on a north-south axis, orienting the primary lobby and guest-room views eastward toward Tōkōen's existing garden and bath structures, rather than northward to the seacoast. Extending ideas he had developed earlier for flexible domestic interior space, Kikutake saw the presence of conventional structural elements within the hotel's guest rooms as incompatible with his mandate to establish an intimate connection to landscape, and so—as he had already done at Sky House and other smaller-scale precedents—the hotel's primary concrete frame structure was banished to the exterior. All vertical bearing was concentrated into six massive "mega-columns" (later divided into grouped columns), spaced 12 meters apart longitudinally, 10.8 meters apart across the building depth. To further exaggerate the hotel guests' sensation of floating in a structure-free zone, the architect proposed suspending the top two floors of guest rooms from a pair of cantilevering girders above (visible on the exterior but unseen from within), using high-strength steel rods. The hotel's program distribution and its innovative technical resolution both follow from these initial spatial concepts.

The program is divided into four primary components—a main lobby and reception area (first and second floors); guest rooms in both Western and Japanese *tatami* style (third, fifth, and sixth floors); a banquet room (eighth-floor penthouse); and service spaces, including circulation, storage, and mechanical rooms (distributed throughout). Particularly noteworthy in relation to his initial spatial-structural concept are the corollary decisions to provide an open-air terrace at the fourth-floor level and to locate an entire floor of closed storage rooms on the seventh floor. Both of these were necessary conditions for achieving and articulating the suspended structure of rooms at the fifth and sixth levels—the seventh floor being enclosed by massive structural girders suspending the fifth and sixth floors, the fourth floor's east-west transparency demonstrating a lack of conventional structural depth and/or support below them.

In response to Kikutake's ambitious spatial-structural concept, Matsui suggested a number of innovative measures. To enhance seismic

Hotel Tōkōen, structural model clarifying the suspension of fifth and sixth floors from slender steel cables.

Hotel Tōkōen, structural steel framing prior to encasement in concrete.

resistance within a visually slender structure, the overall structure would be designed as a steel-reinforced concrete (SRC) frame—that is, its columns and beams would be erected first as a structural steel frame, then encased in concrete. This technique—relatively new in Japan at the time though now in common usage—allows acute bending and tensile stresses to be resisted by the frame's steel core, while surrounding concrete not only provides additional support in compression but also fireproofs the steel. Though the structure must be built twice (first in steel, later in concrete), the process does not typically take longer than conventional concrete frame construction, since the steel frame can be quickly erected in any weather condition, and its presence greatly assists the logistics of assembling temporary formwork and shoring necessary for the concrete construction that follows.[13]

A key refinement of Kikutake's initial parti was to divide each of the six "mega-columns" into one main column and three shorter, thinner bracing columns. Matsui cited a famous icon of Shinto architecture—the *torii* gate of Itsukushima Shrine—as a precedent for this structural model. Just as the gate's primary posts are braced against the ocean's advancing and receding tide by additional posts and tie-beams below, Matsui suggested, a cluster of secondary columns and cross-beams on the lower floors of Tōkōen would help to distribute seismic loads over a broad base while allowing the main seven-story columns to remain relatively slender. Kikutake's final design for the grouped columns resonates beautifully with the wooden architecture that inspired it. Cross-beams that connect the columns are located at staggered heights, as they would be if assembled from notched, interlocking wood members rather than poured together as a concrete moment frame, and in most cases the bracing beams are not used to support slabs above. The concrete formwork has been carefully considered, using cedar boards to imprint wood grain permanently into the concrete surface and imbuing the whole with a sense of fine craftsmanship. On the entrance facade, the lower three floors are recessed from the grouped columns so that these indeed register as freestanding sculptural elements. Throughout the design, in fact, Kikutake took great care to articulate the enclosure walls of each floor as autonomous from the structural frame, either recessed from or protruding beyond it.

The most challenging part of the structural design concerned the thematically critical suspended upper floors. Kikutake and Matsui had experimented together with suspension-based lift-slab technology in an earlier two-story project, but Tōkōen brought this technology to a new and daring scale. Following Matsui's design for the SRC structure, each of the massive seventh-floor girders, which cantilever 6.2 meters beyond their final supports and are responsible for suspending fifth- and sixth-floor slabs, contains a full-story high steel truss. Prior to encasing these trusses in concrete, the steel suspension structure is anchored to their bottom chords. Each tensile member consists of two steel rods—each 24 millimeters in diameter at the sixth-floor level, 16 millimeters at the fifth floor—spaced at 4-meter intervals along the girder length, hence breaking its 12-meter major span into three smaller

Hotel Tōkōen, construction photo of steel rods attached to seventh-floor girder.

spans. The tensile rods are finally encased within interior furnishings and hence cannot ordinarily be detected as "structure" by guests. To support the floor between these tensile supports, shallow steel I-beams are embedded into each floor slab; and to further decrease the necessary structural depth needed at midspan, each suspended slab cantilevers 2.1 meters beyond the line of primary structure. In the case of corner rooms, there is a double-cantilever, its transparency quite effective in expressing the lightness Kikutake sought. Matsui's design allowed the floor slab edges to taper to a mere 120 millimeters, in keeping with the desire for a light expression. To ensure the accuracy and straightness of the final structure, it was necessary during the construction to pre-stress the tensile members using hydraulic jacks until the concrete had reached final strength and its temporary supports could be removed. Nearly floor-to-ceiling glass enclosure in fifth- and sixth-floor guest rooms completed the illusion of a floating structure.

In other areas of the design, Kikutake was eager to experiment with structural and spatial daring: the ethereal "truss-stair" protruding from the garden facade is a fine example of minimally dimensioned, finely crafted concrete (particularly attentive guests may note that the stair enfolds itself around one of the six grouped columns). The steel-and-tensile-membrane penthouse roof structure represents a lightweight version of the concrete HP shell structure topping Kikutake's own Sky House. For the hotel interiors, the detailing talents of the architect's staff (including a young intern, Itō Toyoo) were supplemented by Awazu Kiyoshi's expert graphic design and artwork by Mukai Ryōkichi. Despite the great seriousness of purpose with which Kikutake explains his early projects, it is difficult to imagine that the architect did not consider his Tōkōen project as a bit of an architectural playground—a place where he and his team could freely indulge in design experimentation.

A recent visit to the hotel reinforced this impression. As was the case with the Administrative Building of the Izumo Shrine, published photographs of the work and knowledge of its innovative structural systems had created the illusion that Tōkōen was a far larger building than it seems in person. The main wing houses only 30 guest rooms, and floor-to-floor heights are intimately scaled: 3 meters or less on upper floors, with the exception of the fourth-floor terrace, where greater height was needed for visual clarity. The imposing scale of the four-story-tall grouped columns, exposed on the western entrance facade, is mediated by the addition of smaller, free-standing entrance canopy structures in the same language of post-and-beam, cedar-board-textured concrete. The fourth-floor terrace—which Kikutake had suggested as future expansion space—has remained open, as befits its compositional role in demonstrating the daring suspension of floors above; a glass-enclosed sky-bridge now connects it to the annex's fourth floor.

While his symmetrical structural parti places columns at the center of both east and west facades, Kikutake creates a dynamic ground-floor spatial sequence by displacing the entrance to the north, while locating stairs and elevators to the south of their respective facades. The

Hotel Tōkōen, damage to exposed concrete beams below suspended fifth floor; the slab edge has been clad in metal panels as protective measure.

Hotel Tōkōen, detail of corner guest rooms.

double-height glazed lobby volume pushes out toward the garden, incorporating the east facade's central column group as a sculptural feature of the interior. The contrast of scales—on the one hand, a continuous fabric of low-ceilinged, wood- and plaster-paneled domestic interiors, and on the other, the emphatic presence of a megastructural column group—proves very effective in uniting the visitor's experience of the hotel as an orchestration of several distinct systems.

Predictably, the guest room floors have been altered over the past half-century, but for the most part they remain true to the architect's vision of lightweight interiors inspired by Japanese *ryokan* (traditional inns constructed in wood). Corridors on these floors lack windows and are illuminated by paper lanterns placed along the floor—typical country inn scenery, intended perhaps to intensify a guest's astonishment upon entering his room and discovering its panoramic view. Kikutake's prohibition against robust structural imagery within the rooms is indeed very effective, since it is surprising to imagine a (seemingly) lightweight wooden architecture affording this kind of high-altitude view.

There are other signs, however, that time has not been kind to Tōkōen. Japan's domestic tourism industry has suffered in past decades as younger generations have discovered the pleasures of affordable international travel; remote places like Yonago no longer draw diverse crowds of urban dwellers even for weekend visits, since other rural hot-springs resorts have been made easily accessible by new bullet train and highway routes through Japan's mountainous interior. And despite serious efforts to preserve and promote Kikutake's luxurious and imaginative interiors, the hotel has not fully managed to keep up with the maintenance necessary to preserve an exteriorized concrete structure exposed to corrosive sea air. Instances of spalling concrete and exposed and rusting reinforcing bars are apparent throughout, and particularly notable on the fourth-floor terrace's ceiling (i.e., the suspended fifth-floor slab). Years ago, when replacement glazing was installed on the fifth and sixth floors, the slender concrete slab edges were also clad in aluminum panels to protect against further deterioration—a well-intended but aesthetically disappointing detail revision. The current approach to repairing damaged concrete appears to be rather ad hoc, patching concrete and installing new ceiling plenums to cover and protect as needed. Undoubtedly at some point, a more comprehensive strategy for preservation or replacement will be required.

THE CHALLENGE OF ENDURING: BUILT WORK AND PROFESSIONAL APPROACH

Tōkōen's place in modern architectural history relies very much on its daring structural premise: the suspension of two lightweight floors from an expressive concrete frame exposed to the elements. Yet this very conceit, with the passage of time, appears to have left the building in a precarious state. The hotel has by no means been declared structurally unsafe, but its current condition raises questions about its ability to be adequately maintained. One might conclude that Kikutake's

Hotel Tōkōen lobby.

Hotel Tōkōen, fourth-floor terrace.

ambition, here and in other projects, to create robust, long-lasting structures capable of flexibly accommodating future change should have encouraged a more conservative approach to structural design. But this observation is only possible in hindsight. Had it not been for devastating earthquakes in Awaji-Kobe (1995) and Tōhoku (2011), which demonstrated the vulnerability of many structures built prior to the 1970 revisions to Japan's structural codes, the nation would not be looking with skepticism today at the riches created by its midcentury architects. At this writing in 2014, a great many masterpieces of 1950s and 1960s Japanese modernism, Metabolist or otherwise, have already been torn down or are threatened with imminent demolition.[14] The costs associated with maintaining the appearance of older concrete buildings while upgrading their structural performance is frequently considered too high—meaning by corollary that the societal benefits of architectural preservation are not as widely valued here as in other countries. Whatever intentions Kikutake had for designing Tōkōen as a prototype for open-ended, metabolically adaptable building systems, the building as a whole now faces the same problem of persisting for the enjoyment of future generations that all buildings of that era must confront.

At a deeper level, however, to suggest that Kikutake's pursuit of future flexibility should have dampened his enthusiasm for structural experimentation is to misunderstand the architect's driving ethos. The pursuit of technological innovation was an integral part of his vision for future society; it could not be omitted from an architecture that purported to frame the future. The idea that personal security required living one's life surrounded by rigid concrete walls, reminded of one's own vulnerability by the visual presence of structural elements—this scenario was incompatible with Kikutake's aspirations for liberated modern men and women. In works such as Sky House, Izumo, and Tōkōen, the removal of conventional structural elements from everyday living environments was itself a primary goal, as much as or more than the illustration of a Metabolist narrative.

One of Kikutake's most enduring legacies has been to inspire, through his example, later generations of architects to continue an intensive line of structural research in relation to human spatial perception. The well-known lineage of design mentorship extending from Kikutake through Itō Toyoo, Hasegawa Itsuko, Sejima Kazuyo, and Nishizawa Ryūe to Ishigami Jun'ya, Fujimoto Sōsuke, and beyond has produced a great diversity of innovative structural and architectural expressions in recent years. Though scientifically precise and requiring collaboration with the nation's top engineers, these investigations have been inspired more by the desire to produce particular kinds of spatial experience than by quantifiable (but one-dimensional) measures of progress such as efficiency and economy. The lessons of Kikutake's approach to technological innovation, including both method and attitude, have not been lost on these later practitioners. Emblematic of this approach is the idea that research into new building techniques is an activity worthy of the architect's time and attention, regardless of its direct applicability to whatever program brief

Administrative Building, detail of pre-stressed longitudinal beam ends.

may be on his or her desk at the moment. When the architect is deeply interested in a particular strategy or technique, opportunities for incorporating these into a project narrative will soon suggest themselves. To be tested, structural strategies and construction techniques must be fine-tuned to the requirements and scale of individual projects; but the optimal application of that line of investigation ultimately may occur years down the line at a different scale, and to different effect, from the project in which it was initially tested.

Seen in this light, one is tempted to detect in the work of Kikutake a kind of "loose fit" between individual projects, their specificities (site, program, budget, schedule), and their applied construction techniques, which were under continuous development. While receiving the architect's utmost attention to creating utility and poetry, building projects were also seen as opportunities to experiment with new construction systems of interest; their scales did not always require or even match the technology employed. Was a 40-meter free span essential to the modest requirements of a 10-meter wide Administrative Building at Izumo, or was Kikutake eager to understand the capabilities of pre-stressed concrete beams as he developed a lexicon of innovative structural and spatial strategies? Was Hotel Tōkōen's program an ideal vehicle for showcasing the spatial effects made possible by suspending floors from thin steel rods, or was this just the opportunity that presented itself at the moment? My interest in raising these doubts is not to pursue tautological questions but rather to suggest how, by way of certain slippages, Kikutake was able to develop a research-based architectural practice that (more than) supported itself with real building commissions while developing in parallel a capacity to work at new and challenging scales in the future.

In my own interpretation of his work, it seems clear that Kikutake was not attracted to the idea of completeness in architecture; that he had both an intellectual and aesthetic preference for incomplete, open-ended, and even unstable architectural form. In this sense, he introduced to Japanese modern architecture a new sensibility, different from the controlled compositional approach of the previous generation. The Metabolist urban visions proposed by Kikutake unfailingly emphasized the incomplete nature of the city as a perpetual work-in-progress. But this aesthetic permeated his built work as well, even those projects that at first glance appear classically balanced and distilled to essential elements. Perhaps to the horror of those who saw in the original Sky House a work of perfection, the architect was not afraid to adapt his house over time, according to his own narrative of metabolic evolution. Over the years, he added and subtracted elements, going so far as to enclose the ground plane over which his house famously hovered as an icon of modern detachment.

A preference for expressing autonomous parts at the expense of cohesive wholes is seen in other works as well. In many cases this was a necessary condition for permitting the kinds of technical experimentation the architect clearly enjoyed. Earlier I described Kikutake's ability to work into the design of Tōkōen a number of seemingly unrelated structural experiments; in his account of the hotel's design

evolution, project architect Endō Shōkan writes that the penthouse's shell roof was added as a refinement (and separate design task) only after the project had already gone out to bid.[15] Even within the exquisitely systematic design of the Izumo Great Shrine's Administrative Building, Kikutake could not resist introducing an alien element to destabilize the overall clarity of his composition: the HP concrete shell enclosing an interior ramp that protrudes from the west facade. Unrelated in any sense to the building's structural diagram, its free form added to the project a set of new construction techniques to be mastered and potentially exported to later projects. This attitude allowed the architect some relief from the expectation that every work needed to be a masterpiece; instead all were part of a longer trajectory.

The foregoing analysis should not suggest that Kikutake was endlessly chasing the latest architectural technologies; the families of investigations he launched over his long career were almost exclusively focused on structural configuration in the service of creating structure-free space and enabling construction on sites previously considered unbuildable. Many of the structural experiments of his early years found their way into later projects at larger scales, though increasingly with the actual mechanics hidden from view beneath layers of cladding (exposed structure being disfavored in more recent construction for reasons of maintenance and thermal performance).

The generative Metabolist theory of obsolescence and renewal notwithstanding, one does hope that that the early built works of Kikutake Kiyonori will be appreciated and maintained for many years to come. The best among them—and here should be included many other works beyond those few that I have analyzed—contain experiential riches that can only be fully appreciated in person. Carefully crafted buildings are testaments not only to their architect's imagination and dedication in following through on ideas, but also to the earnestness with which an entire team of builders, material suppliers, and craftsmen approach their tasks. A reluctance to see all of this added human value as expendable is an understandable part of architectural preservation; yet one wonders whether Kikutake himself would be part of such an effort, or whether he saw only new opportunity in the clearing of a future building site.

Administrative Building of Izumo Shrine, ramp volume expressed as concrete HP shell.

Hotel Tōkōen, penthouse detail.

1 Kawazoe Noboru, ed. *Metabolism/1960* (Tokyo: Bijutsu shuppansha, 1960). The proceedings of the conference were published in World Design Conference Organizational Editorial Committee, ed., *World Design Conference 1960 in Tokyo* (Tokyo: Bijutsu shuppansha, 1961).

2 Of the original Metabolists, only Maki Fumihiko (1928–) remains in good health and active in practice today.

3 Particularly important retrospective studies of the Metabolist movement include the Mori Art Museum's 2011 exhibition and associated catalog, *Metabolism: The City of the Future*, edited by Yatsuka Hajime (Tokyo: Shinkenchiku-sha, 2011), and Rem Koolhaas and Hans Ulrich Obrist's *Project Japan: Metabolism Talks* (London: Taschen, 2011).

4 Intended as a literal, technically innovative demonstration of Metabolism's replaceable-part urban architectural theory, the Nakagin Capsule Tower never lived up to its promise of generational renewal and recently, threatened with demolition amid a much scaled-up urban context, has ironically attracted the attention of architectural preservationists.

5 Kurokawa's architecture underwent profound stylistic changes after the 1970s, creating challenges to the interpretation of his own Metabolist writings. Critical interest in Maki's architecture has focused not so much on the early 1960s proposals exploring his theory of Collective Form as on the more mature, materially articulated work of the 1980s and beyond (though Collective Form underlies much of this work). Ōtaka's extensive post-Metabolism design career has so far eluded critical discussion in an international arena.

6 "Sky House," *Kenchiku bunka*, December 1957, vol. 12, no. 12, 134.

7 Much attention has been paid recently, for example, to the architect's claim that the impetus for his lifelong interest in water- and sky-based urbanization arose from his anger at the land reforms instigated after World War II, through which his family lost its lands and hereditary place in local society. His desire to detach architecture from the ground plane has thus been interpreted as an expression of ongoing political protest. But the gesture of lifting structures off the ground is so frequently seen in Kikutake's work—from the 1958 Sky House through to the 1994 Edo-Tokyo Museum and beyond—as to raise questions about the persistence of such a singular attitude, without regard to client or program. Might the idea of raised structure have developed, at some point, its own justification as design trope?

8 Reinforced concrete was also increasingly favored for residential construction, when budgets allowed.

9 The exposed concrete works of Tokyo-based American architect Antonin Raymond were notable exceptions to this rule; his 1924 Reinanzaka House in Tokyo is a famous example.

10 Two decades later, Matsui would help architect Ban Shigeru launch his well-known investigation of the structural properties of paper tubes, corrugated cardboard, and other lightweight materials not previously associated with permanent construction.

11 Buddhist temple roofs differ from Shinto construction in that their ridge beams are not typically supported directly on end posts, but rather on a more complex hierarchy of transfer beams below.

12 Indeed, a four-story annex to Kikutake's building would follow years later, targeting more budget-conscious travelers.

13 The construction of Tōkōen required only 12 months between October 1963 and October 1964, which seems miraculous given the complex coordination of trades and new techniques required of its contractor, Kumagaya Corporation.

14 Among beloved modern masterpieces slated for demolition in 2015 is Taniguchi Yoshirō's 1968 Hotel Ōkura in Tokyo. Sakakura Junzō's 1951 Museum of Modern Art in Kamakura narrowly avoided a similar fate in 2015; and though no longer serving as a prefectural art museum, the structure will be preserved and undergo seismic retrofitting.

15 Endō Shōkan, "Project Management Method and Reality" [*Sekkei kanri no hōhō to jissai*] in "Hotel TOKO-EN by K. Kikutake Arch. and Assoc.," *Kenchiku bunka,* April 1965, 68.

WRITINGS

Text by Kikutake Kiyonori

Sky House 1958.

SKY HOUSE

I have heard that Le Corbusier once grew a garden of weeds, and I imagine that he learned a great deal from them. Weeds are wonderful things, for they are an expression of pure vitality. They don't try to put forth flowers or fruit; they simply thrust their roots into the ground and attempt to stay alive. If they are lacking in what is ordinarily considered comeliness, they nevertheless have energy.

When I started to build my house, the principal question I asked myself was how I would live in it, not how beautiful I could make it. My attitude was something like that of the weed.

The best solution for a livable house, I believe, lies in movable units and movable furniture. Consequently, I designed this house with only one large room and used movable partitions and fixtures everywhere possible. These can, I think, be made to back up my way of life at any given time.

There is still plenty of room for industrial designers to improve the movable furnishings available, to make them more beautiful, more useful, and more comfortable. When mass production of items of this sort develops, new designs should call forth still newer designs, in a sort of chain reaction. When this has happened, I shall exchange my movables for others I like better.

1959

Marine City sketch, 1958.

Diagrams illustrating Kikutake's inspiration from sea creatures for the Marine City structures.

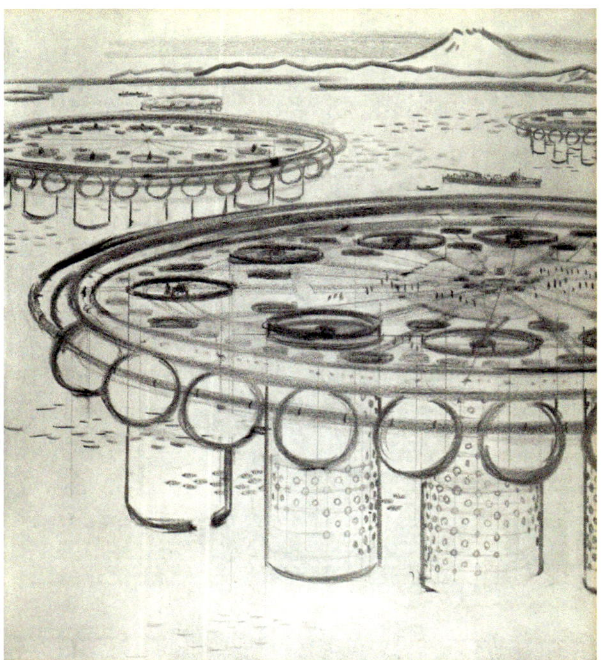

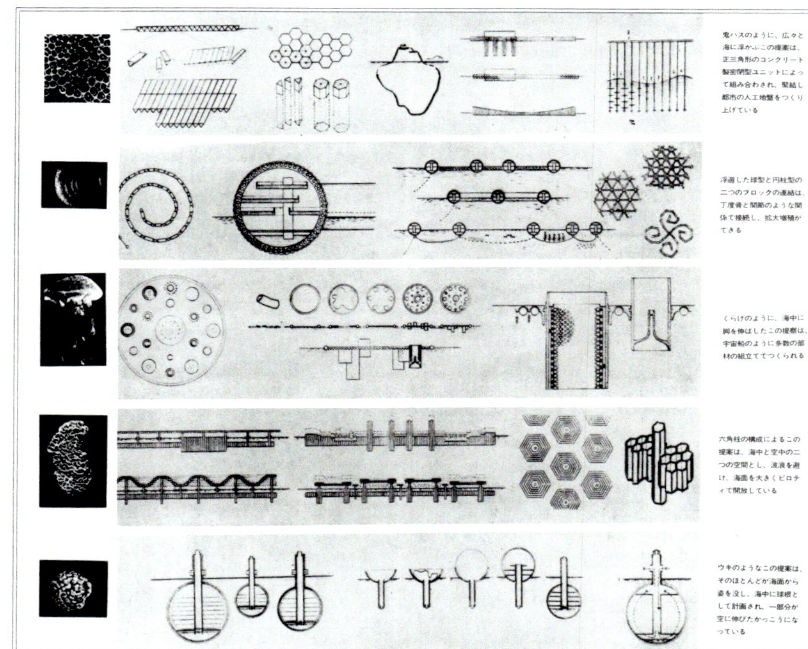

MARINE CITY

It could be said that the history of world civilization has been built on land, discovered on land, and thrived on land as so-called continental civilization. The land has given the human race security, promised happiness and hope, and seemed to meet its expectations. However, is it really the source of happiness and hope now that the human race has been reduced to swarming individual human beings each of whom strives for his own land? No, continental civilization has only generated continuous bloody battles among people in their earthly relationships with one another. The history of land civilization has been nothing but a history of wars. And now, the world is being threatened by the opposition between two continents. It is land civilization that has cultivated, in 5,000 years, this greatest conflict in history. This intense, dreadful conflict, which might cause the total destruction of mankind, could already be predicted when the human race started monopolizing and depending upon land for the source of all its security and hope. The population has grown rapidly, whereas the areas of lands have hardly increased. The clear-cut indication of this is seen in the relationship between the population and cultural products. The model for such a land is certainly Asia. The poverty of the Asian countries is attributed to their excessive dependence on inefficient agriculture and local specialties and the fact that the increase of productivity cannot keep pace with that of population in those countries. No matter how the borders have changed their shapes, and however many different languages and currencies are in use, land civilization can never overcome its internal conflict.

The Industrial Revolution gave man the first important chance to turn his eyes hopefully to the ocean and to feel emancipated from the bondage of the land, with its inherent conflicts.

If a city—a unit of human society—were to be built and developed on the sea and then made to disappear under the water when it becomes unnecessary, it would become something that would save the life of the corrupted, gasping land civilization.

The "Marine City" is a proposition made to build a world for tomorrow.

The "Marine City" is an attempt neither to expand the land nor to escape from it. It is too large a project to become merely a means of escape, and requires too great a unification of powers (technical, economic, and otherwise) just to be considered an extension of land. It is evident that reclaimed land cannot offer the best conditions for human living.

The continental shelf, within 200 meters of the surface of the water, should be, as it is, the site of "Marine City." It does not necessarily have to stay in one place but can be moved to any desirable location. When a "Marine City" becomes unnecessary, unable to meet public needs, it will be sunk into the deep.

The first step toward building a "Marine City" will be the establishment of a floating factory, which will bring a number of marine cities into the world.

The ground of the proposed Marine City is made by combining airtight concrete units of equilateral triangles. To create a space on it, posts will be put up on the datum points—that is, the focal points of triangles, and branches will be fixed to these posts.

To support the upper structure, the units at particular points must be extended downward until necessary buoyancy is gained. The units facing the water are considerably concave, so that, when filled with air pressure after launching, they help increase buoyancy. Furthermore, this concave structure is designed to lessen the up-and-down motion caused by waves.

The most basic question, however, is the treatment of the energy of waves. It has been proposed that special units (air-filled plastic balls and tubes) be attached outside the triangular units, to absorb the waves' energy. This is a proposition to utilize the undulating waves positively, and to cover the water with triangular units, which are stable from the standpoint of statics.

NO. 2

This Marine City is shaped vertically. The body of water inside the vertical line is for the propagation of vegetation. Inside the vertical structure will be processing factories of harvested sea vegetation and stock rooms. Two types of blocks—spherical and columnar—are used, and they are connected in the same manner as bones and joints. These will be made of concrete, but, to lessen the weight, hollow steel balls will be used instead of gravel.

The shape of the city does not need to be vertical. Any shape can be developed if connections are made at the joints. The mooring of the structure will be done by a number of anchors.

NO. 3

This one, in the shape of a jellyfish, will be started by combining small parts.

A circular concrete tube unit will be made to withstand added stress. Taking the maximum advantage of surface tension and buoyancy, slabs made of light concrete will form a "membrane" inside the circle.

The living space will be built downward into the sea by applying the sliding form.

The cylindrical living spaces, like tentacles, will be further extended downward when the population increases.

Inside the cylinder, against the wall will be living units. The membranous portion at the top will be the community center.

NO. 4

This proposition makes use of a great number of hexagonal columns as building material. Plastic columns will be glued or bound together and used for roofs, pillars, floors, etc. If living units were to be accommodated here, they would be shaped like beehives. The space above the water is for people and below that for fish.

When the waves are high and there is a danger that the whole structure will be thrown out of the water, it is designed so that the air in the hexagonal units below the water will be let out and the structure allowed to sink deeper.

NO. 5

This has to do with a structure shaped like a float or bulb, most of which is hidden under the water. To keep the weight and buoyancy in balance, it is equipped with a regulating tank at the bottom, which will also control motion upward or downward, or lateral turning.

This type of Marine City may be used for factories, warehouses, or a lighthouse being moored. As it is quite well balanced, it can be held at so deep a place as to be free from the effects of tides, waves, and weather. This will offer a favorable condition for certain types of industries and experiments. If a "bulb" were dedicated to the sole purpose of distilling water, which is abundant all around, the matter of water supply would be instantly solved.

For the production of a bulb, the projecting portion and a hemisphere attached to it will be first cast and launched. The sphere will next be cast around a plastic balloon. Then, the whole structure will be turned upside down (or, it may be used as it is) and sunk to a desirable depth.

1959

Tower-Shaped Community
sketch, 1958.

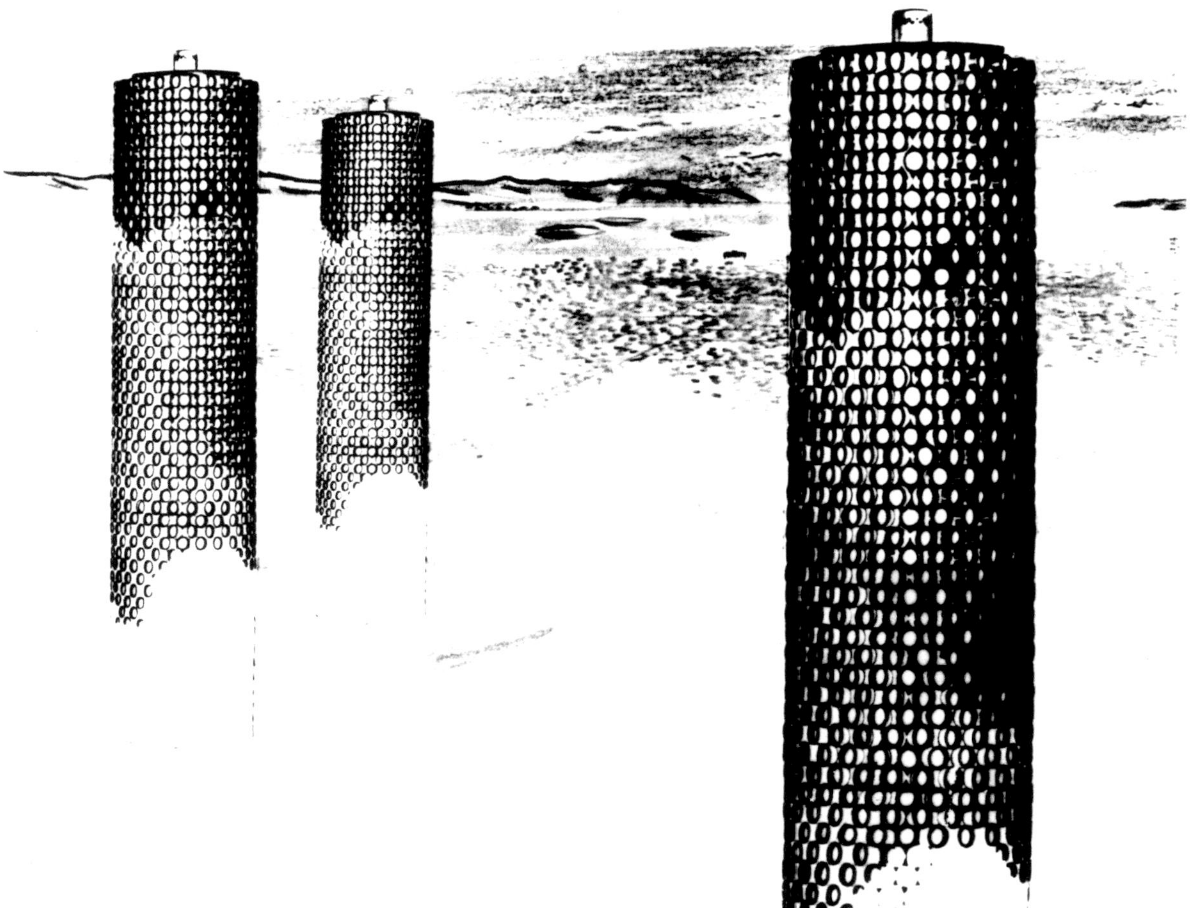

TOWER-SHAPED COMMUNITY

Should city planning be undertaken, it must be done with synthetic considerations to prepare for tomorrow, and it should in no way create restraints on any aspects of the future development of city life.

Tokyo, which has been enormously expanding, has already become sick and fatigued by losing the "control" proper to a city. The limitations of a horizontal city reveal themselves in a chaotic situation of living environments and transportation. Indeed, we should cast light in a new manner on this situation in Tokyo and other great cities.

The significance of the tower-shaped community (or city) I am proposing here lies in the fact that this proposition is based on my incessant search for a space for human beings to live in. I would not say this proposition is the only solution to the space problem in a great city, nor would I say that this is perfect city planning as such.

It is not important that this proposition, if realized, would enable a drastic increase in the density of population by accommodating 5,000 people in 1,250 living units within the 300-meter-high tower-shaped city. What counts, however, is the underlying idea in my proposition to build a modern "Monument."

CONDITIONS TO LIVE IN

A monument ordinarily serves only as a memorial of what is past. But the modern "Monument" I have in mind is to be erected to make people realize what inhabitation is in the true sense of the term. As a matter of course, space planning in view of the relationships between a building and the adjacent buildings, between a building and the city in which the building is located, and between a building and human beings is more important than the internal structure to be designed.

In modern Japan, it appears that these important relationships have oftentimes been neglected, or given secondary attention. Although Japan is surrounded by the sea, people (architects) did not think of the possible harmony that could be attained by the form of a building by the sea in its relationship with the surroundings. This, for example, well explains a failure of the Japanese submission in the international design competition for the Opera House in Sydney.

Tange Kenzō seems to have sought to establish a good relationship between the Municipal Office Building in Toronto and citizens. However, compared with the winner of the first prize in the design competition for the building, Tange's work seems to have fallen short.

On the other hand, the ancient architectures of Ise, Izumo, and Nara (especially Hōryūji) are superior to most modern Japanese architectures in light of the aforementioned.

According to a report prepared by the United Nations Economic and Social Council, the total population of the earth by the end of this century will grow to 6.3 billion from the present 2.8 billion. Japan's population is expected to grow to 900 people per square mile by that time. With this population increase, Japan will be able to rely neither upon the "bedroom town" plan nor upon the idea of multiplying the "satellite cities," both of which, in their intrinsic nature, are horizontal cities. Although the vertical expansion of great cities seems the only solution left, the expansion should not follow the pattern of New York. Any great city should not be denied abundant visibility and vista. Abundant visibility would, to be sure, make the city become aware of its own scale as well as make an individual and a group engage with a concept of the "city."

The large land space left over by the vertical expansion I have proposed would be for planting trees, for the purpose of refreshing the air and also for building similar tower-shaped cities to replace old ones every two centuries.

ARTIFICIAL LAND IS THE WALL

Artificial land for a city needs to have those aspects that natural land has (e.g., agreeable space for human beings, fresh air, sunlight, and so forth), as well as those requisites that are essential to any city (e.g., an orderly supply of electricity, gas, and water and well-planned drainage). Needless to say, it is not enough to reproduce natural land in order to obtain artificial land. It is, therefore, in this sense that Yoshizaka Takamasa's proposition for the strata of slabs is open to question. His concept of artificial land is basically horizontal space, just like natural land.

As is often the case with city planning, private ownership represents a tremendous obstacle, which needs to be eliminated. And this could be eliminated by creating artificial land, which is intrinsically vertical instead of horizontal. By means of today's architectural technology, it is certainly possible for mankind to find a way to live in units installed in a wall, just as the leaves of a tree live comfortably in the air space.

In the past, in China they built a gigantic wall space, that is, the Great Wall of China. The wall structure built for the sake of defense, however, is not suitable as wall space to live in.

Just like a tree, the tower-shaped city would function as an organism, as a whole. It would be self-constructed, by building a factory first in its center. The process of construction might be compared to a process by which a silkworm makes a cocoon around itself.

The tower city would have within it all of the establishments and facilities of administration, health, welfare, and so forth. Those facilities might be shared with neighboring schools and sports centers.

THE LIVING UNIT

Each living unit would be made of steel on the outside and have plastic accommodations and facilities inside the columnar unit. One unit is designed for a family of four members, that is, a couple and two children.

Compared with the space for a couple, the space for children should be suitable for children's growth, both mental and physical.

The iris similar to that of a camera would be set to adjust the amount of light from outside. The cylindrical form was chosen for the sake of getting a better form, dynamic merit, and an easier method of building and attaching the unit to the tower.

Like a movenette, the ceiling and the wall would be changeable according to the necessities of family life. Plastic material was preferred for internal structure. Because plastic is of poor-lasting quality, this would provide a chance for a total replacement before long. A bath, toilet, and sink would be of a compound structure made of plastic.

Each unit would be made in the factory within the tower, and be attached from the outside to the main part of the tower. Magnetism might well be used in this attachment process.

Finally, a spherical form might also be a possibility for a living unit.

1959

Three-step process diagram.

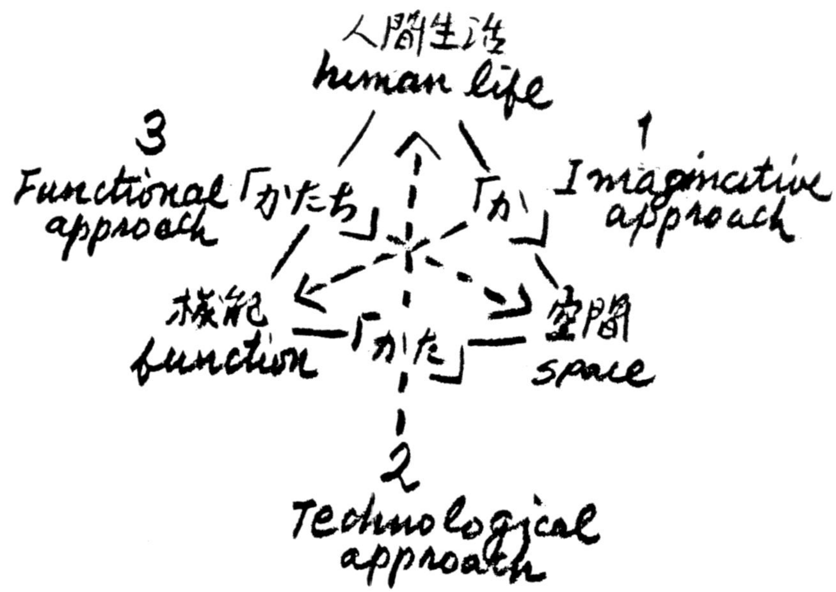

THE GREAT SHRINE OF IZUMO

A certain form—*katachi*—is always inherent in design. There can be no design without form, no design that is inaccessible to cognition through the senses; something that lacks form can under no circumstances be called design. The word "design" can only be applied to something that has some sort of ultimate form, or *katachi.*

Architecture also has its *katachi*, and the *katachi* is the final fruit of architecture. There can be no architecture that lacks *katachi.* Consequently, in order to understand architecture, our first step should be to examine its *katachi.*

It is necessary to approach the *katachi* with all of our senses.

From the *katachi* itself we can sense directly and instinctively whether the *katachi* is good or bad, superior or mistaken. It is possible to decide whether the *katachi* is correct or not, whether it is beautiful or not. Design belongs to people and has a social character precisely because this *katachi* is inherent in design.

For the sake of example, let us take the *katachi* of Japanese architecture. The Ise Shrines and the Katsura Imperial Villa are widely known as representative examples of Japanese traditional architecture.

The *katachi* of these appears to us to be delicate, elegant and feminine.

However, there is another *katachi* in Japanese architecture that is entirely antithetical to that of Ise and Katsura. This one is majestic, powerful and masculine, and is seen in the Izumo Shrine, the Itsukushima Shrine, and the Kiyomizu Temple. Both of these *katachi* must be considered when discussing Japan's traditional architecture.

Since Tange Kenzō has often discussed the architecture of Ise and Katsura, I suppose that they are already only too well known. Therefore, I should like to discuss here the sanctuary of the Izumo Shrine, which is a representative of the sturdy, masculine *katachi* in Japanese architecture, and while doing so I should like to touch on the question of the form and system of *katachi* and *kata.*

The sanctuary of Izumo, located in Izumo facing the Sea of Japan, is the oldest and largest wooden shrine sanctuary in Japan. In the past it was the sanctuary of the Izumo, one of the ancient tribes of Japan. Ise, on the Pacific coast, was the sanctuary of another tribe called the Descendants of the Heavenly Deities. Both of these shrines were outstanding. The vast size of the Izumo sanctuary is indicated by its great height. Historical records attest that the sanctuary was a one-story building 330 feet high. This enormous, awe-inspiring sanctuary had a raised floor and was supported by nine pillars; its shape was a simple geometrical square plan. This simple square plan is said to be a *katachi* that developed from early dwellings.

I have singled out for discussion the sanctuary of the old Izumo Shrine for the following reasons. First, this wooden building with such immense dimensions was built some 1,800 years ago. Amazingly daring techniques were applied in its construction, and the *katachi* resulting from this high technical level has a stirring, lively, and essentially simple nature. It is this that qualifies it to be highly rated as one of the basic *katachi* in Japanese architecture.

Second, the spatial construction of the great sanctuary of the Izumo Shrine is extremely typical. I make a practice of using the word *kata*, or system, to denote the fundamental groundwork upon which a *katachi* is built. From this point of view, one can say that Izumo has the raised-floor dwelling as its *kata*. One indication of the superiority of the Izumo *kata* is the fact that rural dwellings all over Japan have one central column and internal space divided up into four rooms.

By having such a *kata* as its background, a *katachi* is able to have a bigger, wider, and deeper influence. If the *katachi* is merely handed on as a form, it will turn into a lifeless formalism. The life that was in the *katachi* at first will be lost. Hence there will begin the process of elevating the already dead *katachi* to the level of an authoritative formal style. *Katachi* is of the greatest importance in architecture, as I emphasized before.

However, in Izumo I wish to point out how powerful and decisive is the influence of the underlying *kata* that serves as the basic foundation for the *katachi*. One may doubtless evaluate the *kata* of a given design on the basis of its degree of universality and social validity. There are in Japanese culture a number of very deeply rooted *kata*. The importance of these *kata* is indicated by the way in which they have traditionally pervaded everyday life. For instance, *kata* reach into all phases of daily life in such things as etiquette, flower arrangement, dance, the martial arts, and so forth. It is for this very reason that the architecture of Japanese dwellings has won such positive evaluation as being highly compatible with Japanese living patterns.

It is not true that Japanese dwellings are merely a *katachi* to which such things as the *toko-no-ma*, the *tatami*, the *shōji*, are attached. If the Japanese dwelling were merely a *katachi*, there would not have been so much variation and such extensive penetration into society. It was only because the Japanese dwelling has been handed down as a *kata*, not as a mere *katachi*, that it was able to survive to the present day, adjusting itself so successfully to the successive modifications in patterns occasioned by the vast historical changes that occurred from period to period.

Consequently, one should recognize that the Japanese dwelling has perfected and possesses a dwelling *kata;* and the most original architectural expression of this *kata* of the Japanese dwelling is none other than the great sanctuary of the Izumo Shrine.

It is not a mistake to assert that the final test determining the success or failure of a design is its *katachi*. Nevertheless, I believe that the task of design today is to find a *kata* that will make it possible to give free expression to individuality, which will allow individuality to reach its highest possible development. This also is, I think, the fundamental task of contemporary architecture.

A THREE-STEP METHODOLOGY

If we were to define *katachi* as the stage of concrete phenomena, we might say that *kata* corresponds to the stage of the underlying substance. I believe it is very important to understand the *kata* as the substance in which the individual *katachi* are realized.

Concerning *kata*, we are further confronted with the questions: How is a *kata* born? What, exactly, is the basic groundwork on which the *kata* is built? In other words, we are moving on to the deepest and most elusive problem of architecture: What is the essence of *kata*?

One moves from *katachi* to *kata*, and finally to *ka* or Order. Going through this three-step process, one reaches the essential in design.

The essence of architecture is spatial order.

This process of cognition from *katachi* to *kata* and then to *ka* is extremely important in design.

A deep cognition of this type will help us to judge and to select *katachi* correctly.

However, cognition alone, although it may help us to judge a *katachi*, cannot create one.

Since the duty of architects is to engage in practice, to produce concrete *katachi*, we must understand the structure of practice together with the structure of cognition.

I regard the process of practice to be the opposite of the process of cognition; that is, I regard it as a three-step process starting from *ka*, then leading to *kata*, and finally arriving at *katachi* by applying the *kata* in actuality. In this case, *ka* is not merely an Order attained as a result. *Ka* means the conceiving of an Image. It is the process in which new functions are discovered from the contradictions of real life, and these new functions are projected into the unknown world of the future.

It has often been said that an airplane does not fly because of the resistance of air. First of all, it was necessary for man to grasp the new function of flying from the contradiction arising from the fact that man wished to fly through the air. If this new function had not been discovered, it would have been impossible for the airplane to be realized in actual practice.

Kata come into being when the *ka* are realized in concrete form through the medium of techniques. In the case of the airplane, the invention of the engine a well as technical achievements such as light alloys and other new materials, hydrodynamic theory, and other techniques were unearthed by Image. When backed up by the techniques discovered in this way, the *kata* of the airplane came into being. When this *kata* is applied to various real situations and different functions are fulfilled, different concrete *katachi* such as jet airliners or helicopters are obtained.

This three-step process of *ka—kata—katachi* is what I mean by the structure of cognition and practice. It is my basic methodology.

There are, it is true, many different theories of design. However, any theory that possesses no process for actual practice is nothing more than formal logic. Formal logic can play no effective role at all in promoting actual design activities. When a theory of practice has been faithfully carried out, one must evaluate whether the theory was correct or incorrect by the *katachi* obtained as a result. Theory is cultivated and developed by this constant process of evaluation.

SPACE AND FUNCTION

The Izumo and Ise Shrines have been rebuilt every 60 and 20 years, respectively. It should be noted that the method of periodical rebuilding was adopted as the form of transmission of wooden architecture, which is limited in its durability in time. However, rebuilding does not mean any changes in the architectural function of the shrine sanctuary. Today many excellent synthetic materials are being produced as substitutes for wood. Today we have the task of deciding how to utilize these materials correctly, and how to combine and systematize them. Besides, the question of changes in man's demands on his spatial environment, and the question of changes in social function, have come to the forefront.

Unlike the architecture of the past, contemporary architecture must be a changeable, movable, and comprehensible architecture, capable of meeting the changing requirements of the contemporary age. Therefore, it is my view that the *kata* of contemporary architecture must be metabolic.

With the static theory of the unsophisticated functionalist, to the effect that *form follows function*, it is impossible to discover a *kata* capable of corresponding to functional changes. In order to reflect dynamic reality, what is needed is not a fixed, static function, but rather one that is capable of undergoing metabolic change. Therefore, naturally, our ideas about architecture are also bound to change. We must stop thinking in terms of function and form, and think instead in terms of space and changeable function. It is for this reason that the *kata* of metabolic architecture is defined as the unity of human space and of service function. By distinguishing between these two elements, I believe it will be possible to make a new and more meaningful unity. The consistent objective of metabolic architecture is to explore new methods of obtaining human space.

The process of separation will make it possible to define even more clearly the goal of architecture.

The method of constant rebuilding whenever there is a change in the function is no longer realistic, and it will become less and less realistic in the future.

Thus, I believe that if we think of space and function as two opposing elements, it will be possible for the human environment to attain a metabolic order instead of a static beauty.

This will make it possible for the human environment to respond truly to the requirements of a dynamic reality.

When I say concerning architecture that *space discards (pure) function*, I have in mind two different meanings. First of all, I mean that the objective of architecture is to attain human space. Second, that the objective is to enable the auxiliary functions to assist and to liberate humans through daily life.

1965

Floor sets off space diagram,
columns define space diagram.

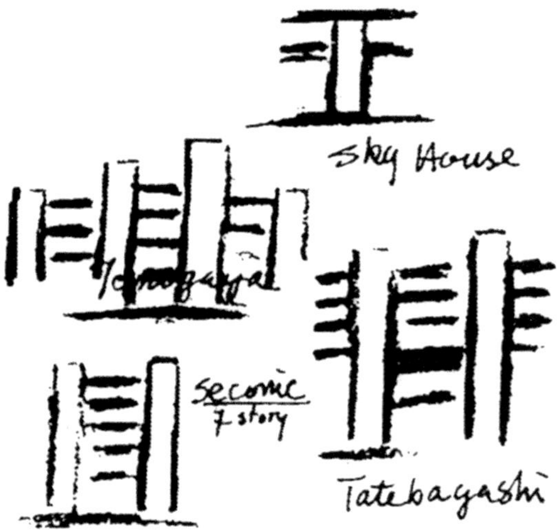

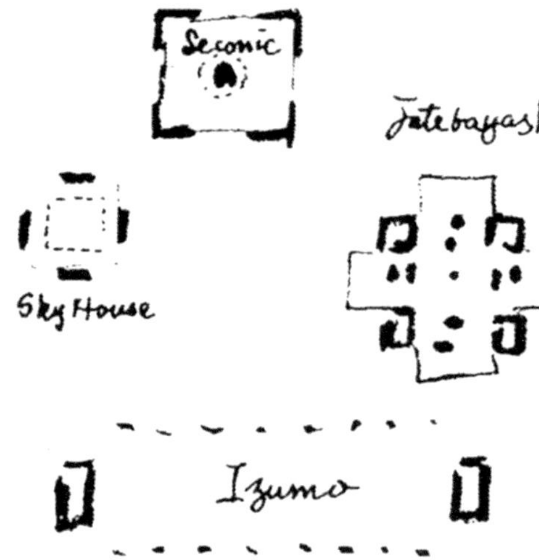

THE ORDER OF THINGS ONE CAN SEE: FLOORS AND COLUMNS

FLOOR SETS OFF SPACE

The first-floor surface has a deeper significance than its plain, physical meaning as the base supporting human living. In our country, we have been trained to attach a definite psychological significance to the floor, which is relied on as a source of stability.

Even in outdoor Noh stages and balconies, we sense the existence of a clearly defined spatial arrangement. It must be emphasized that the floor is able to define and limit space far more strongly than the ceiling or the walls. The sense of space created by the floor is neither an infinite one nor a mere idealistic, subjective limitation. The problem of "platform," which we have been pursuing from the outset—although it indeed involves the defining of space—by no means involves interrupting it or dividing it up into small units. Here we are pursuing the floor area as a term of definition of space, we are investigating the relation between floor and space. The scale of the floor is not confined merely to architecture. It applies also to the city as a whole. The proposal of "decks" in the Ikebukuro Plan was made in order to win new space for man. This was, in a word, a proposal of a "City Floor." The Marine City project also was a proposal of the creation of an artificial and intensely human "City Floor."

COLUMNS DEFINE SPACE

In our country we often encounter huge old trees with ropes tied around their trunks to denote that these trees are treated as objects of veneration. When we see a sacred tree like this, we are impressed not only by the venerable age of its trunk. We are also frequently moved by the feeling of tension implicit in the trunk, which links into a single unit two worlds: the heaven-like microcosm formed by the superstructure of the branches and leaves, and the supporting substructure formed by the roots that spread out in all directions underground. Even if the trunk has been cut down and remains but a stump, we may still be struck with the same emotion when we imagine the superstructure as it ought to appear. This is so because the trunk sets off a certain space, marking it off from the endless expanse of surrounding space. Columns perform the same function as trunks in this sense. If one wishes to set off spatial divisions distinctly, one ought to make the columns clearly visible. I think that columns, which are impressive expressions of power itself, are probably the most suitable elements for setting off space.

1969

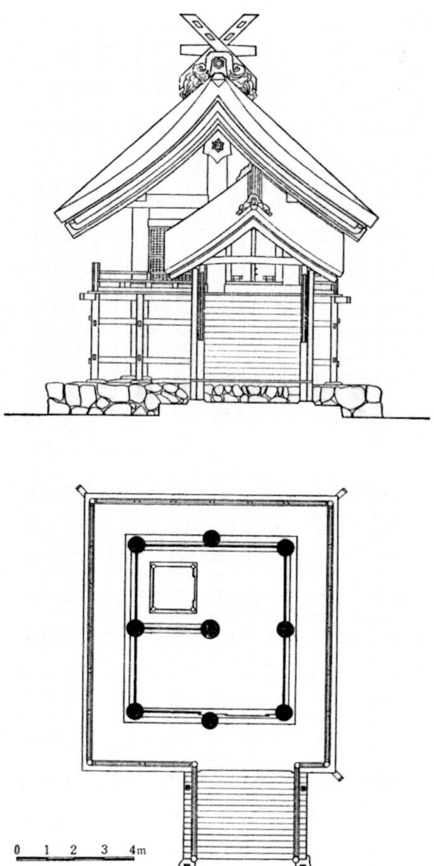

Izumo Shrine elevation and plan.

NEW FORM AND OLD TRADITION

Whenever a new form is created, it is always created on the basis of tradition, in rejection of tradition. In time, the new form will create a new tradition in its own right. Tradition, particularly when it has a long history, does not act to restrict forms. But traditional forms have no power to give birth to new forms. Nevertheless, the traditional spirit is, I think, a power that supports new forms.

Ideas have changed with the times, and forms have become diversified with the progress of history. However, the spirit that links ideas and forms has become refined and condensed gradually from ages past. As tradition, this spirit plays a stimulating role upon the present and provides an orientation for the future.

Therefore, the important problem in history is this: what spirit is to be discovered in the old tradition? This is a question closely connected with the question of the creative process, and it also develops into the question of how creation is to be verified in human society.

In my thinking about contemporary architecture, I use three basic viewpoints: "new forms," "technology as an impetus," and "development of order." First of all, what is the basis on which new forms are created in contemporary architecture? I like to consider this basis as the harmony of two different functions: "spatial equipment" and "living equipment." Second, I believe that contemporary architecture must find a new orientation with respect to the clash existing between technological conditions and local conditions.

Technological progress has brought about a universal elevation of the values of countless multitudes. It has immeasurably raised our levels of civilization. However, architecture is still restrained by local restrictions. For this reason, I believe, the personality has not yet been freed to develop fully on the basis of technology. We must correctly utilize technology as an impetus in building a contemporary architecture that will be more abundant, more individual, and more human.

Third, with regard to "development of order," I believe it essential to create a new order in the relations between architecture and nature and between architecture and man. For the essence of architecture is order. An old tradition is an old order. In creating a contemporary order, we must apply ourselves to learning order within the historical framework. The Metabolism Group of Tokyo is a group attempting to seek such a new order for man. This order will be founded on human values. Human values are the matrix out of which new forms will grow. I will try to elaborate on my basic concepts by using the Izumo Shrine as an example. My involvement with designing the Administrative Building of the Great Shrine of Izumo began in 1958, when I first saw the shrine sanctuary. It moved me deeply.

This involvement began with an "encounter" or what we call *de-ai* in Japan. An encounter of this type must be either too early or too late. It occurs purely by chance, but it is a decisive happening in one's life. An encounter had occurred between myself and Izumo. I was astonished by the form concept of the Izumo Shrine. What was it that fascinated me in this sanctuary building, a building that does not even adhere strictly to all of the ancient traditions? No doubt it was the great shrine sanctuary of the fourth century rebuilt and restored through my imagination.

In fourth-century Japan, a system of production centering around culture had already been perfected in the Izumo area. This fact is reflected in the existence of a technological context capable of carrying out extensive irrigation projects, building river embankments, and constructing large bridges. This was an era of greatness that might well be the birth of the Agricultural Revolution. It was during this same period that the Tomb of Emperor Nintoku was constructed larger in size than the pyramids! The people, at last liberated from dependence on daily searches for food, must have cherished great hopes for the future. This was the historical background that made possible the construction of the great shrine sanctuary, in which the technology of the time was utilized to its optimum limits. I think the high technological levels were utilized to express the hopes and aspirations of the people of that serene and tranquil period.

I came to think that, if a building is to be located near the present sanctuary, it must be one expressing the hopes and aspirations of contemporary man. It must make bold and judicious use of contemporary technology in a manner not inferior to the manner in which technology was used here in antiquity.

In the book *Dwellings of the Gods*, critic Kawazoe Noboru regards the sanctuary of Izumo as having been a "dwelling place of the deity." I myself prefer to regard the ancient sanctuary as having been a symbolic representation of a storehouse for rice. Such significance in building a sanctuary with these vast dimensions and with such boldness and strength could only be interpreted by this symbolism.

It is also for this reason that the sanctuary was able to become the symbol of the Izumo region. To preserve rice in a storehouse year-round, the primary necessity would be that the storehouse be kept dry. In this case, the *inakake* or gridded stand construction was adopted, enabling the seasonal winds to dry out the storehouse. This construction is a typical one in the Izumo region; everyone is familiar with it and fully acquainted with the functions it performs. This is why I selected the *inakake* as the motif for the design of the Administrative Building at Izumo.

Another pertinent thing to consider was the religious factor: Shintoism. There are various interpretations of Shintoism, the religion of which Izumo is a symbol. In my own interpretation, there are two basic concepts. The first concept is the idea of rebirth, a way of thinking that accords with agriculture, in which new buds sprout forth from the grains of rice and come to fruition in the rhythmic process repeated annually. In a sense, this concept is very similar to the ideas of Metabolism.

The second concept is the idea that all men are gods. In Japan, the term "myriad of deities" is often used and Japanese mythology is unequaled in the vast numbers of deities. Of course, Japanese mythology originated in the matriarchal family system; nevertheless, this concept is strikingly similar to the ideas of democracy.

And man's emotion plays another role in these Shinto shrines. A common feature that can be seen in all Shinto shrines is the use of unpainted and untreated raw materials. As a result, the expressions and forms utilized in the shrines are characterized by simplicity and plainness. The roofs thatched with tree bark, the columns, the beams, the walls and staircases are made exclusively of wood. The shrine architecture is thus one based entirely on these materials. For this reason, there is absolutely no distinction between the structure and the finish, between the basic unit and the decoration. Here, all of the parts must not only form a part of the basic structure, but must also contain within themselves the final finish. At the same time, they must satisfy the aesthetic requirements.

This uniform reliance upon materials may be said to be the basis of Japanese architecture, and its characteristic feature. Hence, how can we justify the use of modern materials in shrine construction? In his *Aspects du XXe siècle*, André Siegfried emphasizes that "technology is a means, and being a means is its reason for existence." This basic attitude toward technology always causes one to ponder. Siegfried goes on to mention Americans and Asians as dangerous people who are liable to make technology an end rather than a means. If Siegfried were to have known that the main theme of this [AIA California chapter's 1964] convention is the "Aesthetics of Technology," I am sure that he would deplore our lack of culture.

At the same time, when dealing with beauty, we should first recall the contrast between the classical Greek view of art and the Romantic school. The Greek view of art as outlined by Aristotle was a concept of technology and imitation. The artistic thought of the Romantic school emphasized genius and creation. Goethe says that "life is the ideal of art." Thus, the question of contemporary technology and aesthetics—as long as it is a question of technology and aesthetics—is without a doubt also the problem of contemporary architecture. At the same time, I also think that the contrasting views of art—the technological and the aesthetic—contain a suggestion of a new development.

In terms of the Izumo Administrative Building, all of the technological conditions are those imposed by contemporary technology. This includes the designing methods and the methods of production. This is a technology, a mechanism, and a system moving toward mass production. Large beams of pre-stressed concrete and louvers of precast concrete are merely examples. Although they are the products of universal technology suited to standardized production, one is forced to produce individualized items that are unique to the Izumo Administrative Building.

There is another local condition that makes this so. However, in the final analysis, one wonders whether it is still desirable to start out in architecture from local conditions simply because this was the practice in the past. When he sets out from definite given conditions, the architect often neglects to ask the question: Why precisely have these conditions come into being? The technological conditions tend toward universality, while the local conditions demand uniqueness.

The louvers are among the standardized parts used in the Izumo Administrative Building. However, there are gradual changes in their cross sections as one proceeds downward from the top and the louvers are definitely not standardized. The large beam, which appears to be a simple form, is really quite complex and specialized. Although fundamentally I cannot say that the Izumo Administrative Building has provided an entirely satisfactory answer to the conflicting claims of these two sets of conditions—technological conditions and local conditions—I can say that it gave me a strong awareness of the tasks that contemporary architecture faces and will face in the future.

No matter whether the Izumo sanctuary was meant to be a dwelling or a storehouse, its primary architectural space still exists. The space—10 meters square, surrounded by nine columns and supported high above the ground—has, to be sure, very human dimensions that would not be at all inappropriate for a dwelling. If one were to use it as a dwelling, all that would be necessary would be to install the various facilities needed for modern living. The sanctuary would then serve admirably well as a dwelling place.

It seems to me that there are two elements in architecture: first, the spatial equipment, which determines the space itself; and second, the living equipment, which corresponds to living patterns. Not only in the Izumo sanctuary but in all historical edifices, we view the spatial equipment. On the other hand, in viewing contemporary architecture, we place considerable weight on the living equipment. These two elements, each corresponding to its respective functions, will create new forms.

In the Izumo Administrative Building, the spatial equipment is comprised of two columns on both sides, a large beam with a 40-meter span, roof plates attached to the large beam, and a mezzanine slab. These determine elevation, expanse, and orientation. Living equipment composes the other features—the entrance, the outer walls of the horizontal louvers, the staircase wall made of a hyperbolic paraboloid shell, and the finishing of the interior.

The spatial equipment is thought of as the spatial skeleton, which is not subject to temporal changes or changes in function. The steel structure was covered with a concrete layer 100 millimeters thick. However, in the living equipment, which occupies the subordinate position, we adopted the method of installing onto the spatial equipment those fixtures necessary to satisfy current requirements. We believe it quite permissible if their positions change in the future, if they are replaced by other fixtures using different materials, or if they are replaced in order to meet changes in function.

As one example of this, I might mention that at the beginning I designed the horizontal louvers to be of colored reinforced glass. This was abandoned when it was learned that pieces of reinforced glass with odd-shaped cross sections could not be made by present production techniques. Therefore, precast concrete was substituted. However, I think it quite probable that there will be advances in glassmaking techniques in the near future, which will make it possible to realize the original plan. When this has become possible, I should like to replace the entire outer wall section with glass.

When I use the term "Metabolism," I mean the introduction into architecture of such a method of replacing and changing the living equipment in accordance with living patterns. At the same time, this method helps us to delineate clearly the main portions of the building that will not change and that will continue to be the center and predominant part of the building. This also will help the architect to formulate his own goals clearly.

Thus, it becomes necessary to devise a metabolic system making possible variations between the two elements. Since in this way of thinking no final form is envisioned, great care is necessary in putting it into practice. However, I regard this method as advantageous for contemporary architecture for a number of reasons: First, it permits the accumulation of aggregates of spatial equipment on the human scale; also, it provides forms that can be changed as time goes on; lastly, it allows for the future developments that will be achieved in living equipment as contemporary technology makes further advances.

Order and its role in architecture: I am always amazed at the differences in the aging of old, traditional architecture and new architecture. The former increases its gracious refinement, while the latter seems to become dirtier. This distinction between architecture that gradually becomes more fascinating and beautiful as time goes on, and architecture that gradually becomes uglier and shabbier, is not merely a question of the life expectancy of a building, nor is it a question of cleaning. It seems to be that there is a problem here concerning the fundamental humanity of architecture.

In Japan, with its rainy monsoon climate, the Izumo area is noted as one area with the greatest rainfall. The buildings constructed here are constantly exposed to rain and attacked by dampness. This makes it necessary to adopt special techniques. At the same time, I believe that the architecture of Izumo must display not merely a technical solution but also a solution of beauty to the problem of architecture in this environment of so much rain, fog, and snow.

The ancient sanctuary of Izumo, with its big roof and raised floor, presented a remarkable and vivid solution. For this reason, it was referred to in song and poetry as a building "towering among the clouds." In the Administrative Building, which is on a low level, I used insulation materials, and the floor is almost on the same level as the ground. However, it also adopted the method of allowing rainwater to drain off from the upper parts of the horizontal louvers gradually down to the lower parts. The path of the rainwater was incorporated in the design of the outside of the building. This is probably reminiscent of the common sight in Japan of rice paddies arranged in step-like patterns down a mountain slope.

With this design, whenever the rain starts to fall, and whenever it stops falling, the water path will remain; and in time, the designs carved by the water will be added to the shape of the horizontal louvers. The same concept was also followed to emphasize further the variations of color made by the rain. The length of the eaves was adjusted with this in mind, and the provisional frames were made of two different materials: wood and plastic. The sand used in the concrete contained large amounts of iron. It is expected that with the passage of time, the concrete as a whole will assume a reddish hue.

These problems of the effects of aging are not easy problems that can be solved simply by using a weather meter. I believe that the problem of aging is a question of a gradual dialogue between architecture and nature, and it can be solved only by learning many things from the old, traditional architecture.

In addition, the relation between man and architecture is of the utmost importance. The question of scale is often brought up. In the Administrative Building of the Izumo Shrine, it was decided to adopt an external appearance with deeply carved features and a surface texture with many wrinkles and creases. In this way, one can produce variations in the shadows depending upon the sun's angle, and the appearance of the building changes as one approaches it. Graphic designer Awazu Kiyoshi designed the steel grille doors in front. These doors change their appearance from moment to moment as one approaches them. The striped design has great depth. The flat, smooth design on the front surface of the building is plain. The building resembles a desert; it shimmers when the sun rises and becomes cold when the sun sets. However, I think that this method of adopting deeply carved, wrinkled features in architecture will produce warm, deeply refined buildings like the bark of a huge tree that has long withstood the ravages of wind and snow. Such a building will undoubtedly have much to say to man. However, not all parts of a building need to have such a profoundly refined design, and not all parts need to be able to endure for equally long periods of time. In some parts, one ought to adopt the method of periodic replacement and renewal so that they will always be able to shine with a newness and to have a delightful design. In the Izumo Administrative Building, the uses of concrete and wood are based on this concept. Wood was used in finishing the interior, which was treated as living equipment, having a more human warmth. In the final analysis, the beauty of space must be a stable, dignified, refined beauty, and the beauty of things on the living dimensions must be something delightful and kaleidoscopically changing.

Finally, I should like to say a few words concerning the relations between the several buildings standing within the sacred precincts at Izumo. When one designs buildings, there are always superior and subordinate buildings; only when this is so can any order come into being. By "order" I mean mutual relations and hierarchical relations. Mutual and hierarchical relations are necessary in all parts: in the grouping of the buildings, in the basic structures, in the choice of materials, and in the coloring. I believe that human values play a very important role in seeking out this order, which determines what is the center and what is in a subordinate relation to it.

At Izumo, the sanctuary building is definitely predominant, and all the other buildings are subordinate. In like manner, the Izumo Administrative Building must also be subordinate. The relations between superior and subordinate are relations between large and small, between strong and weak, between high and low. However, the relation must also be a mutual one. The superior must be made to stand out by the presence of the subordinate, and the superior must enable the subordinate to fulfill its functions well. There must be a relation of high tension between them.

I think that only great human values will be able to produce a great order. It is this order that is the very essence of architecture. In other words, we may say that human values are the determining factors that give orientation to architecture. They are order and concept. Consequently, technology devoid of human values and function lacking human values are both meaningless. Similarly, human values lacking technology and human values ignoring function are equally meaningless. This is why a design methodology becomes necessary, and why one must take cognizance of technology and function in their correct perspective within the framework of the methodology.

It is my view that human values are elevated and enriched as history advances. Old tradition is old order, and new order will create a new tradition. That which we must learn from old tradition is this order. And we are required to display a new order by means of new forms.

In conclusion, I would like to devote a few thoughts to new forms and old tradition in Japan. As representative examples of Japan's traditional architecture, one might mention the Ise Shrines and the Katsura Imperial Villa. These buildings each have in common their qualities of delicacy, refinement, and freshness. I agree that they are superb examples of Japanese traditional architecture. But I also think that there is another genealogical line, characterized by daringness, simplicity, and vastness of scope. This line is presented by Izumo, Itsukushima, and Kiyomizu.

Not only are these two trends antithetical in their forms, but they are also antithetical in the order that they display. If one is more symbolic, then the other is more rational. If one is sensuous, the other is more technological. And if we examine the historical background of the periods in which these buildings were constructed, we note that the Ise Shrines and the Katsura Imperial Villa were constructed in the periods of ripe maturity of their respective epochs, while Izumo, Itsukushima, and Kiyomizu were constructed at the dawning of their respective eras.

When we bear this in mind, it becomes self-evident what we contemporaries should select from the old tradition, what we ought to learn from it, what we ought to inherit from it, and what new elements we ought to add to it. Here we should not confine ourselves merely to form alone. We ought to devote ourselves to the technological actualities and to deal with tradition as a whole, including also the essential order.

If we are to deal with architecture for man in the new democratic society, we can say that the new forms should be established on the basis of a rejection of old traditional forms. The new forms should be neither for the gods nor for the powerful, but must be merely for man.

Therefore, the architecture of tomorrow should not be an architecture for the machine. It should not be an architecture for the sake of technology. It must be an architecture created for the sake of man in a truly organized state. This is the task of Japanese contemporary architecture and our responsibility in creating new forms.

1964

PROJECTS

Text by Ken Tadashi Oshima

Diagrams of the Sky House transformation, 1958–85.

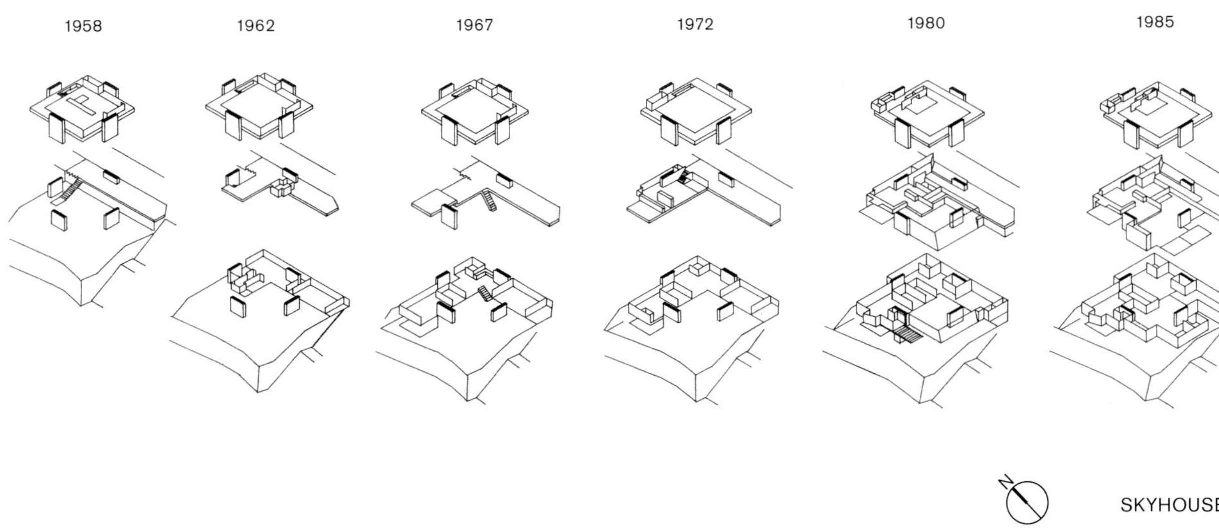

SKY HOUSE

Tokyo, 1958–85

An architect's ability is said to be best judged from the house he lives in. I think there is some truth in the saying, and so I decided to make the building of my own house the very first project of my career as an architect.

—Kikutake Kiyonori, 1960

At age 30, Kikutake gained international acclaim for the design of his own 10-square-meter Sky House, which addressed the basic requirements of dwelling. The concrete waffle-slab platform suspended 6.6 meters above the ground by four piers originally afforded lofty views of a low-rise residential district adjacent to Gokokuji Temple. For Kikutake, the reconsideration of family life was the revisiting of the dwelling as a "fundamental resistance unit" to protect against earthquakes, floods, typhoons, fire, emergencies, illness, noise, and pollution. During the period of post–World War II reconstruction, Kikutake conducted research on the traditional Japanese wooden house, focusing on aspects of its replaceable elements that became a basis for his Metabolic thinking of an architecture able to embrace change. While maintaining the human-scale proportions of his family home in Kyūshū, Kikutake kept the main square living platform free of internal structure and permanent utilities as a single room covered by a hyperbolic paraboloid concrete shell roof, with a movable furniture unit ("movenette") system. This included kitchen and bathroom units, kept to the edges of the plan and easily replaced as necessary. In addressing the challenge to adapt traditional *tatami*-mat living within a modern house, Kikutake embraced movable elements include sliding *shoji* screens, which together with the verandahs on all four sides evoke a distinctly Japanese domestic character while maximizing light, air flow, and view.

Kikutake's home embodies his quest "to create an environment that nurtures rich sensibility within the local culture and climate by looking at dwellings with a broader vision."[1] As a composition of "served" and "servant" spaces, Kikutake's design found resonance with Louis Kahn, who visited the house in May 1960 while attending the World Design Conference in Tokyo; the two became close friends. Although Kikutake noted that they did not talk extensively about the Sky House, its close connection with Kahn's designs can be seen in the basic plan structure of his Richards Medical Center (1957–65) and combination of concrete platforms with wood infill in the Salk Institute (1959–65). The Sky House's primary living space has served as a platform for architectural discourse with other Kikutake guests, including Peter Smithson and Rem Koolhaas.

Over time, the Sky House came to epitomize Metabolist ideals of an architecture built for change. Originally Kikutake lived with his wife on the upper floor and ran his design office from space tucked under the parking area. Upon the expansion of his family, he hung a children's movenette on the structure in 1962, accessed by a ladder through the living platform above. In 1977, the main level was converted entirely into a living room, the middle floor was expanded, the kitchen and dining room became an entrance, and the area underneath was remade as a sunroom and bedrooms. In 1985, the sunroom became the main living room, with various private rooms arranged around it. After more than half a century, the Sky House continues to stand robustly, served well by critical details including its 25-centimeter overhang to protect the wooden screens below.

1 Interview with Kikutake Kiyonori by Imamura Souhei, June 19, 2009, "Sky House," in George Wagner, ed., *Tokyo from Vancouver* (Vancouver: UBC School of Architecture, 2014), 89.

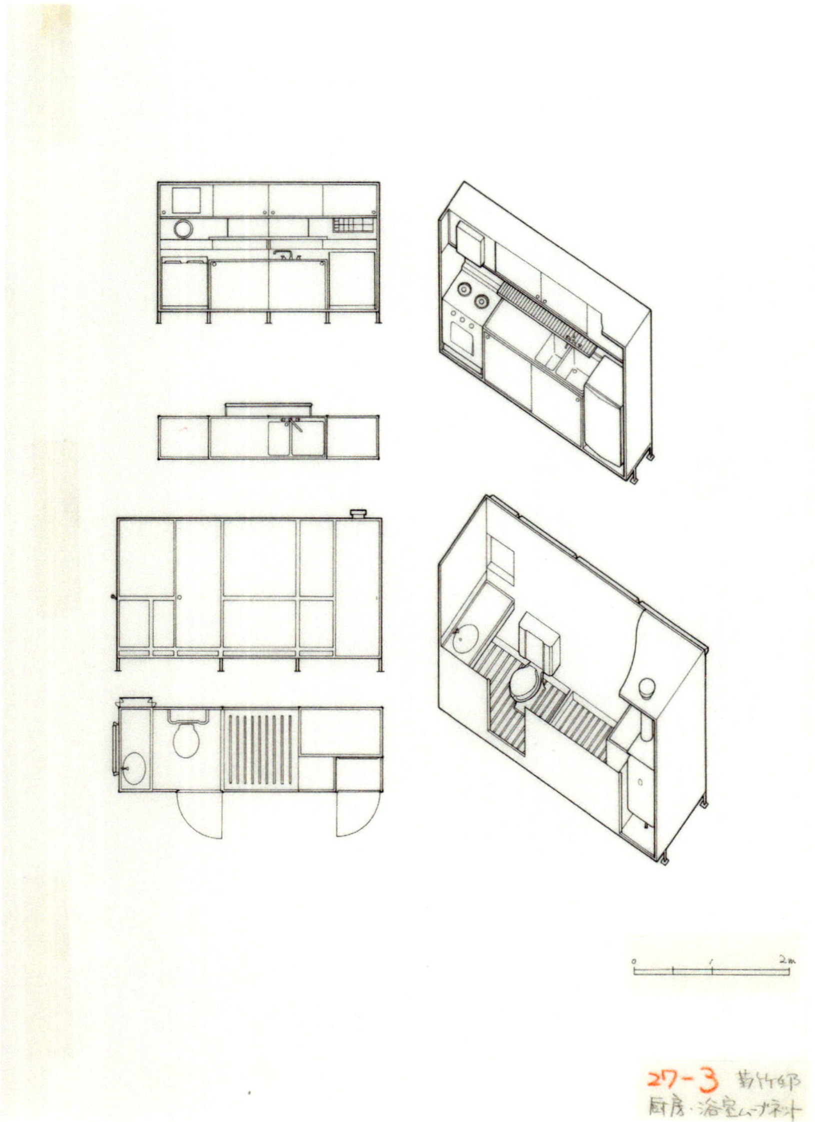
0
1
2m
27-3 菊竹邸
厨房・浴室ムーブネット

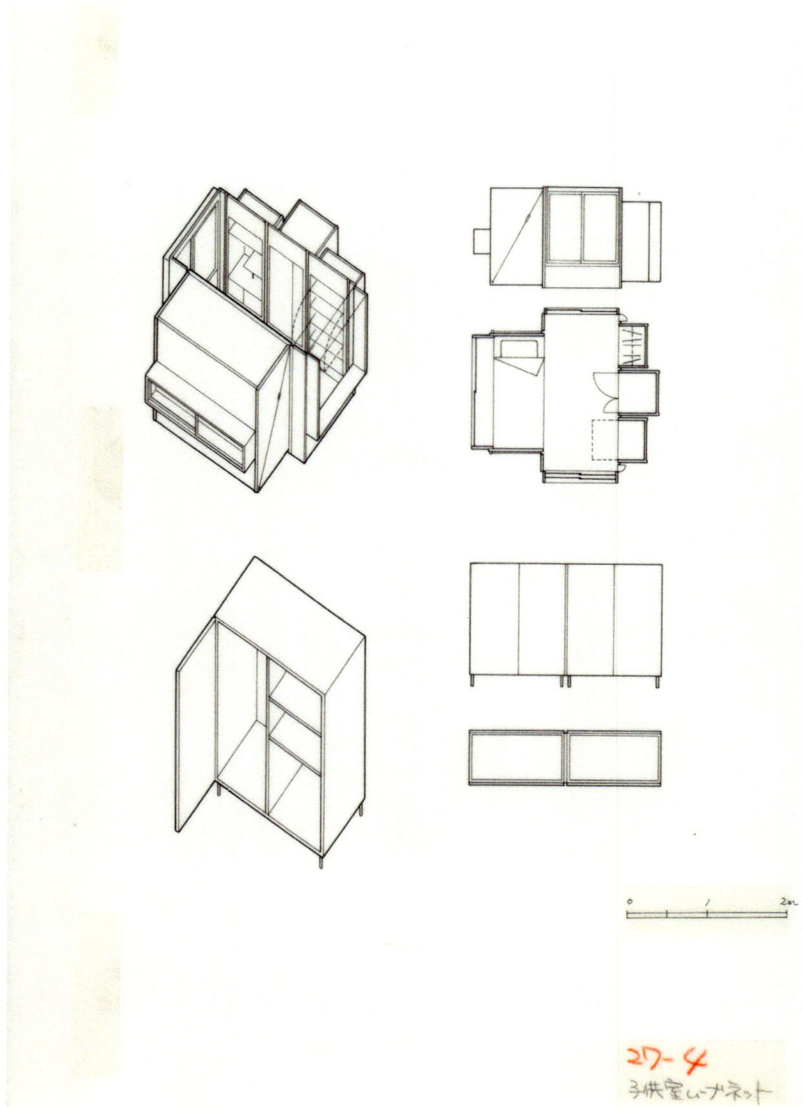
0
1
2m
27-4
子供室ムーブネット

Kitchen and bath movenettes.

Children's room movenette.

First-floor plan.

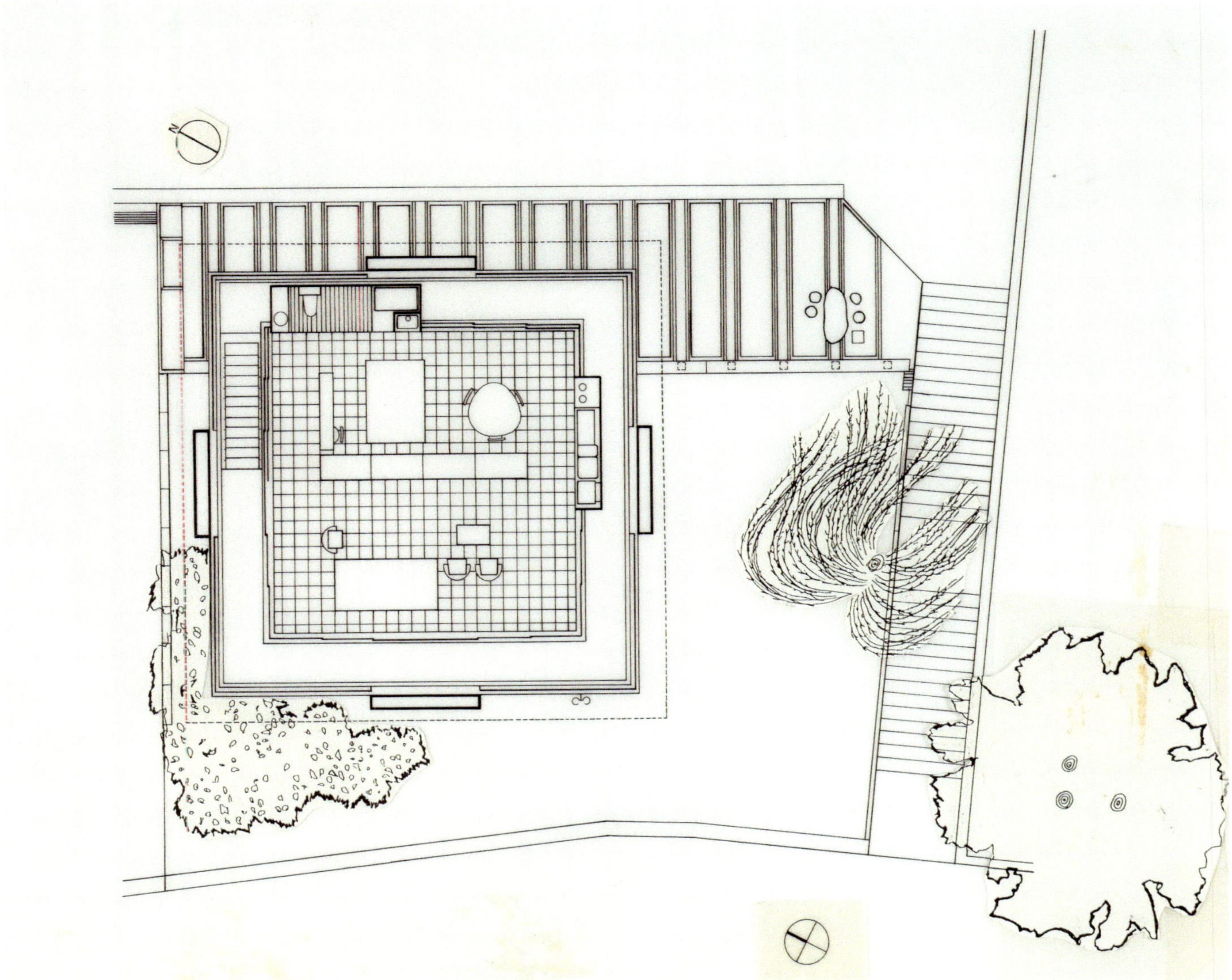

View of model from west
with children's room movenette
below.

Aerial view from south.

Southwest elevation.

View from north circa 1958.

Southeast elevation circa 2014.

View from south.

View from east with children's movenette.

Verandah.

View of living room circa 1958.

View of living room circa 2008.

Axonometric view of structure.

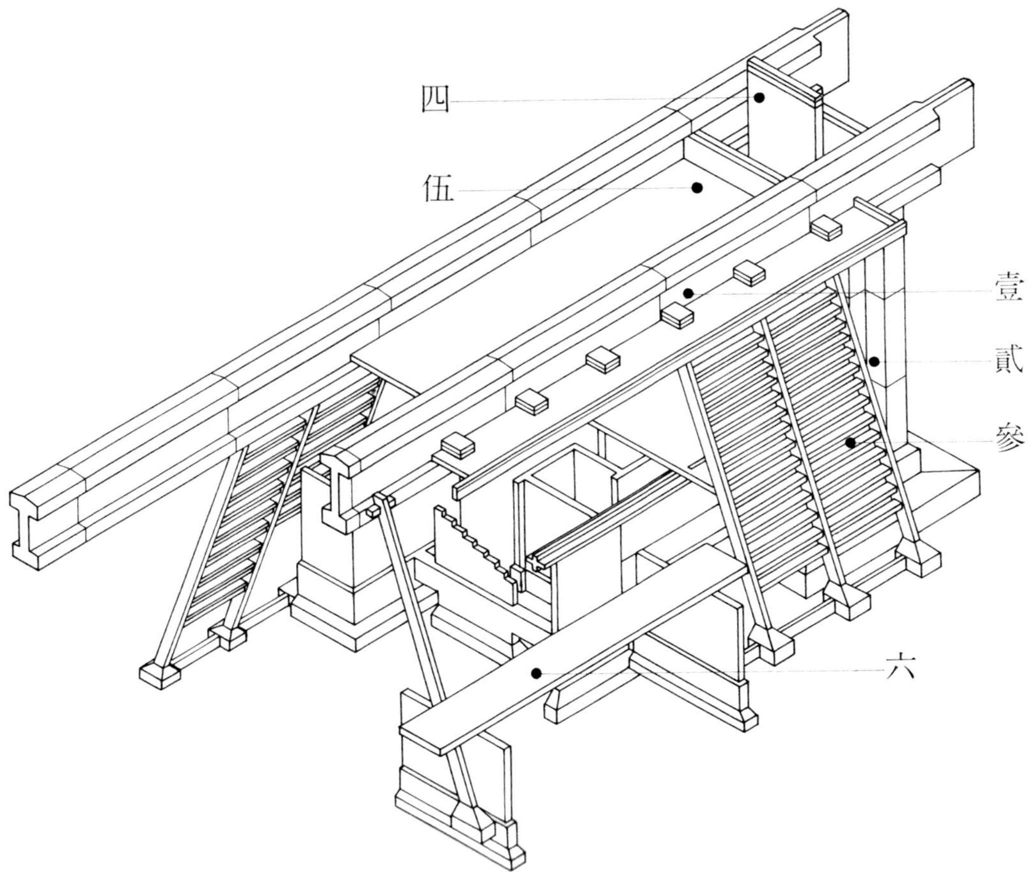

ADMINISTRATIVE BUILDING OF IZUMO SHRINE

Izumo, Shimane Prefecture, 1963, 1980

For this structure adjacent to one of the oldest and most important Shinto shrines in Japan, Kikutake's scheme used state-of-the-art construction technology of pre-stressed precast concrete to rebuild the original administration building, which had been lost to fire. Two 50-meter super-beams span rectangular blocks at each end of the building, with a cascade of precast concrete members forming a curtain wall, producing a vast columnless interior space. The curtain wall is a cascading rain gutter inspired by the irrigation technology of rice-paddy agriculture, and the overall form takes inspiration from the traditional *inakake* rice-drying rack. In contrast to the horizontality of the overall composition, Kikutake employed a hyperbolic paraboloid concrete shell adjacent to the promenade to the upper level and a curvilinear grill entry by Awazu Kiyoshi, evoking images of clouds through line patterns based on fingerprints. Changes to the area since completion include additional adjacent buildings that block the full view of the front horizontal elevation, Kikutake's design of the Shrine Repository (1981), and the reconstruction of the main shrine in 2013.

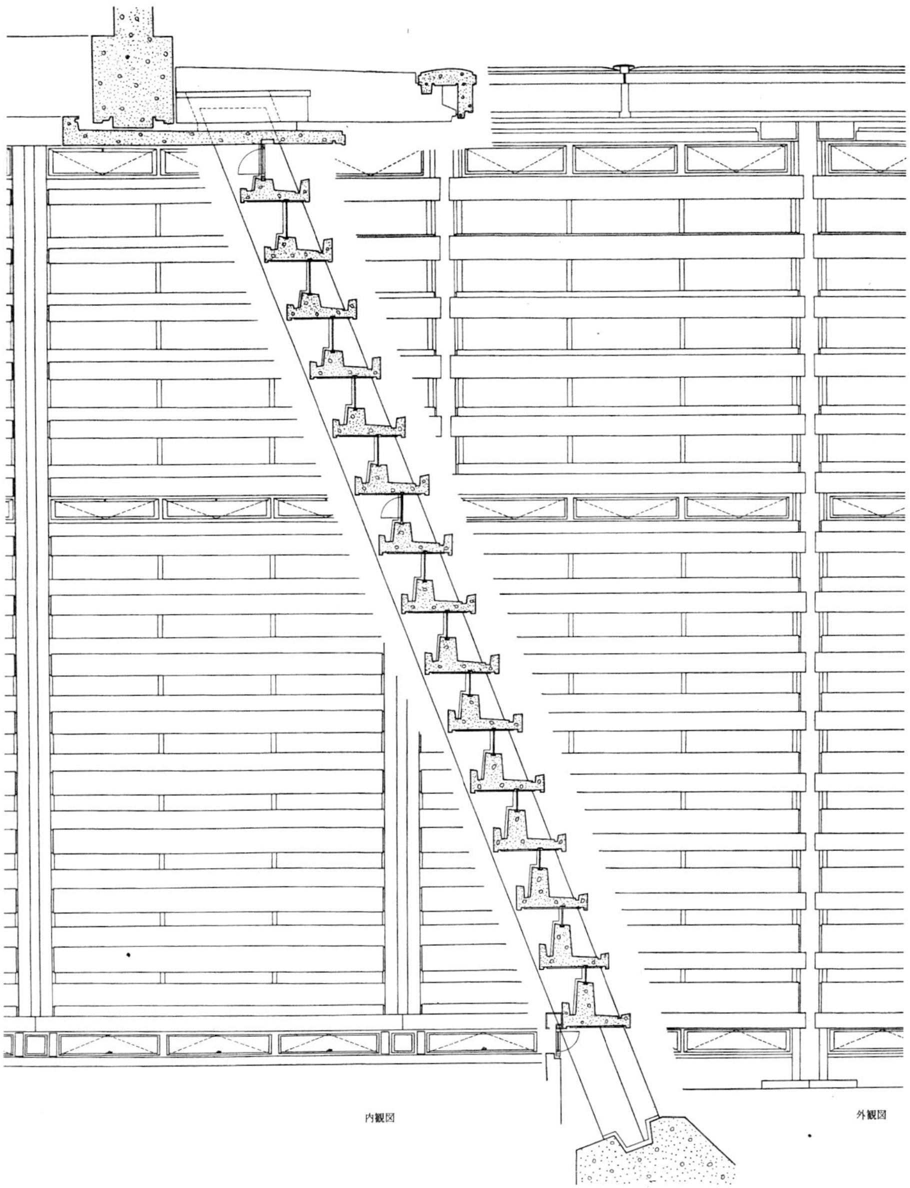
内観図
外観図

Precast concrete screen section, detail.

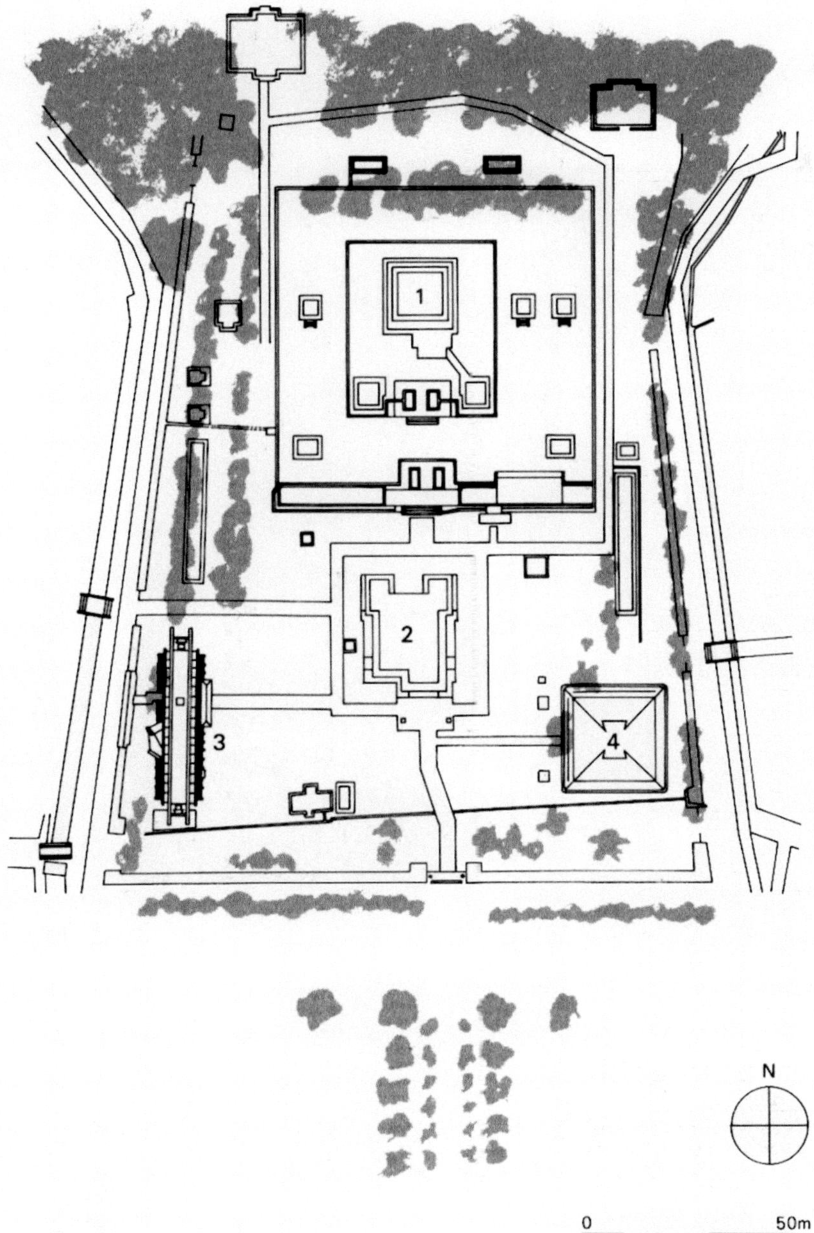

Site plan. 1: main shrine, 2: front shrine, 3: Administrative Building, 4: Shrine Repository.

View of model from south.

View from northeast.

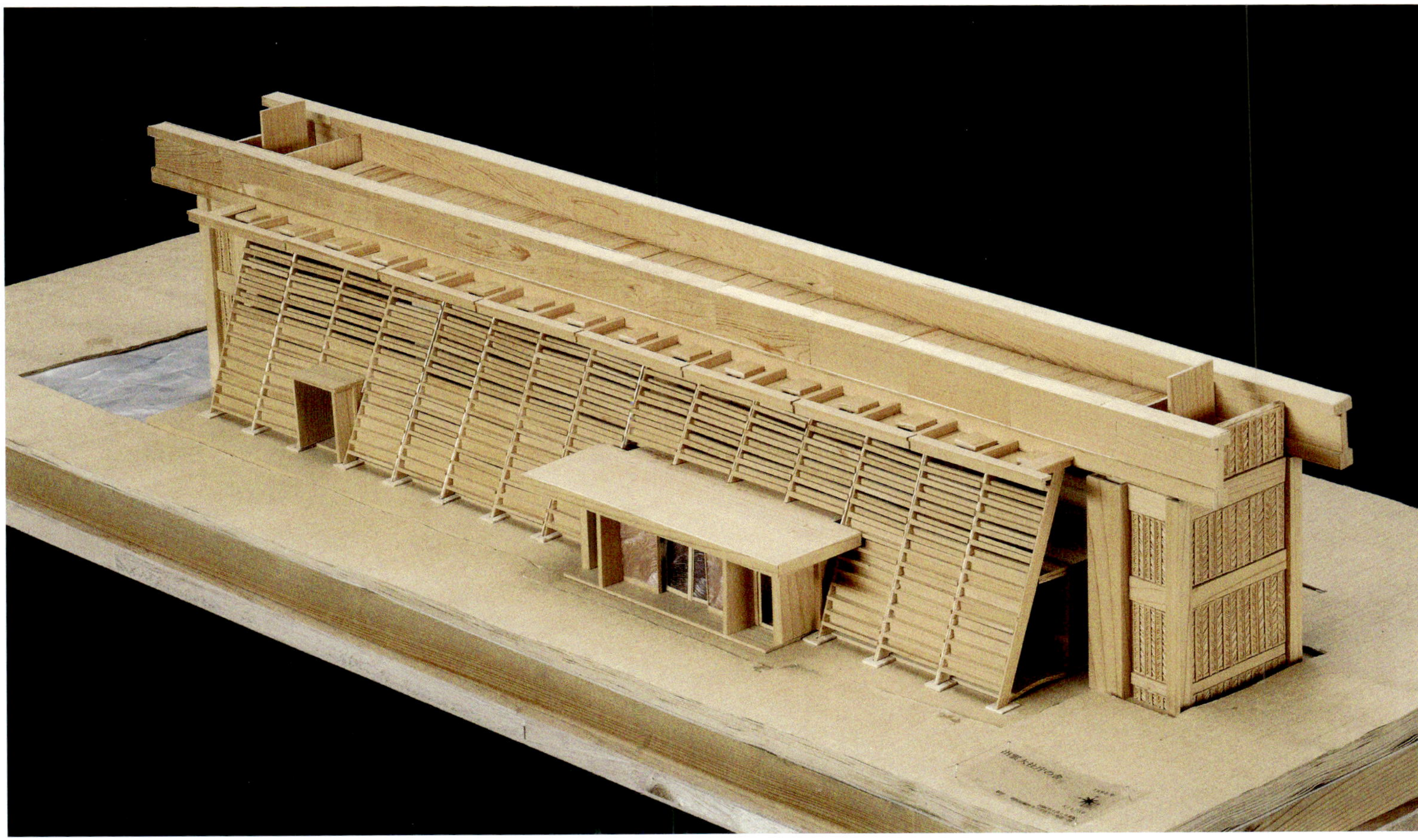

Chief priests returning from the opening ceremony of the Administrative Building.

Interior looking south.

East screen door by Awazu Kiyoshi.

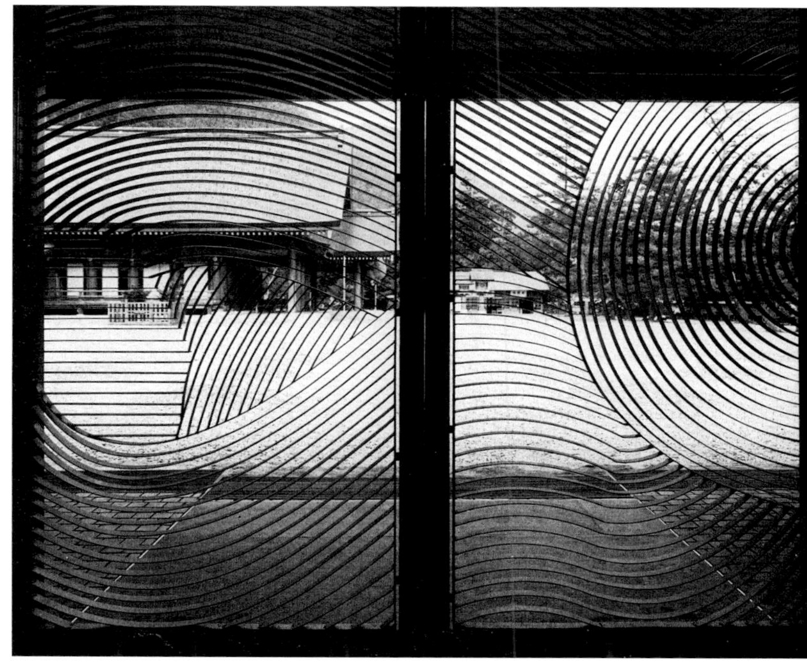

Planning model for competition.

KYOTO INTERNATIONAL CONFERENCE HALL COMPETITION PLAN

1963

In developing this scheme for elevated conference halls around a cloister-shaped lobby, Kikutake extended the conception of the elevated ground plane from the domestic realm of the Sky House to the truly public realm. The design is based on the notion that a continuous elevated plane would both provide spectacular views of the surrounding Kyoto landscape—akin to the Tatebayashi City Hall (1963)—and promote productive adjacencies between the conference hall, organizers, secretariat personnel, delegates, reporters, and other observers. In an inverted square pyramid with the greatest floor area above, administration offices are located below. The superstructure of pre-stressed concrete beams, columns, and bracket arms recall the *hijiki* traditional Japanese wood-frame bracketry system as an open-ended metabolic strategy of transformation. Although Ōtani Sachio (1924–2013) won the competition, Kikutake's drawings express a high level of design refinement, including seat and skylight details.

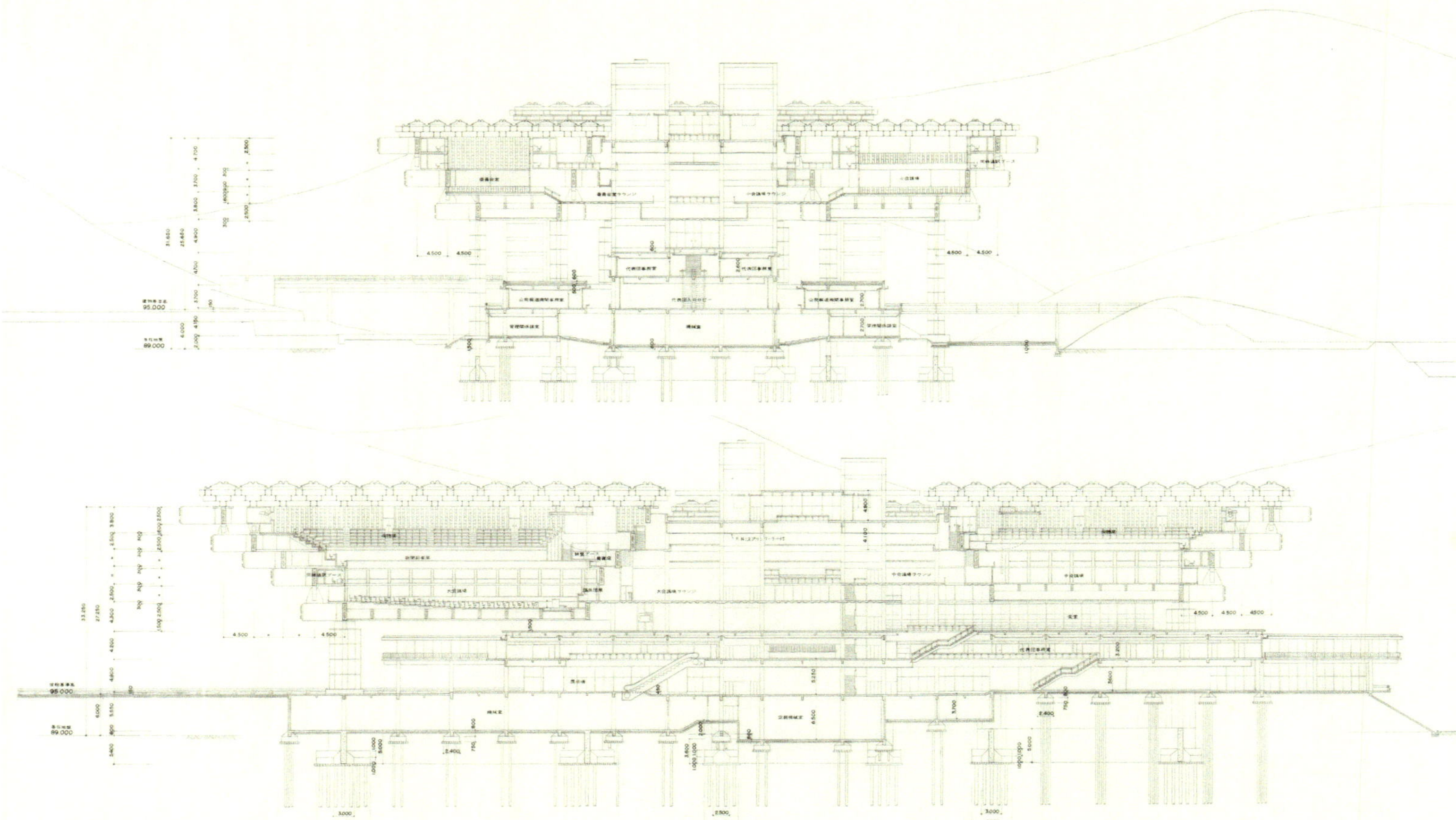

17 断面図 — 1:200
国立国際会館設計競技応募図案

Sections.

Section detail.

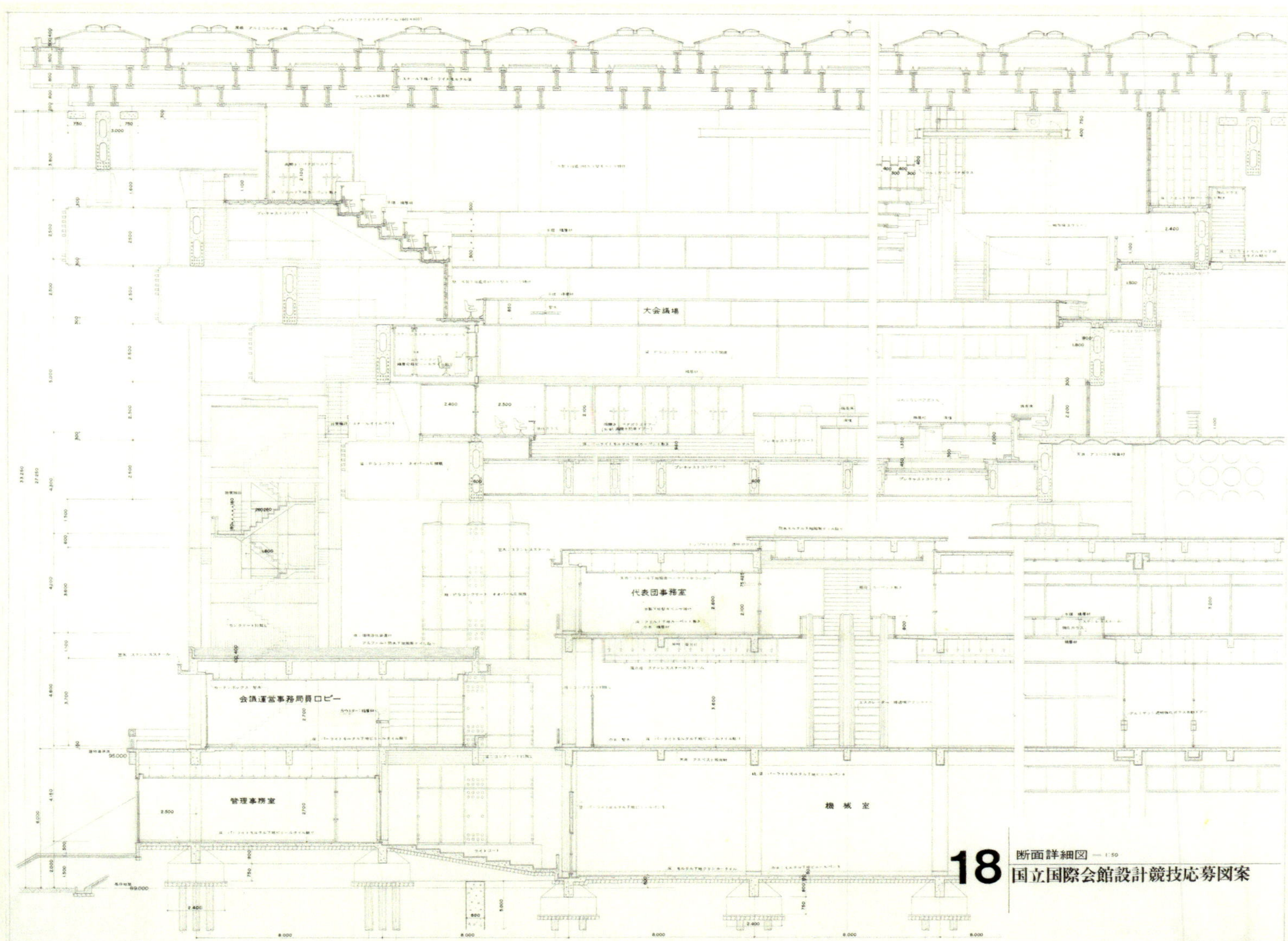

Model, detail of roof structure.

Model, entry view.

HOTEL TŌKŌEN

Yonago City, Tottori Prefecture, 1964

Located on the coast of the Japan Sea at the Kaike hot springs, this monumental hotel links Metabolic architecture with the broader social and environmental context. To avoid the unsightly and undesirable spatial effects of concrete columns within *tatami*-mat interiors, Kikutake collaborated with structural engineer Matsui Gengo (1920–1996) to conceive of this eight-story hotel structure as an assembly of six primary columns, each with three auxiliary tie-beams—a new framework for a modern Japanese hotel. Such an ingenious arrangement finds precedents in the *nukibari* wood-frame super-assembly of the *torii* gate at Itsukushima Shrine and the beam assembly of the Heian-period Byōdōin. At Tōkōen, the seventh-floor superbeam supports the fifth and sixth floors, providing for suspended platforms open to the surrounding views of the sea and mountains. The hotel's tripartite organization consists of guest rooms as the "main space," vestibules and lobby as the connective public "subspace," and the interstitial infrastructural space for administrative functions. From the main entrance, one passes through the gateway of the double-height lobby that is shaped by the character of the column assemblies and the Japanese garden designed by Nagare Masayuki (1923–) to the north. The ingenious cantilevered open-truss stair features landings that serve structurally as a balancing moment, while glazed elevators offer views of the garden and surrounding terrain to the guest rooms, fourth-floor open terrace, and a rooftop restaurant capped by a hyperbolic paraboloid shell roof, which presents a complementary peak to the surrounding landscape. The hotel design is completed as a total work of art by wall murals of oversize *kanji* characters by Awazu Kiyoshi (1929–2009) and sculptures by Mukai Ryōkichi (1918–2010).

The hotel has expressed its Metabolist character over time, as Kikutake's hotel design first expanded on the tradition of an existing Japanese inn, which was then extended through the addition of auxiliary wings over subsequent years, while interior room configurations have been modified to suit the changing demands of guests.

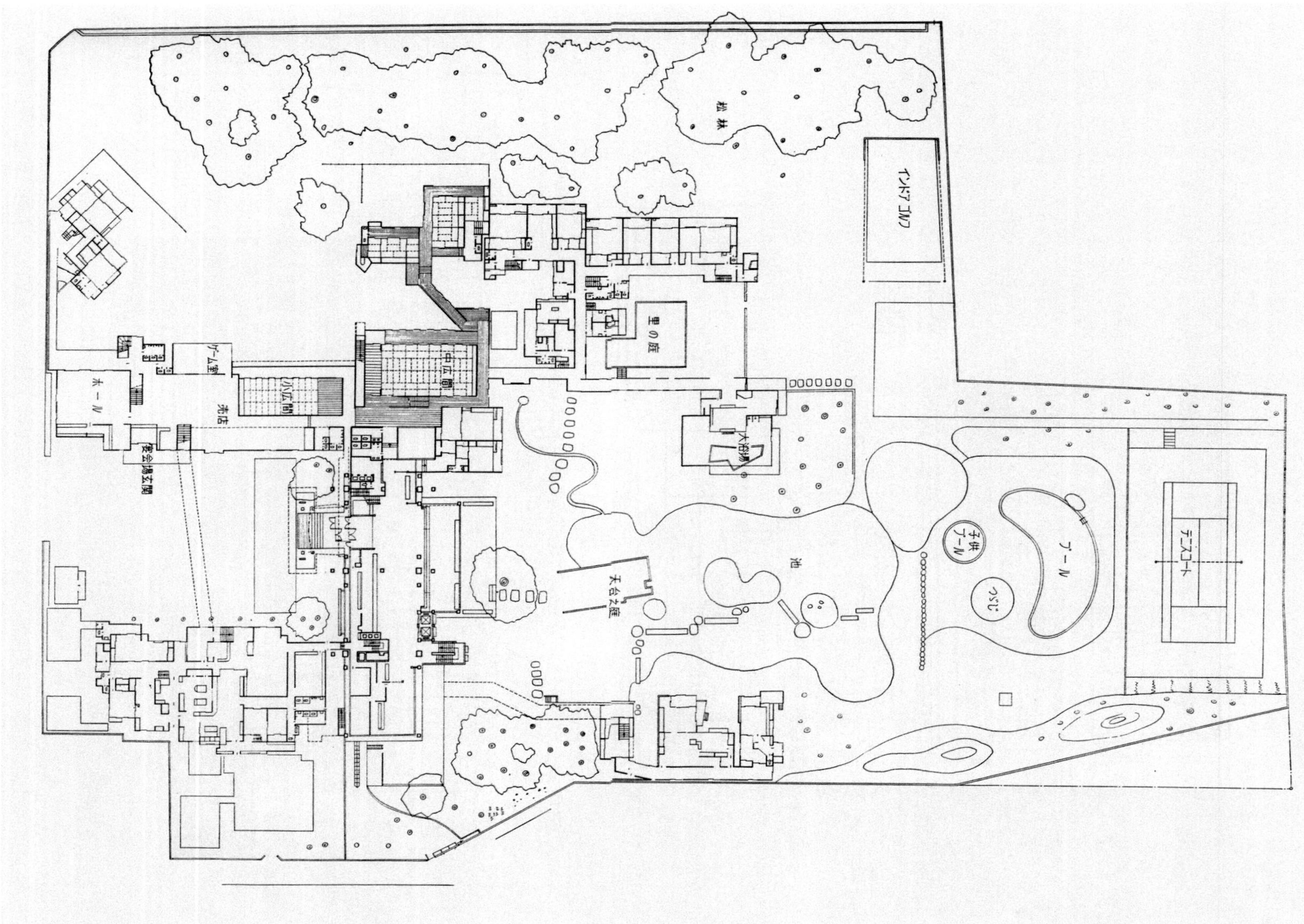

松林
インドアゴルフ
里の庭
中広間
小広間
ゲーム室
ホール
売店
宴会場玄関
大浴場
池
天台之庭
子供プール
プール
テニスコート

Ground-level floor plan and site plan.

First-, third-, and fifth-floor plans.

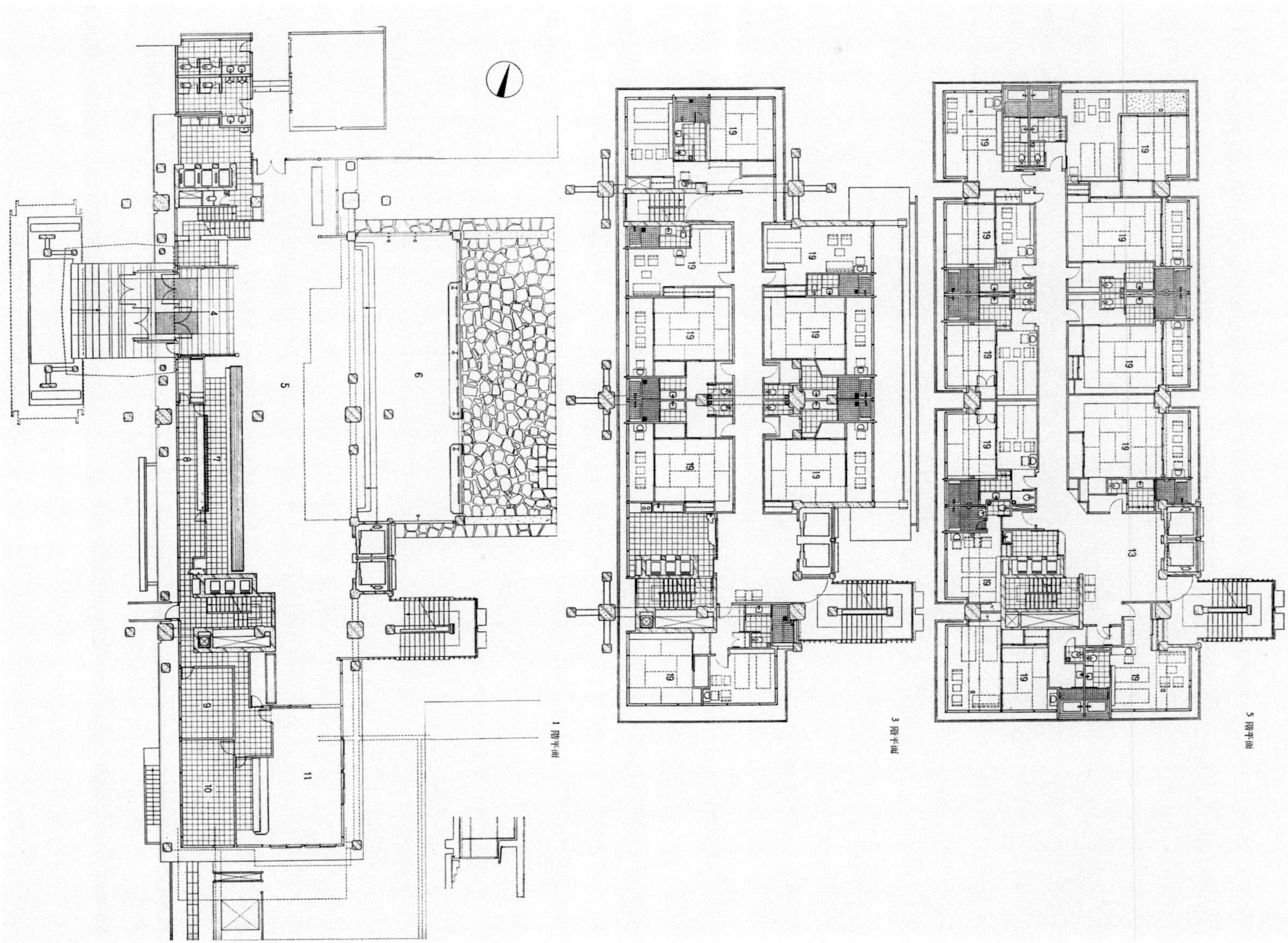

断面図

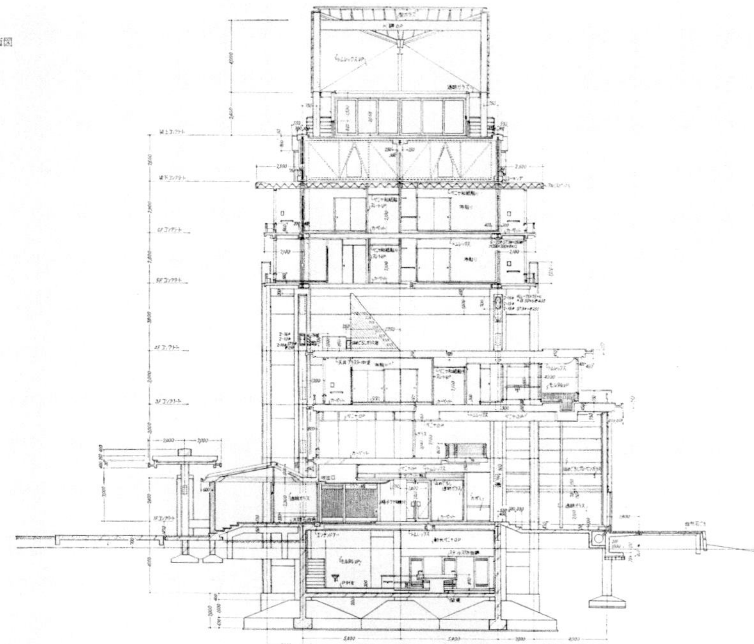

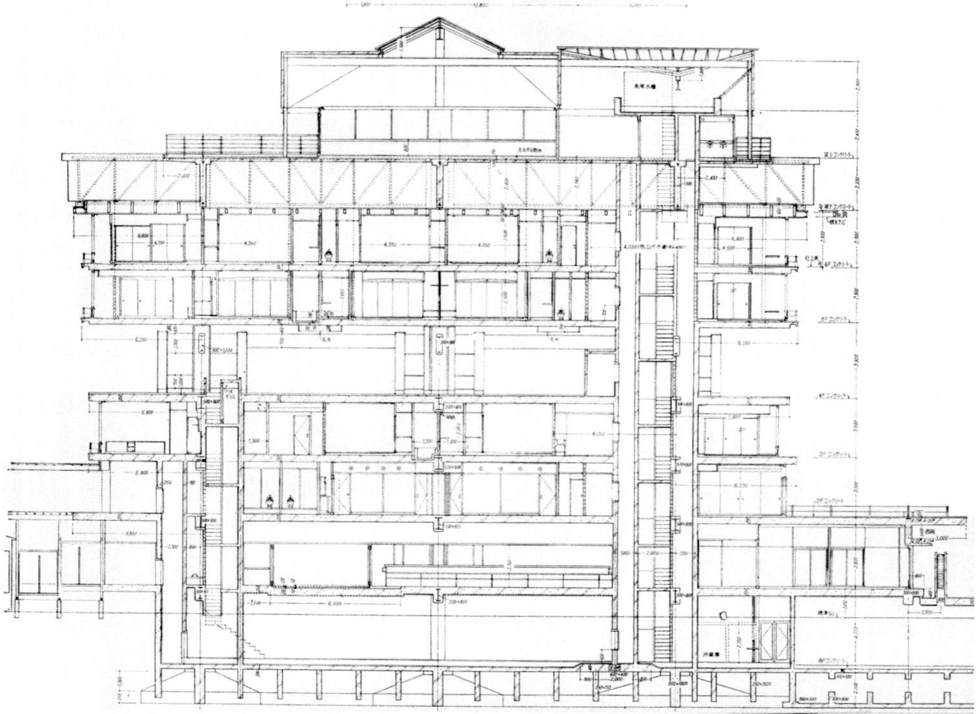

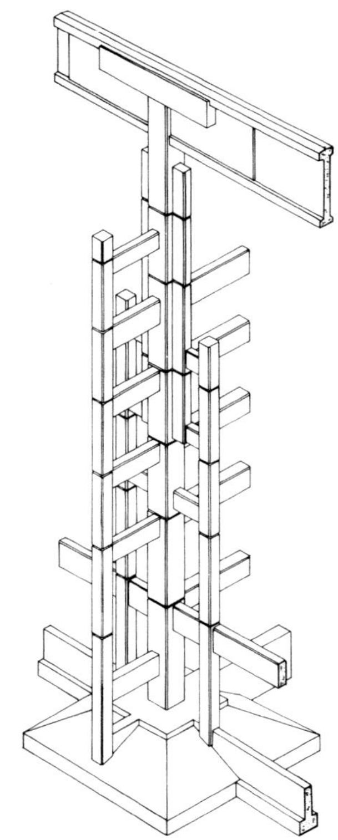

Sections.

Isometric column diagram.

East elevation.

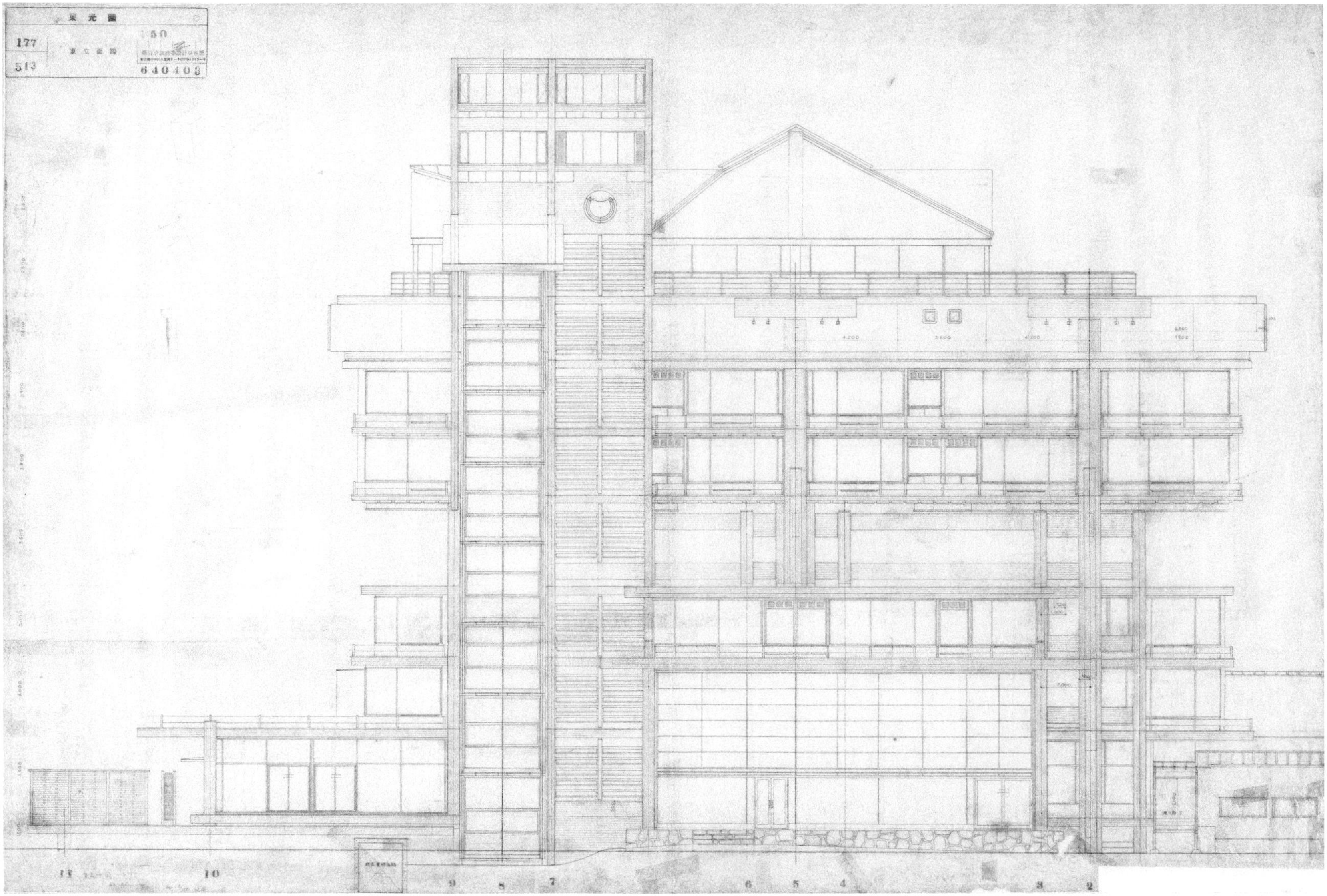

East facade with garden by Nagare Masayuki.

View from west with the Mt. Karasugasen and Daisen in the distance.

TOKUUNJI TEMPLE COLUMBARIUM

Kurume City, Fukuoka Prefecture, 1965

Located in Kikutake's hometown, this columbarium at the back of the Tokuunji Temple complex provides a space to contemplate death and life through the encounter with the souls of those housed within niches for 170 families in this concrete structure surrounded by greenery. The visitor confronts a 25-meter-long rectangular volume, with its concrete floor slab hovering 1.2 meters above a reflecting pool. Kikutake effectively dematerializes the mass of the concrete walls; 60-millimeter concrete walls hung 1.8 meters from the ceiling hover above the floor, leaving a 0.3-meter gap. Visitors who experience this floating sensation may either approach in peace or in dynamic dialogue: kids may play in the water or families picnic on site, especially during Buddhist services held at the equinox.

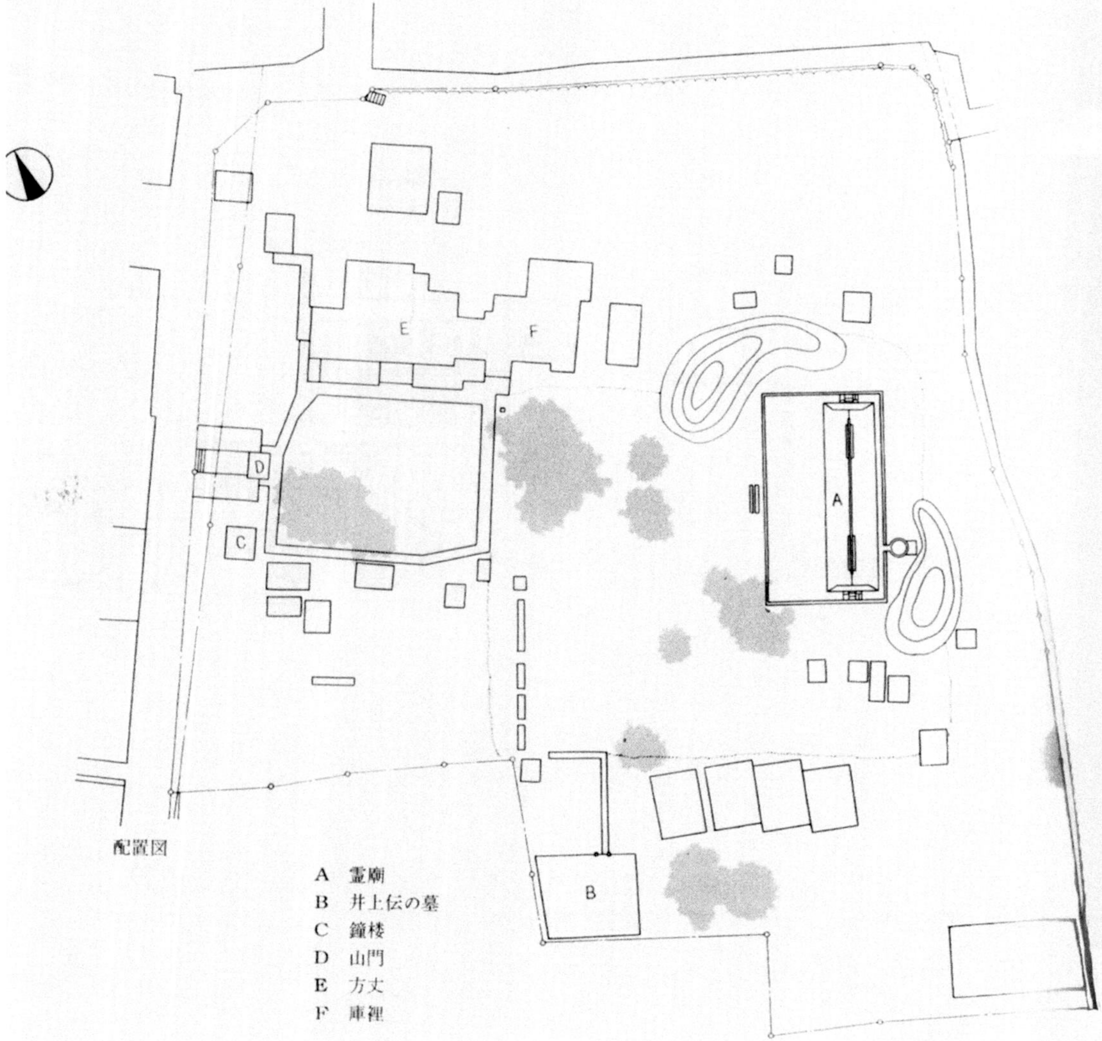

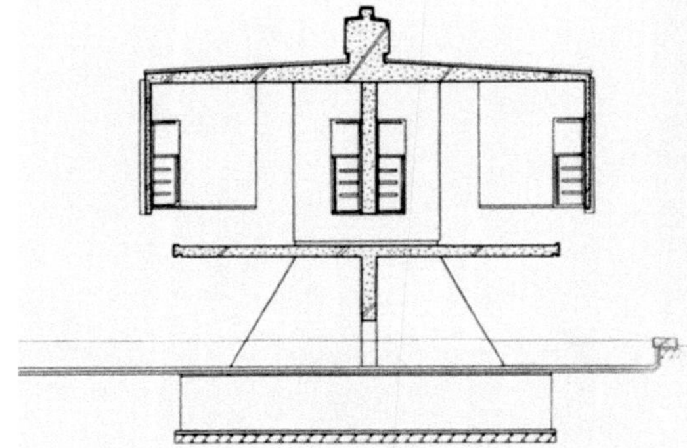

配置図

A 霊廟
B 井上伝の墓
C 鐘楼
D 山門
E 方丈
F 庫裡

Site plan.

Section.

Plan, longitudinal section.

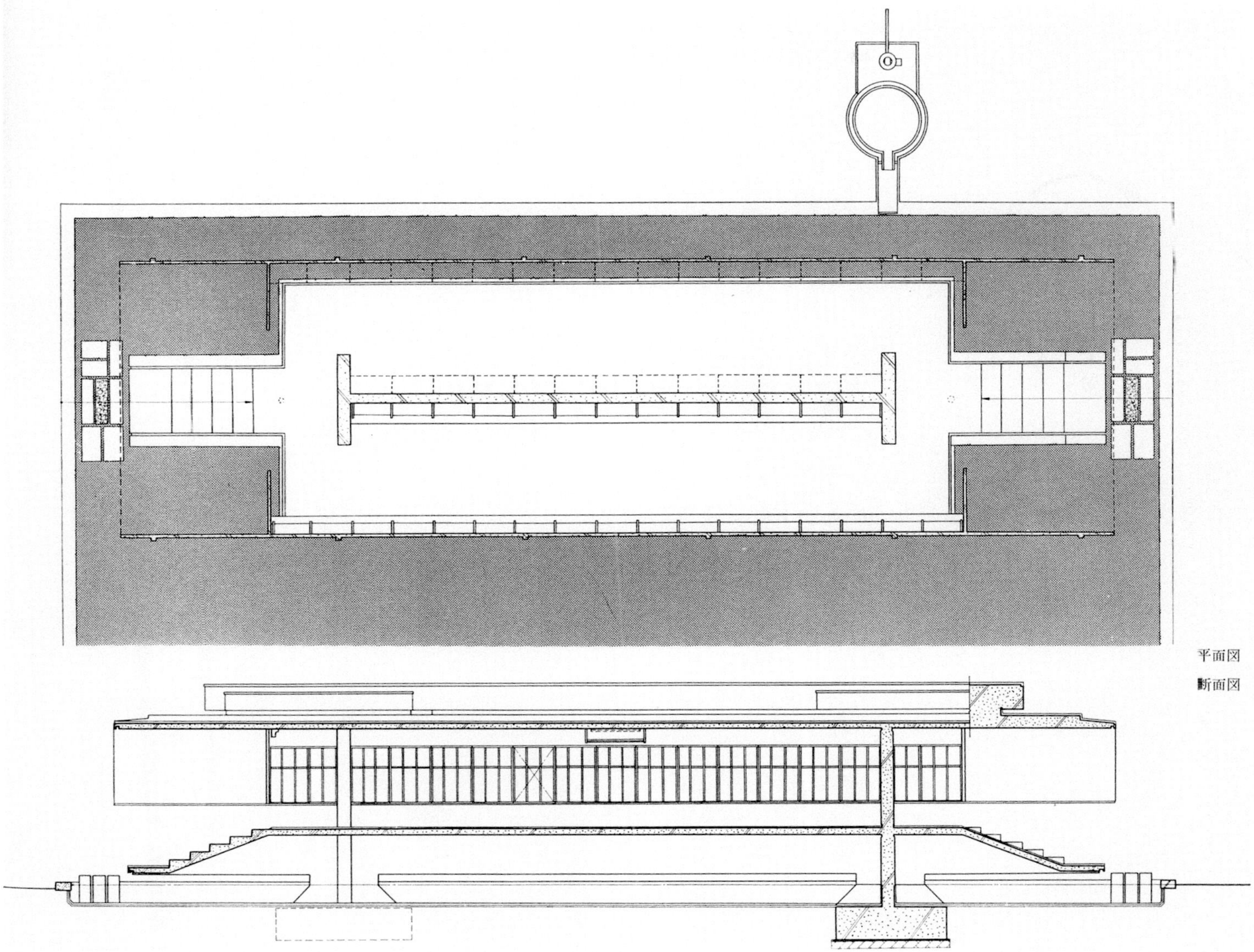

View of entry circa 2013.

View of entry circa 1965.

West elevation.

Photo collage.
Sectional perspective of
Tree-Shaped Housing.

PROTOTYPE OF MASS HOUSING/ TREE-SHAPED HOUSING

1966–(unbuilt)

Houses and housing were integrally linked for Kikutake, whose schemes envisioned elevated living platforms with common gardens and gathering spaces below. To maintain social cohesion, Kikutake limited groupings to five levels and conceived the spaces in-between as sites of social interaction.

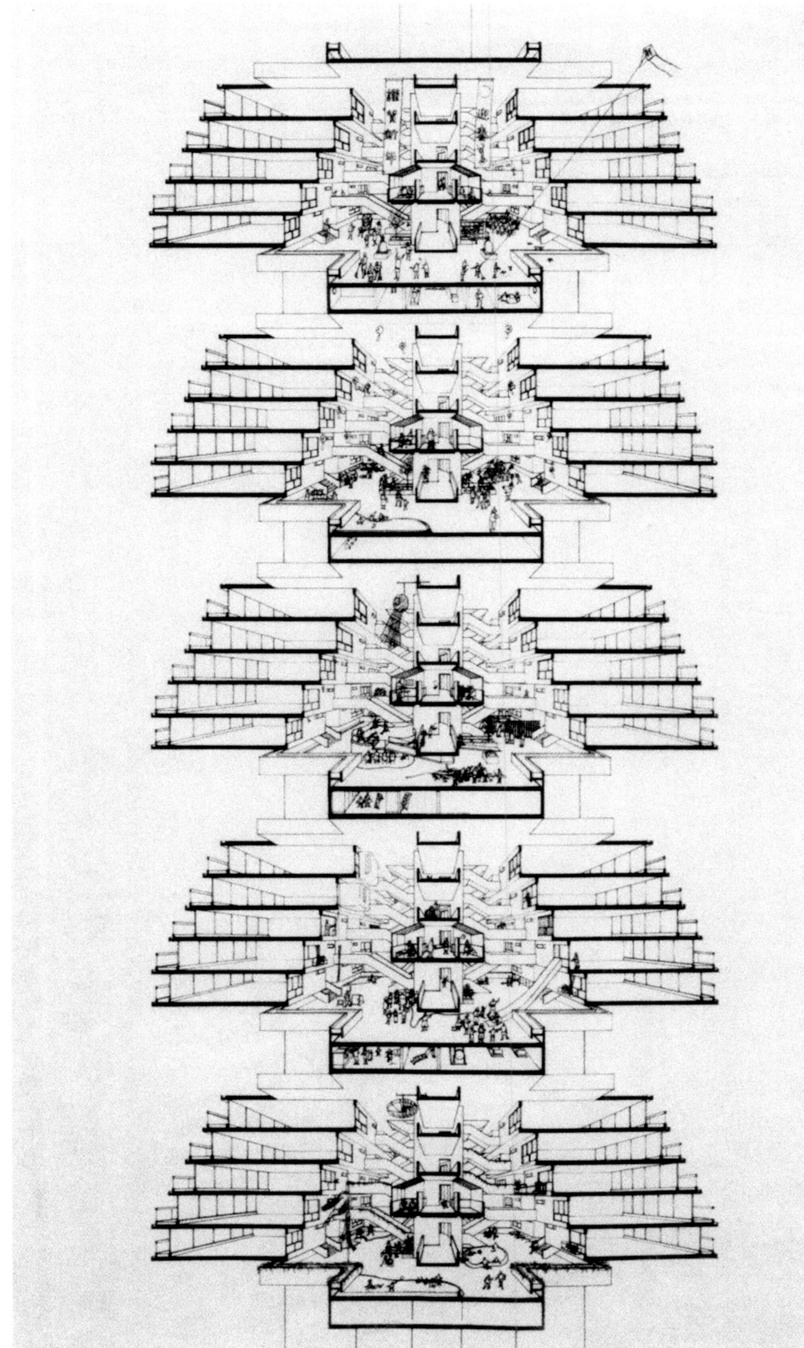

Sketch.

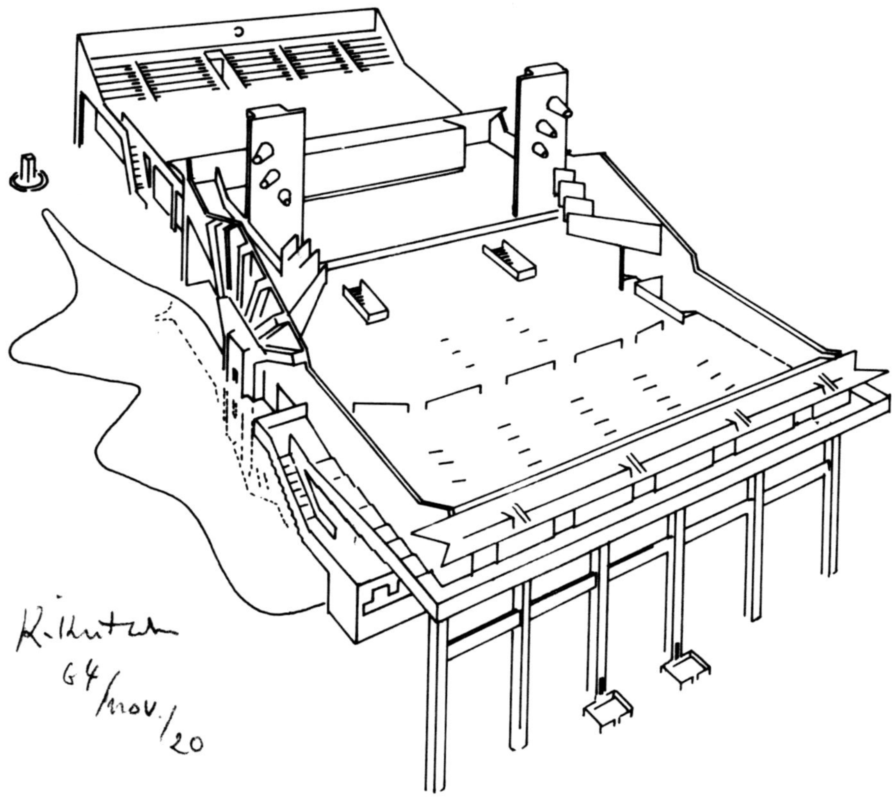

MIYAKONOJŌ CIVIC CENTER

Miyazaki City, Miyazaki Prefecture, 1966

Kikutake sought to differentiate between changing and unchanging elements in designing this civic center with a 1,400-seat auditorium for this provincial capital on the island of Kyūshū. The profile of the baby-carriage-like steel-frame roof volume, rising above a reinforced concrete platform, defines the city's skyline in contrast with the surrounding mountains. The roof structure was constructed primarily using standardized components (including truss tension bars and wooden window mullions) and left structural members exposed to allow for ease of replacement according to technological and social changes over time. The concrete column structure supporting seating above defines the lobby space, akin to the structure of Kiyomizu Temple. Based on a consideration of what should be seen and what not seen, the primary form derives its shape from considerations of sound, light, and space, with the servant functions (including mechanical systems and audio equipment) concentrated in the central concrete base. Following a campaign to preserve the hall in 2007, it is now under the jurisdiction of the Minami Kyūshū University.

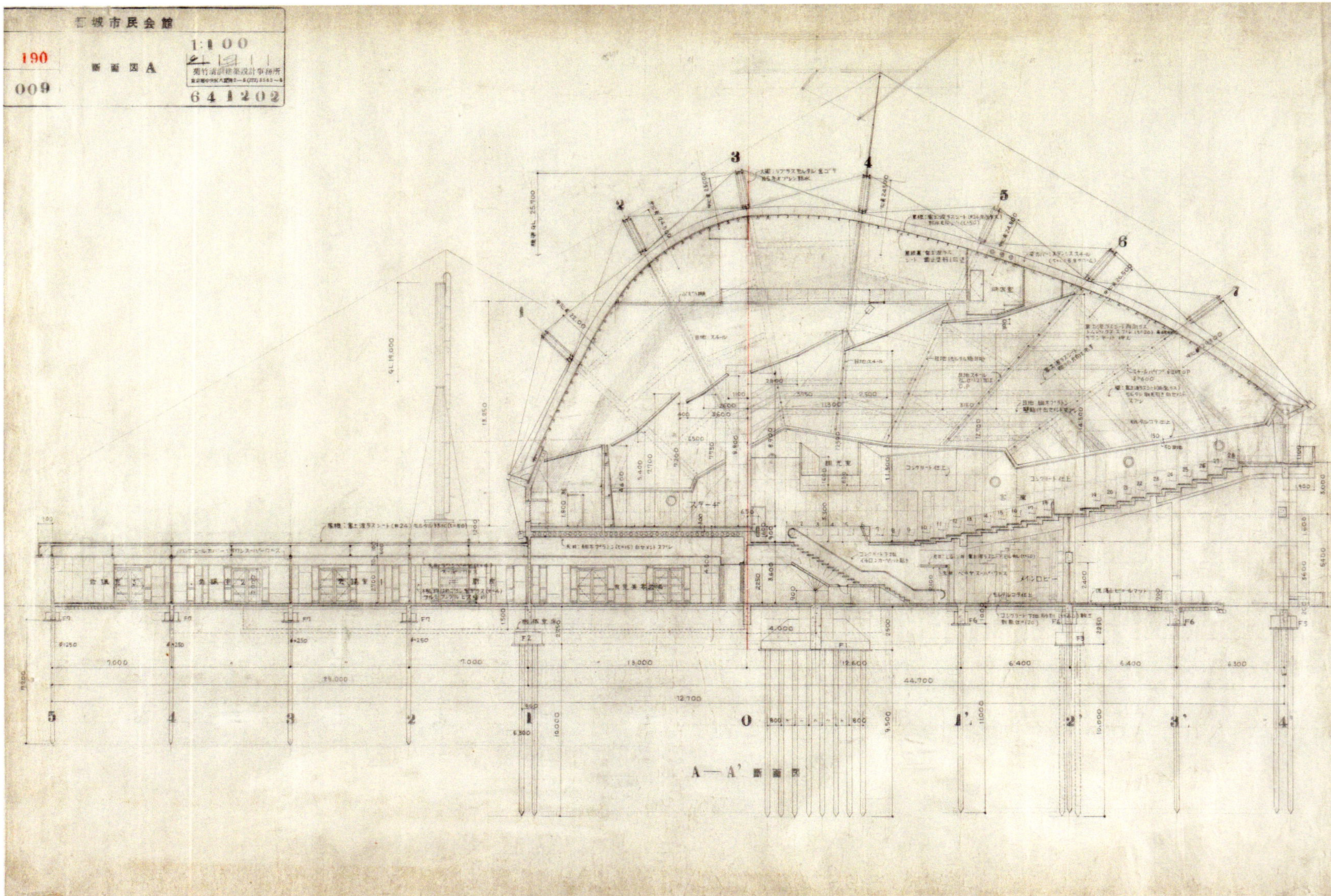
都城市民会館
190
009
断面図A
1:100
菊竹清訓建築設計事務所
641202
ステージ
メインロビー
A—A' 断面図

Detailed section.

Section concept.

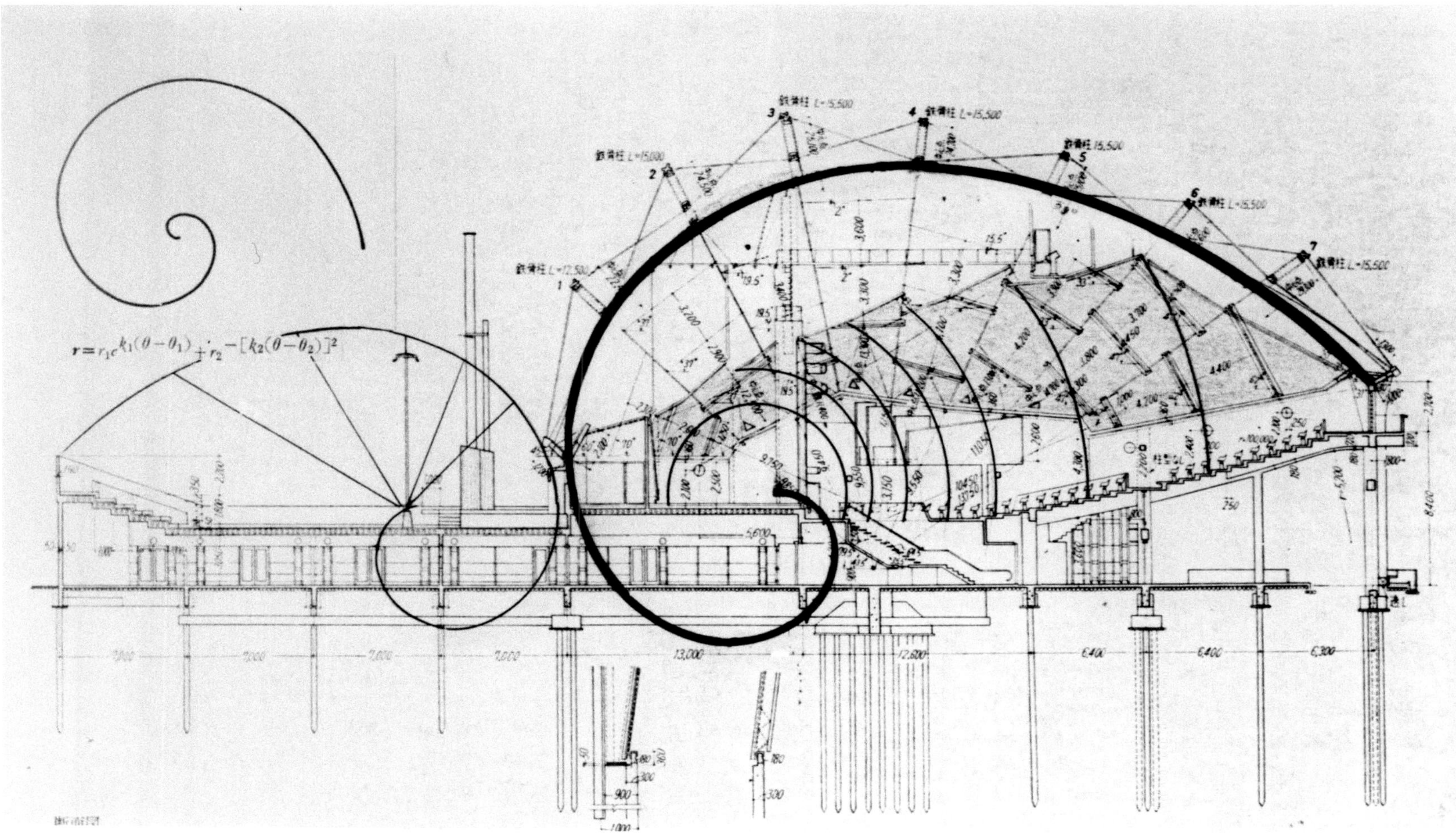

Model, view of entry.

View of hall with amphitheater and garden.

View from northeast.

タイヤ

View from west.

Interior view of hall.

Sketch.

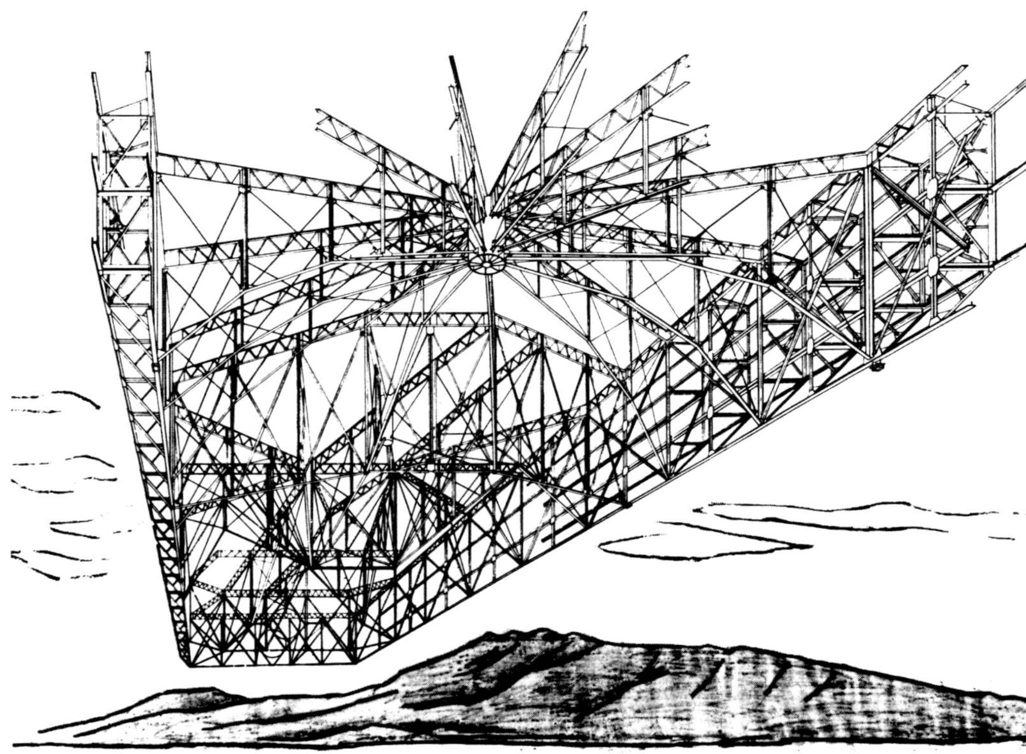

HAGI CIVIC CENTER

Hagi City, Yamaguchi Prefecture, 1968

This civic hall, located in this former castle town in southwest Japan along the Japan Sea, recalls the so-called Black Ships from the United States that arrived in this coastal city and eventually led to the opening of Japan and the start of modernization during the Meiji Period (1868–1912). Although the design went through a number of schemes and transformed radically in the final stages, the finished hall expresses the image of a steel-frame ship floating above a reinforced-concrete base. The design embraced the most advanced shipbuilding/welding and steel production technology of the time, while the exterior walls resonate with the white plaster walls of historic houses from the area.

This design yielded a shortened construction period and was economically efficient. The space of the open steel-frame canopy is illuminated by a spectrum of bare lightbulbs designed by Ishii Motoko and conditioned by exposed air-conditioning ducts. Employing the latest audio technology for microphones and loudspeakers, the hall maintained its open, airy character. The lobby spaces are designed to maximize natural light and ventilation, to reduce reliance on mechanical systems; they are conceived as a space of information exchange and informal encounters through community events such as art exhibitions and tea ceremonies. The project was the collaborative effort of many individuals, including Itō Toyoo on the schematic design team and Hasegawa Itsuko on the design development team.

Since the completion of the hall, Kikutake designed the adjacent black steel-encased city hall (1974). Additional changes include the replacement in 2011 of the original lightbulbs with LED bulbs that have slightly different diameters; the effect of the illuminated constellation above, however, continues to impress visitors to the hall and meeting space.

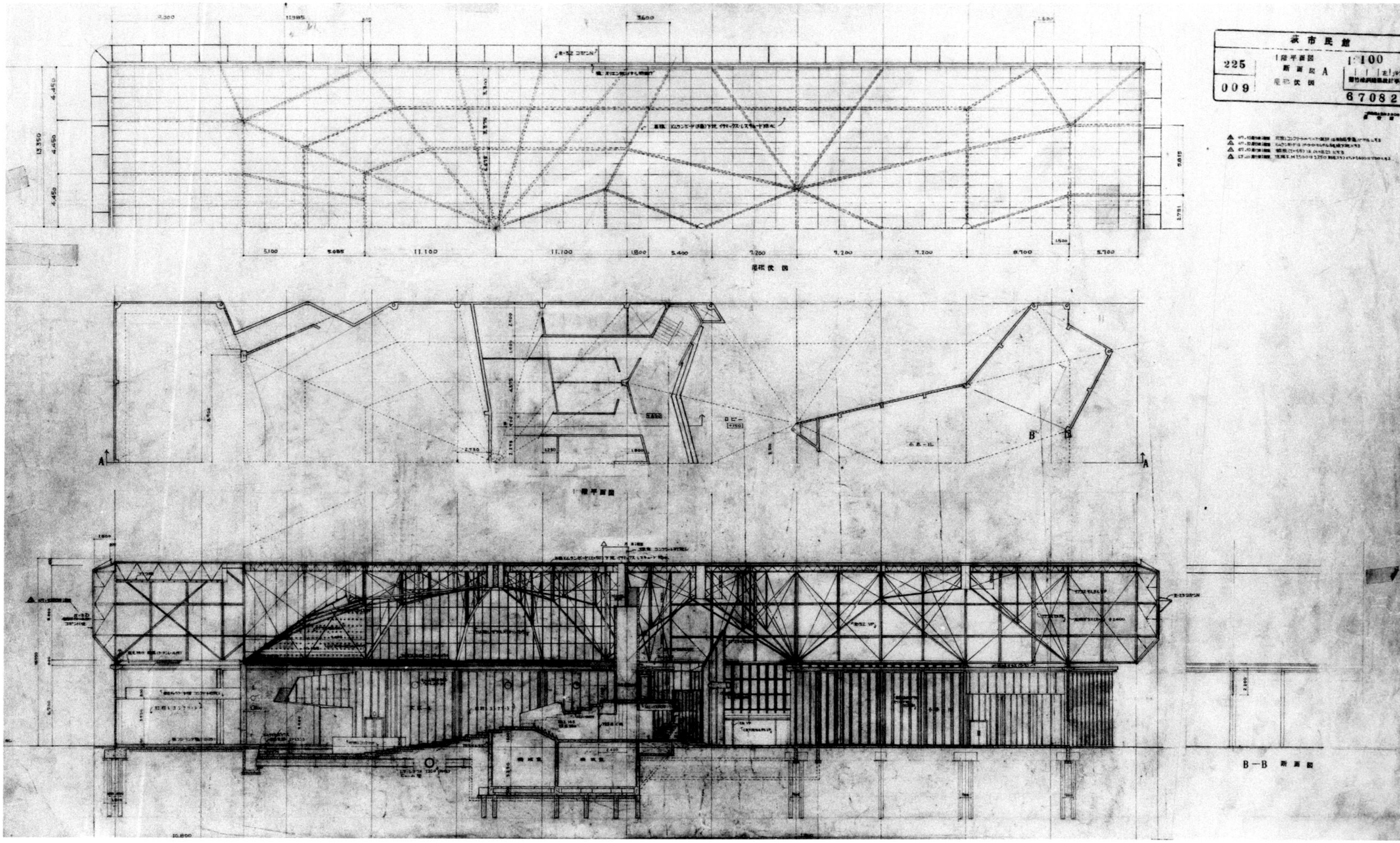
萩市民館
225
009
1階平面図
断面図 A
屋根伏図
1:100
670821
屋根伏図
1階平面図
B−B 断面図

Section, structural details.

Cross section.

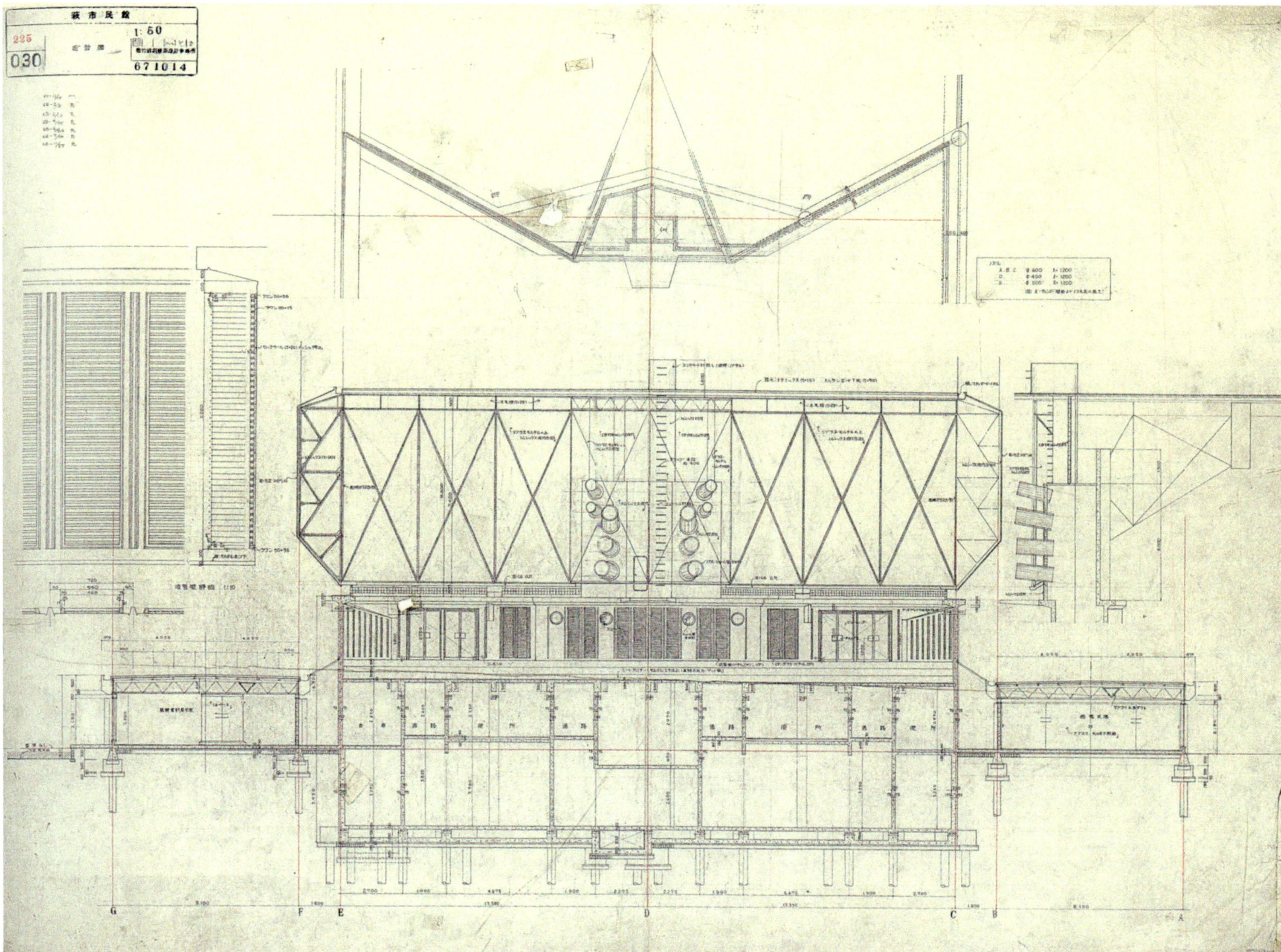

Model, view from northeast.

Aerial view from northwest.

Ceiling structure.

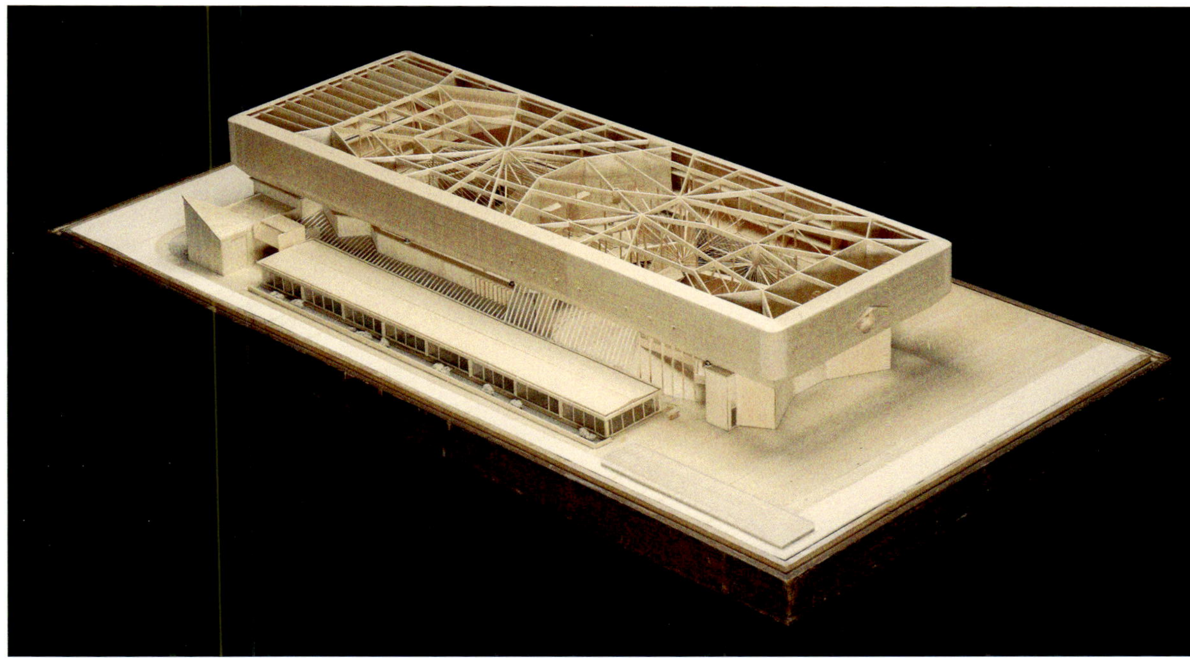

South elevation.

Southeast corner.

View from small hall.

Movenette capsule hoisted
up during construction.

EXPO TOWER

Expo '70 Osaka, 1970

Symbolizing "a new living environment in the city," this 127-meter (417-foot) observation tower stood at the south end of Expo '70's main "symbol zone" axis, as the exhibition produced architectural reality. Kikutake sought to address the era's increasing environmental problems with an open, flexible frame in realizing ideas from the Tower-Shaped Community 1958 and the tower of Ocean City 1968. The three-column steel-lattice structure soaring high into the sky supported geodesic "movenette" capsules of cast aluminum and glass to house observation decks, exhibition space, a VIP room, elevator mechanical space, and radio machine rooms—much like grapes on a vine. Based on a module of 360 cubic meters, the capsules were constructed as prototypes of prefabricated residential units. The tower featured two "high-speed" elevators and a spiral stair with the upper portion offering both open and closed stair circulation to enable multiple routes and shortcuts. Following the close of the Expo, the structure continued to stand as an observation tower until being disassembled in 2003.

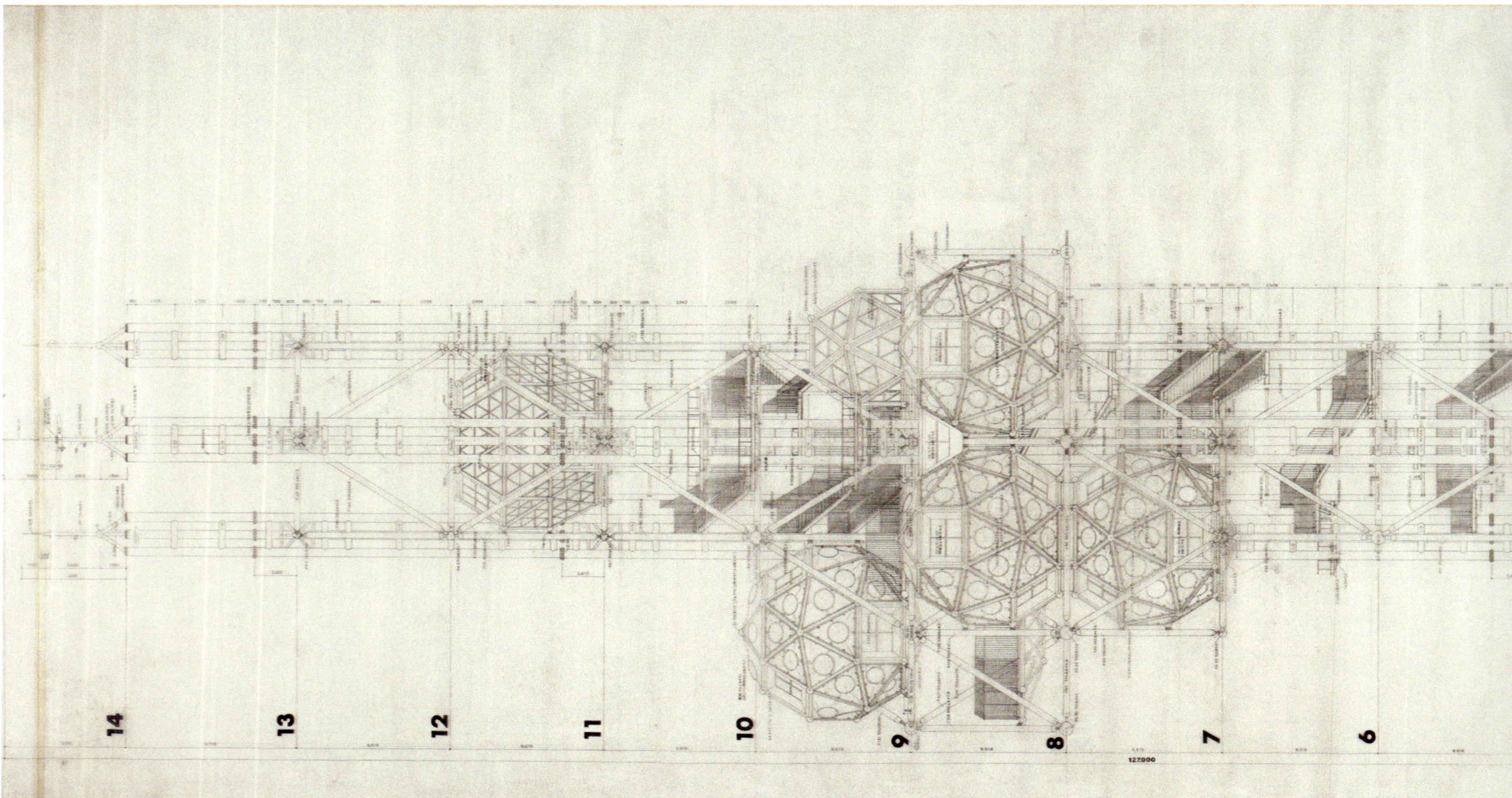

Elevation.

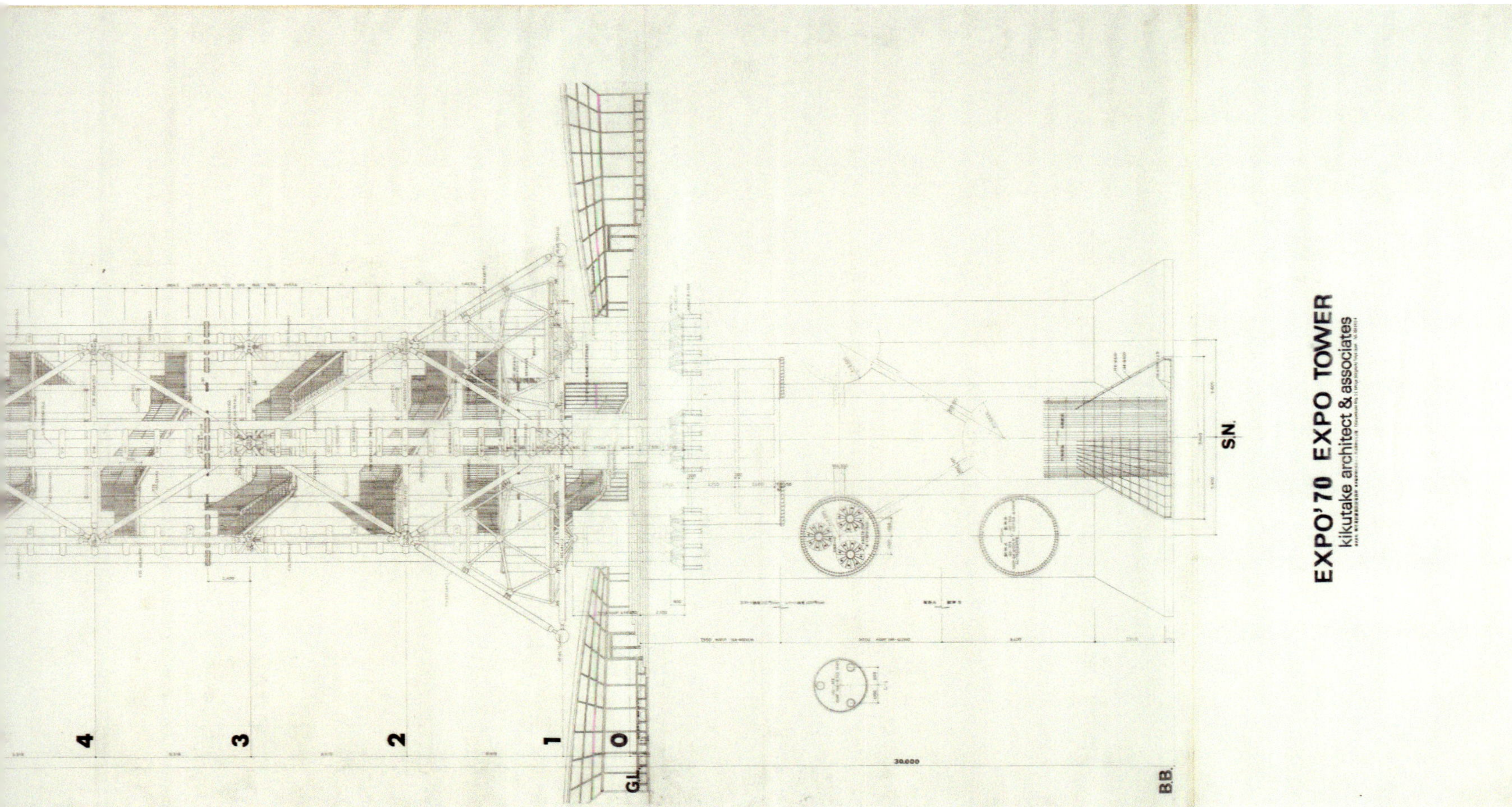
EXPO'70 EXPO TOWER
kikutake architect & associates
S.N.
B.B.
G.L.
4
3
2
1
0
30,000

Night view.

Expo Tower with Festival Plaza below left.

Marine City 1962–63, model.

OCEAN URBANISM 1956–1975

"The ocean knows no borders. The world can finally get rid of borders. The Marine City could speed up this process."

"When the Marine City gets old and is no longer needed, it could simply be sunk into the sea."[1]

"Two-thirds of the surface of the Earth is ocean. Over these past fifty years, from the beginning to the end, I have held fast to the dream of making a residential environment upon the splendor of the sea. This is what gave birth to the vision of the Marine City."[2]

Kikutake's vision to develop the possibilities of living on the sea emerged during Japan's postwar era of recovery and rapid, intensive economic development. Through Japan's defeat and Occupational Reforms (the 1947 Land Reform Act), Kikutake's family had lost ownership of their land-holdings in Kurume, on the southern island of Kyūshū, which they had for fifteen generations. Kikutake had witnessed the destruction of bay-front areas and beaches such as at Yokkaichi in Mie Prefecture through the development of heavy industries. From 1956 he saw the ocean as a more appropriate site for the expansion of new communities on a constructed ground, open to the aquatic environment and "waiting for a new discovery … which will promise true happiness (for human beings)."[3] The floating city offered an alternative to urban sprawl generated by the lack of land in urban areas, which often resulted in one-hour commutes. Other explorations of ocean urbanism can be seen in Tange Kenzō's 1960 Tokyo Bay Plan or Buckminster Fuller's Triton floating city from the early 1960s and Sea City 1971, developed by Pilkington Glass, but these ideas would not be pursued with Kikutake's lifelong zeal. As Rem Koolhaas relates: "Through an alchemy of ambition and technology, Metabolism transforms what was previously felt as a limitation—Japan's islandness—into an opportunity."[4]

1 Kawazoe Noboru, *Kenchikuka—hito to sakuhin* [Architect—man and work] (Tokyo: Inoue Shinsho, 1968).
2 Kikutake Kiyonori, ed., *Megastructure: Atarashii toshikankyo wo motomete* [Megastructure: In search of a new urban environment] (Tokyo: Waseda University Press, 1995), 142.
3 Kawazoe Noboru, ed., *Metabolism/1960* (Tokyo: Bijutsu Shuppansha, 1960), 23.
4 Rem Koolhaas and Hans Ulrich Obrist, *Project Japan: Metabolism Talks* (London: Taschen, 2011), 354.

Sketch.

MARINE CITY 1958–

The launch of *Sputnik* in 1957 inspired an era of looking to modern science to realize people's dreams. Kikutake's vision calls for floating urban surfaces resembling water lilies, kept afloat and stable by spherical and cylindrical factory/sea farm volumes below. The concept was first published in 1958 in the journal *Kokusai kenchiku.* Kikutake wrote: "The idea was to create an artificial industrial city in the Bay of Suruga (characterized by deep waters)—a floating city to replace the conventional industrial complex on land combining petrochemical, steel, chemical, and electricity-generating industries. The principal production-related systems will be fixed deep enough in the ocean where temperatures and other environmental conditions are relatively stable. On the surface of the ocean there will be afloat several circular platforms with a diameter of 4 kilometers, which will not be affected by waves of any size."[1] Set on the sea, "the Marine City is moveable, autonomous, and climate controlled."

1 Kiyonori Kikutake. "Metabolist Kiyonori Kikutake," *SD: Space Design*, October 1980, 31.

Sketch.

TOWER-SHAPED COMMUNITY

1958 (unbuilt)

The Tower-Shaped Community, 300 meters tall, is conceived as a "vertical ground" with an infrastructure of utilities into which 1,250 living units can be plugged. The steel units can be attached magnetically and be replaced like new buds on a tree. Kitchens, toilets, and bathrooms are to be manufactured as integrated units. In contrast with the congested land of Tokyo, here residents would gain wide perspectives of the city.

Sketch. General view of Unabara.

OCEAN CITY

Unabara, 1960 (unbuilt)

This scheme extends the Marine City/Tower-Shaped Community concepts to incorporate high-density, high-rise housing, accommodating around 30,000 residents in a structure 300 meters tall. This serves as a production center for cultivating seafood, included facilities for generating electricity from solar and wave power, with harbors for flying boats and submarines. All components are connected organically, and when required, the city could propagate and split off a new community in a manner akin to cell division.

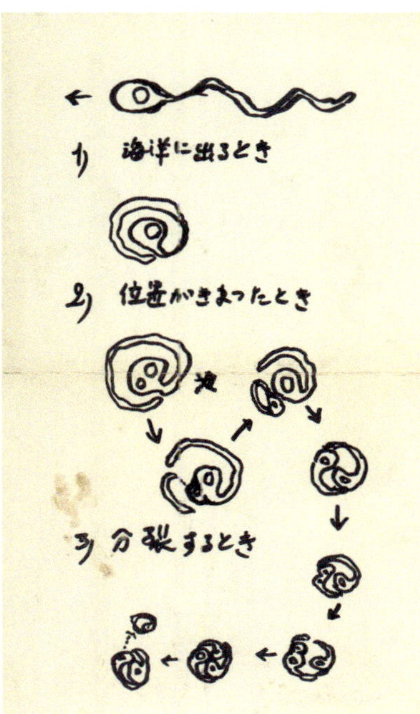

Unabara expanding through cell division.

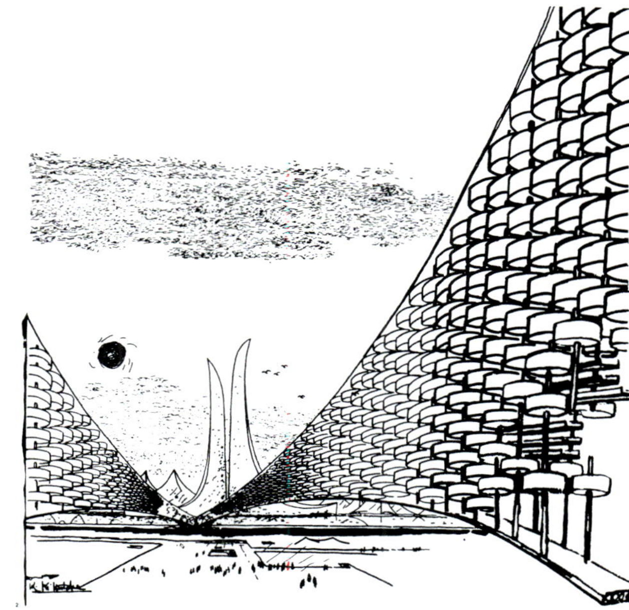

General view of housing structures.

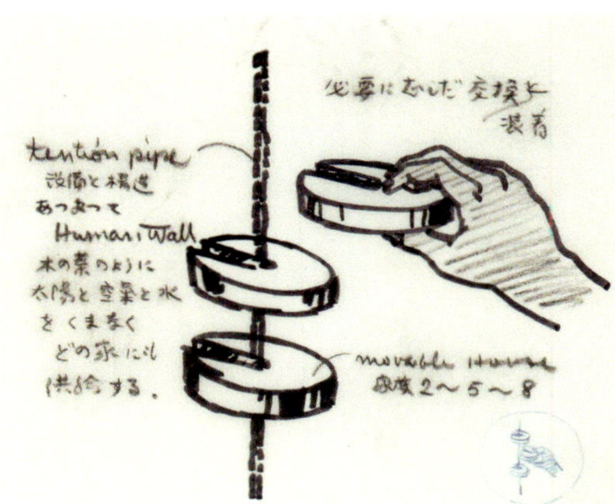

Basic concept of movable house.

Site plan of Tokyo Bay Project.

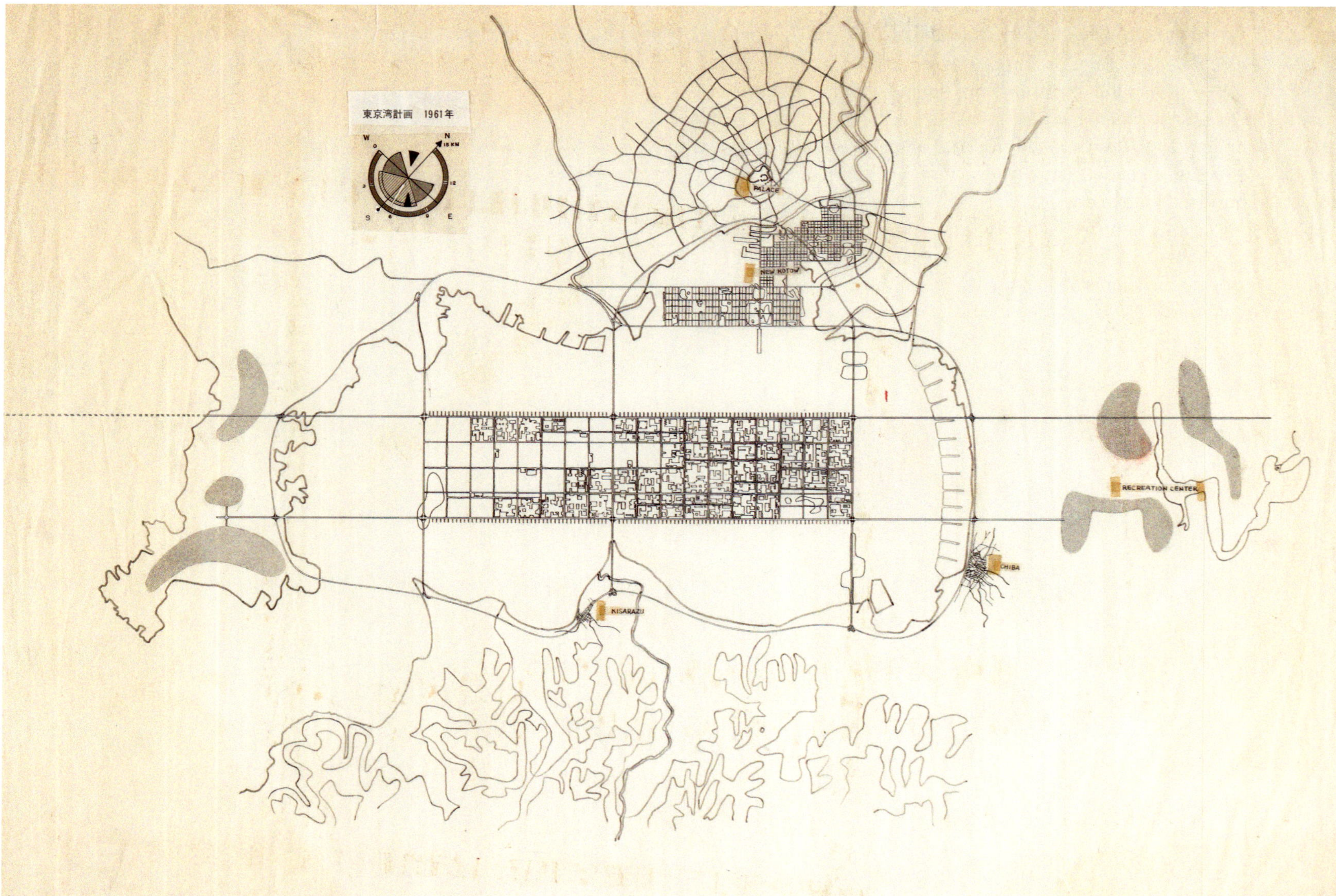

TOKYO BAY PLAN

Kōtō Ward, 1961 (unbuilt)

In contrast to Tange Kenzō's Tokyo Bay Plan of a linear spine extending out from the city center, Kikutake proposed multiscalar bands across Tokyo Bay, including the band covering the low-lying Kōtō Ward, to house 1 million people within a grid of towers atop an artificial ground at or below sea level. In this scheme, urban functions could continue even in the event of major flooding. The Tetra City Project employs a tetrahedral structure to integrate solutions for collective housing and circulation for both people and goods. Kikutake envisioned links between other Tokyo Bay Projects and his own Ocean City Unabara adapted from the site of Sagami Bay located southwest of Tokyo. This plan remains schematic as an individual proposal envisioning the possibilities of the future city, rather than one commissioned or developed with the help of students.

Block section.

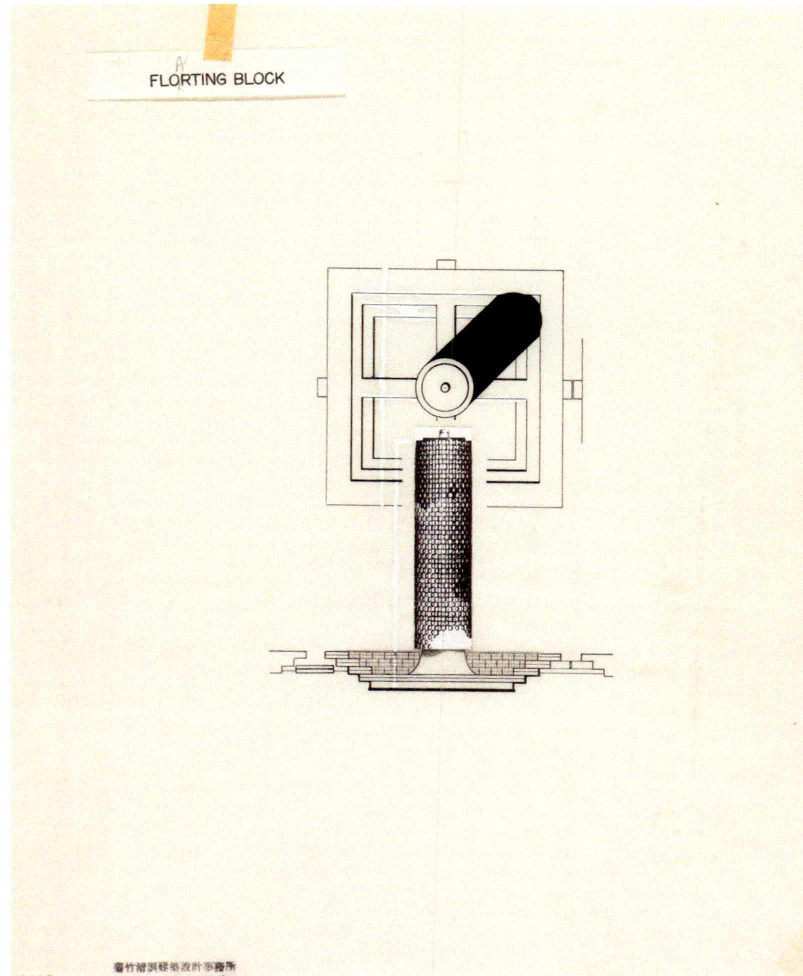

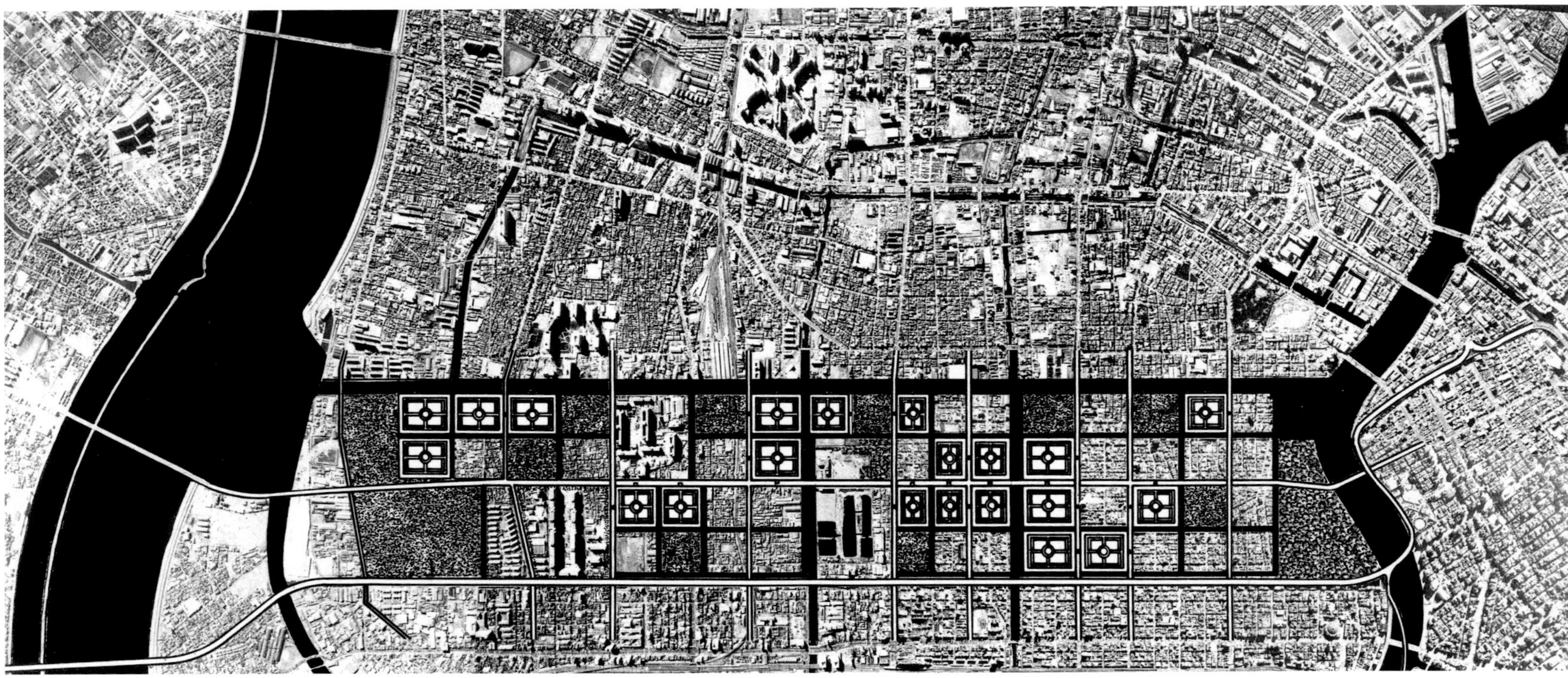

Floating blocks connected
by canals and bridges.

Model.

Sketch.

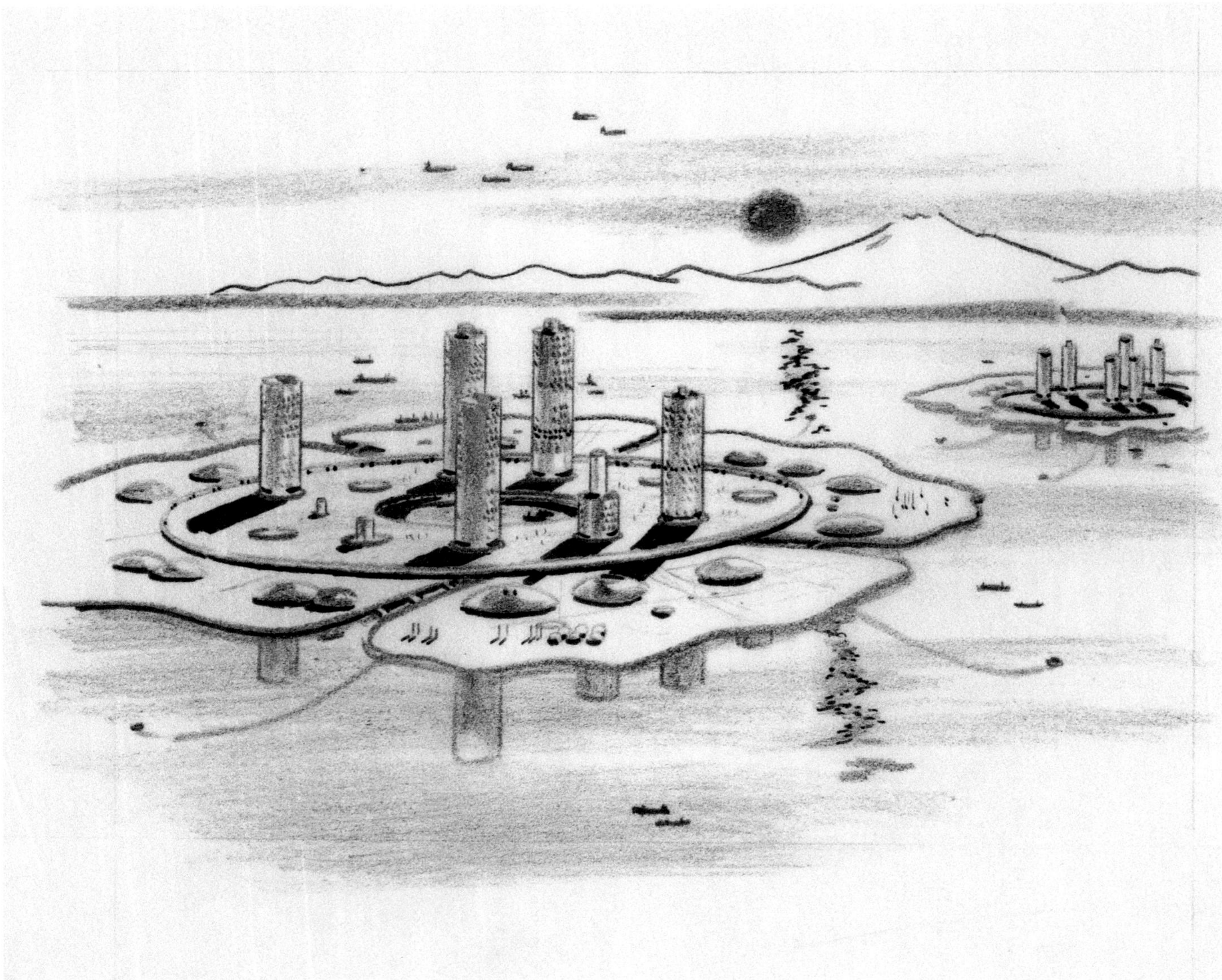

MARINE CITY 1963–

As a further development of Ocean City, Unabara (Marine City 1960) that combines Tower-Shaped Community and Marine City 1958, this fragmented scheme presents tower-shaped housing on irregular-shaped islands rather than on a single large loop platform. This plan for a floating community proposed the banning of cars in favor of moving belts and submarines. The supershaft structures are now designed to withstand the heavy seas, no longer requiring platforms underneath. Individual residential units can telescope in and out as needed.

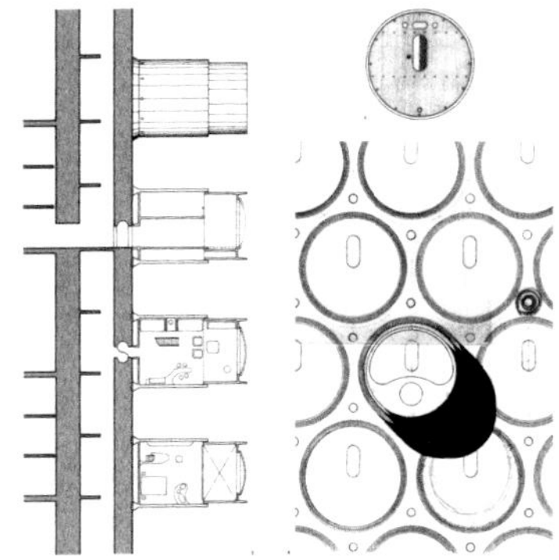

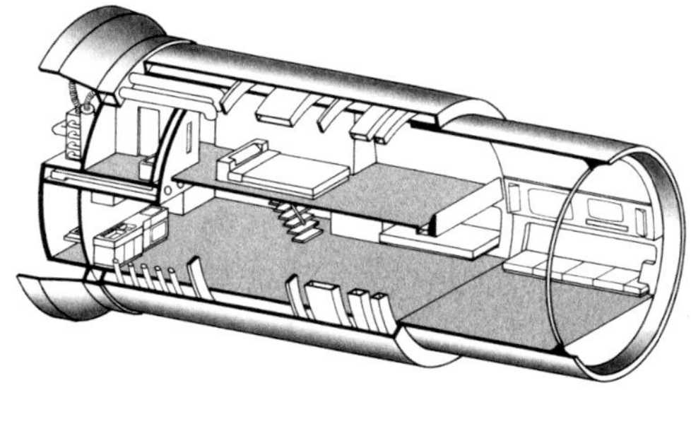

Model photo.

Elevation and section, floor plan for residential unit.

Isometric section, interior view of housing unit.

Model photo.

Photo collage.

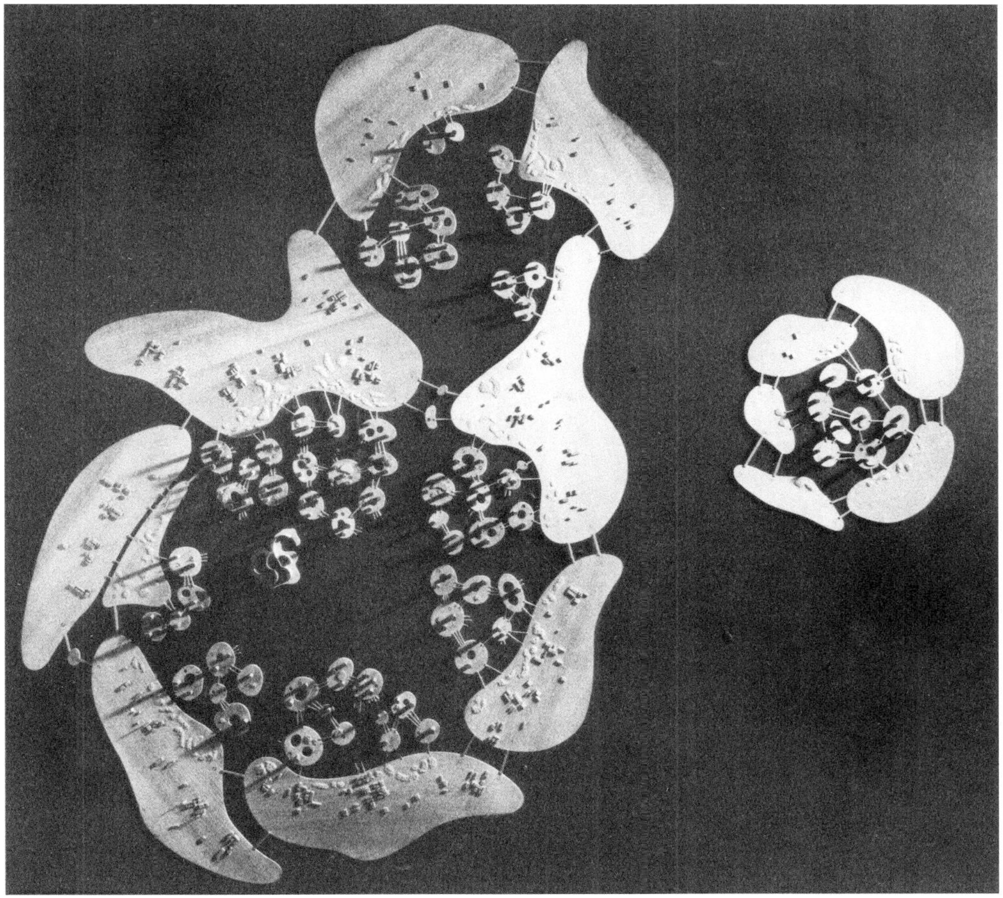

Model photos.

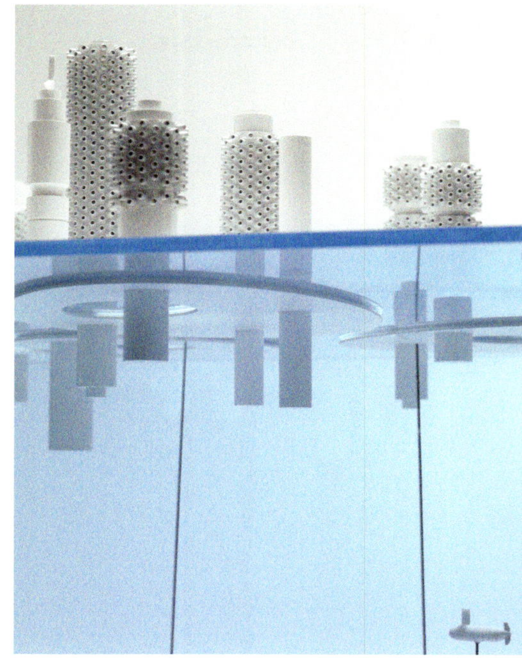

MARINE CITY 1968

Model photos.

Here cranes are installed at the top of the towers, facilitating constant metabolic change. Later proposals include midair connections between towers to facilitate three-dimensional circulation.

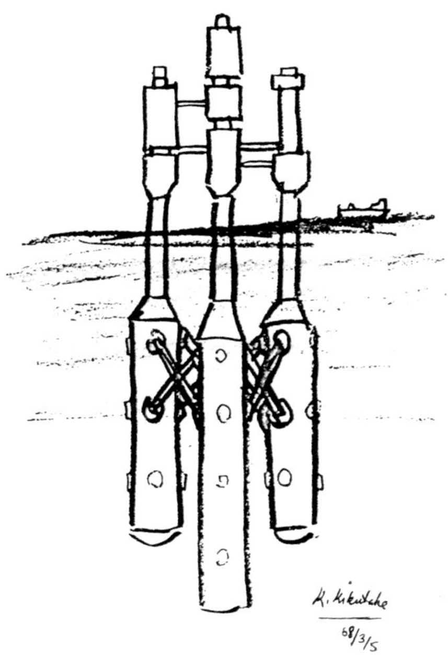

Axonometric drawing,
inner ring.

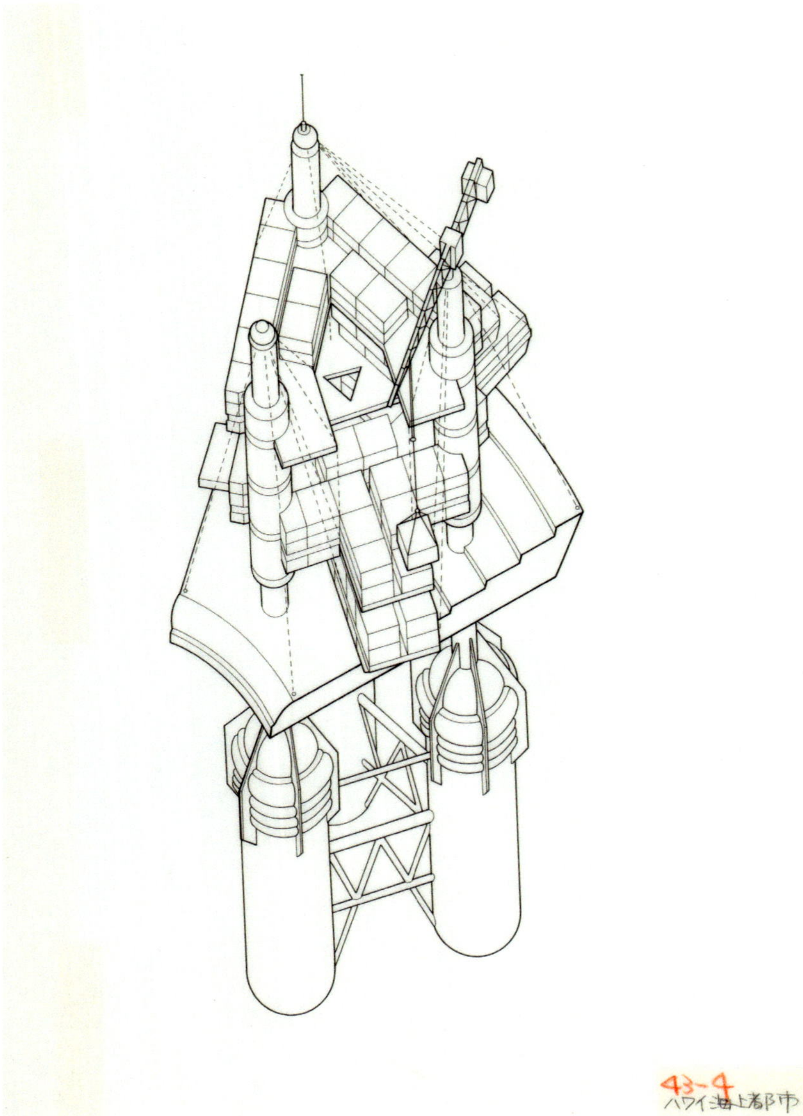

MARINE CITY 1971–75: FROM HAWAII TO OKINAWA

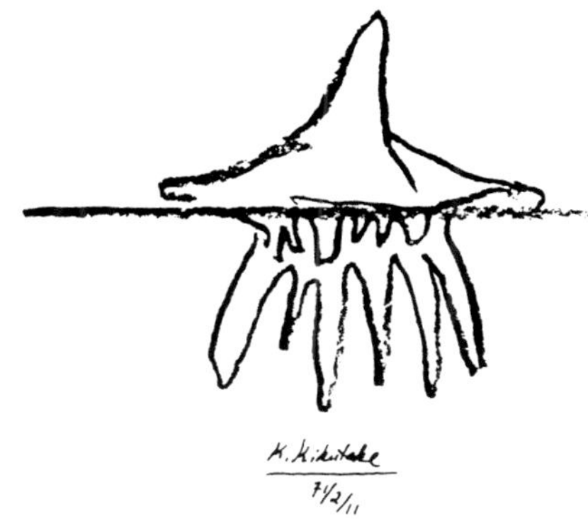

Sketch of jellyfish.

The early 1970s marked the concretization of Kikutake's Marine City ideals. Upon his appointment as visiting professor at the University of Hawaii in 1971, Kikutake led an international research team of scientists and engineers to create "Marine City 1971—Project in Hawaii" as a floating city set on two concentric rings. Kikutake found particular inspiration in the RP (Research Platform) FLIP (Floating Instrument Platform) as a 355-foot-long ocean research vessel that could pitch backward 90 degrees, with the depth of the partially flooded vessel able to withstand wave currents. The inner ring of high-rise buildings contained housing, hotels, offices, and shops, and the low-rise outer ring served as the platform for the Ocean Expo. The rings sat upon cylindrical "milk bottle" floats, bundled in groups of three as an open-ended, extendable system.

Marine City found its final realization in Kikutake's Aquapolis design for the Japan Pavilion at the Okinawa Ocean Expo '75, which celebrated the return of the Okinawa Islands from the United States to Japan. Kikutake's floating city was towed more than 1,000 kilometers by boats to Okinawa from Hiroshima, where it was built. With a capacity of 2,400 people, the semi-submersible floating Aquapolis was the size of a city block: 100 square meters in plan and 32 meters high, containing exhibition spaces, a banquet hall, offices, an infirmary, a communication room, a post office, residences for 40 staff members, and a computer room. The primary structure termed the "lower hull" consisted of four giant floats that could be pumped with seawater to adjust the draft. In the event of rough seas, the Aquapolis could anchor offshore and partly submerge to protect the structure. Following Expo '75, Aquapolis could not find a suitable owner and was dismantled.

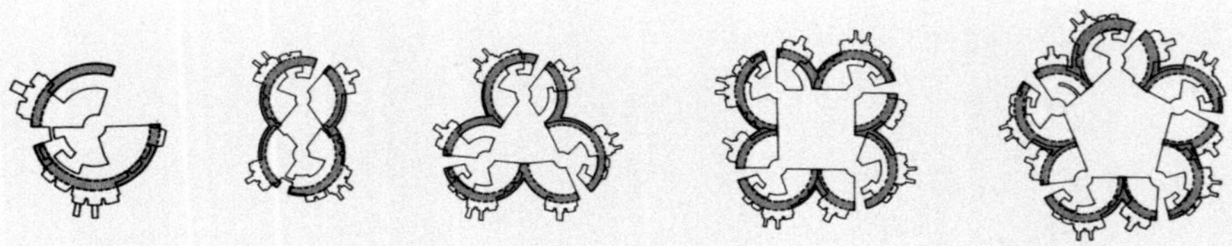
21

Model of Floating City
with expansion diagrams.

Site model.

2 may '83

2 may '83

Aquapolis sketches.

Delivery of Aquapolis pavilion by tow ships.

Night view.

Bird's-eye view.

OCEAN URBANISM 1976–

Kikutake's schemes for Ocean Urbanism continued to find form through the subsequent decades, in seas far beyond Japan. In the year following Aquapolis, for an invited competition, Kikutake designed a crescent-shaped Abu Dhabi Floating Hotel that floated independently of its interior courtyard, rotating 360 degrees every 8 to 10 hours. In continuing his early scheme for Ocean City, Unabara, he proposed prefabricated plug-in rooms inserted in a semi-cylindrical structure as a vertical ground. In suiting this context's increasing appetite for luxury and leisure, the interior courtyard includes a waterfall, woods, and a swimming pool that moves along with the hotel, while the square platform remains static. As part barge and part hulking cruise ship, Kikutake's 500-room Saudi Arabia Floating Luxury Hotel (1977) was to be constructed by shipbuilders and towed to shore. This was to be both a "free zone" with legalized gambling and a microcosmic city with its own water, waste, and energy systems. Related developments include an "urban belt" of floating precast concrete factories and residences along the Mediterranean coast from Tripoli to Benghazi in 1977, and the "infracassette project," a small-scale version of early Marine Cities to be exported to Iraq for flood protection along the Tigris and Euphrates in 1978.

Section.

FLOATING HOTEL 1977

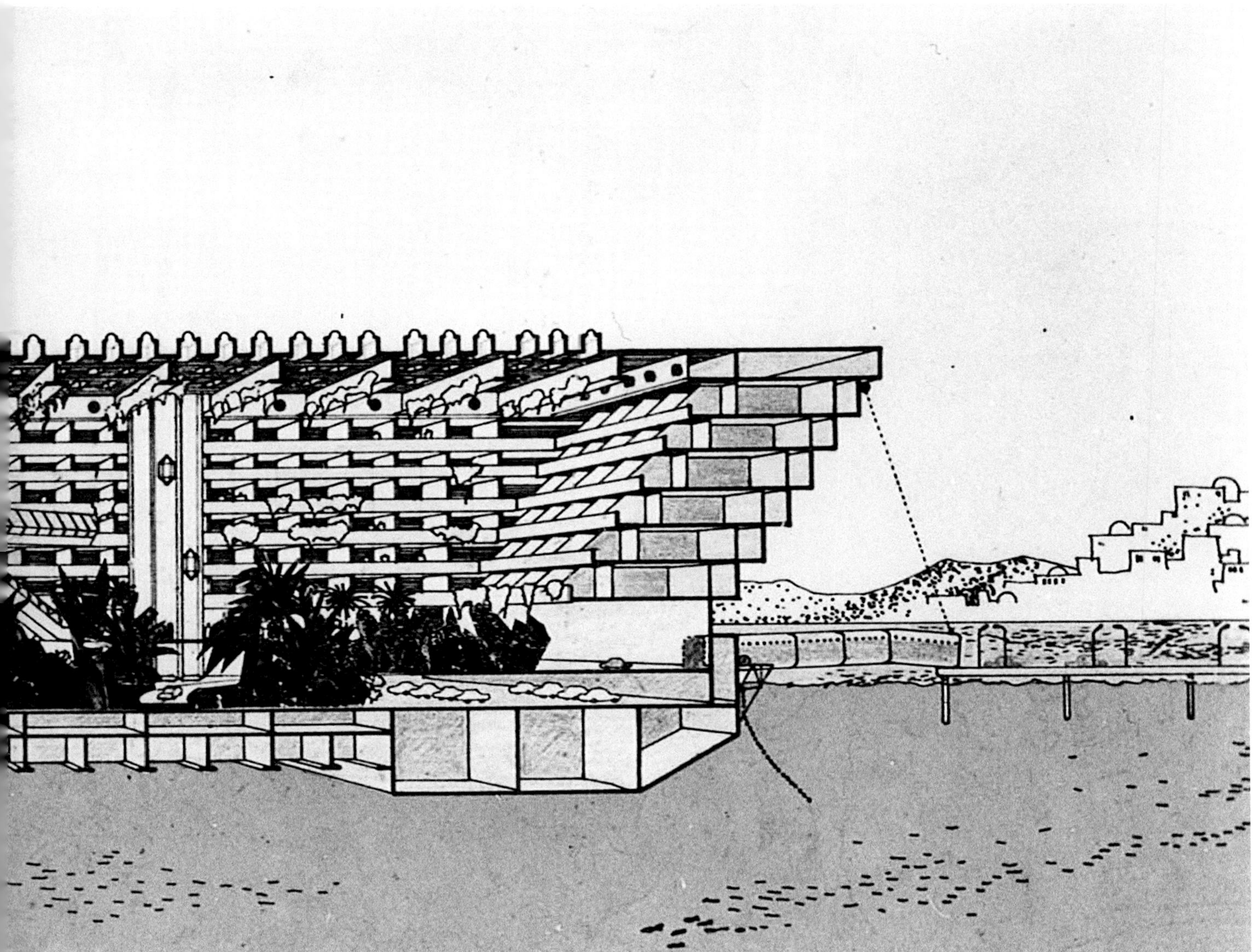

KIKUTAKE KIYONORI

1928 Born in Kurume, Fukuoka Prefecture, Kyūshū, into a family that had been large landowners for 600 years.
1944 Enrolled in architecture program at Waseda University.
1948 Won third prize in the Hiroshima Peace Cathedral design competition.
1950 Graduated from Waseda University.
1950–52 Employed by Takenaka Corporation.
1952–53 Employed by the office of Murano and Mori Architects.
1953 Established Kikutake Architectural Research Office (renamed Kikutake Kiyonori Architectural Office in 1962).
1956 Began work for Bridgestone Corporation.
Ishibashi Cultural Center/Cultural Hall and Eifukuji Kindergarten completed.
1958 Proposed Tower-Shaped City 1958, Marine City 1958. Sky House completed.
1959 Tokyo Bay Plan 1959 exhibited at CIAM 1959 in Otterlo, Netherlands.
Became lecturer in architecture at Waseda University.
1960 Exhibited Ocean City, Unabara, at the World Design Conference as part of the launch of Metabolism with Kawazoe Noboru and others.
Exhibited in "Visionary Architecture" at the Museum of Modern Art, New York.
1962 Became director of the Japan Institute of Architects.
1963 Received Award of Excellence for competition plan for the Kyōto International Conference Hall. Proposed Marine City 1963. Administrative Building of Izumo Shrine and Tatebayashi City Hall completed.
1964 Awarded 7th AIA Pan-Pacific Prize. Lectured on "Contemporary Architecture and Metabolism" at the University of Hawai'i Kennedy Theater along with the installation of the "Kikutake Kiyonori" exhibition. Visiting Professor at the University of Southern California.
Awarded 14th Bunka Senshō Prize from the Japanese Agency for Cultural Affairs.
Received 15th Award of the Japan Institute of Architects. Hotel Tōkōen completed.
1965 Awarded 6th Architects Association Prize. Tokuunji Columbarium completed.
Pear City Plan 1965 presented.
1966 Miyakonojō Civic Center, Pacific Hotel Chigasaki completed.
1967 Sado Grand Hotel completed.
1968 Hagi Civic Center and Shimane Prefectural Library completed.
1969 Kurume Civic Center completed.
1970 Awarded special distinction for the Expo Tower by the Japan Institute of Architects.
1970–80 Kyoto Community Bank branches completed.
1971 Visiting Professor at the University of Hawaii where he presented the Hawaii Marine City.
Became an Honorary Fellow of the American Institute of Architects
1974 Pasadena Heights completed.
1975 Aquapolis completed for Expo 75, Okinawa.
1976 Seibu Ohtsu Shopping Center completed.
1978 Awarded the 8th Union Internationale des Architects' Auguste Perret Prize.
1979 Received the 21st Mainichi Arts Prize. Tanabe Art Museum completed.
1980 Visiting Professor at the University of Virginia and RWTH Aachen University.
1982 Elected Vice President of the Japan Institute of Architects.
Became lecturer in architecture at Tokyo University.
1985 Became Honorary Professor at the University of Buenos Aires.
1987 Became Honorary Professor at Peru National University, Visiting Professor at Hōsei University. Hotel SEIYO Ginza completed (closed 2013).
1988 Nara Silk Road Exposition producer. Became Professor and Academician of International Academy of Architecture.
1990 Became Visiting Professor at Waseda University and Chiba Institute of Technology.
1991 Member of the International Academy of Architecture, Visiting Professor at Kōgakuin University. Awarded 4th Nara City Architectural Culture Prize.
1992 Edo Tokyo Museum completed.
1994 Member of Académie royale d'architecture. Honorary Professor at Beijing University of Technology. Hotel Cosima (demolished 2003) and Kurume City Hall completed.
1998 Director of the Nagano Olympics spatial composition.
Elected President of Japan Federation of Architects & Building Engineers Associations.
Kita Kyūshū Media Dome completed.
1999 Shōwa Kan and Shimane Art Museum completed.
2004 Kyūshū National Museum completed.
2005 General producer for Expo 2005 World Exposition, Aichi, Japan. Global Loop completed.
2006 Awarded the Order of the Rising Sun, Gold Rays with Neck Ribbon by the Japanese Government.
2011 Died in Tokyo on December 26 at the age of 83.

CONTRIBUTORS

ITŌ TOYOO worked in the office of Kikutake Kiyonori from 1965 to 1969 and established his own studio named Urbot ("Urban Robot") in 1971, renamed Toyo Ito & Associates in 1979. He received the Pritzker Prize in 2013.

SENG KUAN is Assistant Professor of Architecture at Washington University in St. Louis. He is co-editor of *Kenzō Tange: Architecture for the World* (2012). His curatorial work includes "Utopia Across Scales: Highlights from the Kenzō Tange Archive" (Harvard Graduate School of Design, 2009) and "On the Thresholds of Space-Making: Shinohara Kazuo and His Legacy" (Mildred Lane Kemper Art Museum, 2014).

MARK MULLIGAN is an architect based in Cambridge, Massachusetts, and Associate Professor in Practice at the Harvard Graduate School of Design, where he teaches courses on construction technology and modern Japanese architecture. He is editor of *Nurturing Dreams: Collected Essays on Architecture and the City by Fumihiko Maki* (2008) and co-author of *The Thinking Hand: Tools and Traditions of the Japanese Carpenter* (2014).

KEN TADASHI OSHIMA is Professor of Architecture at the University of Washington, Seattle. He received a PhD in architectural history and theory from Columbia University and an MArch from U.C. Berkeley. He is author of *Global Ends—Towards the Beginning* (2012), *International Architecture in Interwar Japan: Constructing Kokusai Kenchiku* (2009), and *Arata Isozaki* (2009).

SEJIMA KAZUYO is an architect with Kazuyo Sejima & Associates, established in 1987, and SANAA (Sejima and Nishizawa and Associates), established in 1995. She worked for Itō Toyoo from 1981 to 1987 and received the Pritzker Prize together with Nishizawa Ryūe in 2010.

FRED THOMPSON is Professor Emeritus at the University of Waterloo. He worked in the office of Kikutake Kiyonori from 1961 to 1964, and in the office of Aarno Ruusuvuori from 1965 to 1968.

ACKNOWLEDGMENTS

The effort of making the extraordinary work of Kikutake Kiyonori better known to an English-speaking audience through the publication of this book has drawn on the crucial contributions of many people.

At the Harvard Graduate School of Design, Dean Mohsen Mostafavi advanced the School's engagement with the topic through his support for an exhibition, symposium, and now, published volume. These activities were all made possible through the generous collaboration of Mrs. Mutsuko Smith Kikutake/Kikutake Architects, tireless contributions of Tsukamoto Jirō, and insights of Kikutake Yuki. The symposium was highlighted by the remarks of Fred Thompson, Mark Mulligan, Seng Kuan, and Florian Idenburg, and the closing lecture by Itō Toyoo.

The exhibition team for "Tectonic Visions between Land and Sea: Works of Kiyonori Kikutake" included Dan Borelli and David Zimmerman-Stuart. Iwan Baan, Justin Knight, and Adam Kellie provided photographic documentation. In the GSD's Frances Loeb Library, Ann Whiteside, Mary Daniels, Inés Zalduendo, Irina Gorstein, and Johanna Kasubowski provided invaluable support. I thank Seng Kuan and Yukio Lippit for their foundational work *Kenzō Tange: Architecture for the World.* Among the GSD staff who deserve special thanks are Executive Dean Pat Roberts, Associate Dean Beth Kramer, Assistant Dean Benjamin Prosky, Editor in Chief Jennifer Sigler, Deputy Director of Development Sarah Bordy, and Public Programs Manager Shantel Blakely. I thank Melissa Vaughn, the GSD's Senior Editor, for bringing to this project her remarkable critical voice, wisdom, and patience.

The contributing authors to this volume are owed my sincere appreciation for their engaged collaboration. This publication builds on the invaluable insights of Kikutake associates Endō Shokan, Hasegawa Itsuko, Naitō Hiroshi, Tsukamoto Jirō, and Ōmura Ayako, and the foundational scholarship of Hasegawa Takashi, Matsukuma Hiroshi, Iso Tatsuo, and Imamura Souhei. The Japan Foundation and Japan Studies at the University of Washington provided research funding to survey extant Kikutake buildings. Elizabeth Cummings provided additional editorial assistance.

I am grateful as well to Yoshida Nobuyuki, publisher of *Shinkenchiku,* along with Muto-Hayashi Natsuko at the Digital Archives for Architectural Space consortium, Maeda Naotake of the Mori Art Museum, and photographers Murai Osamu, Fujitsuka Mitsumasa, Kawasumi Akio, Oyama Takashi, Arai Masao, and Iwan Baan for the contribution of key images. Itō Toyoo, along with Ōta Yuma and Uono Miki at Toyo Ito & Associates, and Sejima Kazuyo, along with Komura Harumi and Fukuhara Tomoko, provided generous assistance. I would also like to acknowledge Yamana Yoshiyuki, National Archives of Modern Architecture, and Furuya Nobuaki, who realized the exhibition "The Spirit of Architecture: Kiyonori KIKUTAKE in Architectural Archives" in 2014.

It has been a pleasure making this book with Lars Müller and his team at Lars Müller Publishers in Zurich, including Natascha Kuhn, Martina Mullis, and Esther Butterworth.

—Ken Tadashi Oshima

THE GSD AND JAPAN

Since the 2012 release of *Kenzō Tange: Architecture for the World,* the previous collaboration between the Harvard University Graduate School of Design and Lars Müller Publishers on a visionary Japanese architect, the GSD has extended its fruitful engagement with Japan through a range of activities.

Faculty and students have continued to undertake projects in Japan to further the recovery from the tragic events of March 2011. A 2012 study-abroad studio led by Itō Toyoo, Thinking about Home-for-All, responded to the destruction in the Tōhoku region. Ken Tadashi Oshima led the accompanying seminar on Metabolic Tokyo. In 2014, a student team advised by Jerold Kayden, Frank Backus Williams Professor of Urban Planning and Design, was awarded first prize in the Toyo University Tōhoku Recovery invitational academic competition, aimed at generating ideas for public-private partnerships to advance recovery. The multiyear Sanriku Project in Minamisanriku engaged Harvard students and faculty, including GSD Community Service Fellows, in helping that community to plan its rebuilding.

Other studios with a focus on Japan take up varied themes in architecture. Robert P. Hubbard Professor in the Practice of Architecture Toshiko Mori led two successive fall Kyoto Studio sessions on the responsive nature of architecture. Visiting Professor Ishigami Junya addressed Another Nature in his options studio in 2014. Innovative Construction in Japan was the title of a course taught by Mark Mulligan, Associate Professor in Practice of Architecture, in spring 2015. At the time of publication, Itō Toyoo is continuing his collaboration with the GSD as the 2015 Kenzo Tange Visiting Professor, leading a group of students for a second studio abroad in Japan, with a focus on Omishima Island. In spring 2016, Atelier Bow-Wow will conduct a studio.

A two-week design workshop for students from Japanese architecture schools, Tokyo: A Synthesis of Scales, took place in that city in summer 2014, led by Felipe Correa, Associate Professor of Urban Design. A second session on Archipuncture Urbanism in Tokyo was held the following summer, engaging students from the GSD and Japanese universities, instructed by GSD alumni.

A cross-disciplinary student team advised by Mark Mulligan and Kiel Moe, Assistant Professor of Architectural Technology, won the 3rd LIXIL International University Architectural Competition to build a sustainable house in the Taiki-cho province of northern Japan. Called the Horizon House for its 360-degree views, the building was constructed in fall 2013

Other programming at the GSD reflected the School's abiding interest in Japanese design culture. The Frances Loeb Library was honored in 2013 to receive the Kenzō Tange Archive; this important collection is being conserved, cataloged, and digitized to provide worldwide access. The Takenaka Corporation's gift of a collection of museum-quality traditional Japanese woodworking tools was displayed as part of "The Thinking Hand" exhibition co-curated by Mark Mulligan and Yukio Lippit, Harvard University Professor of the History of Art and Architecture.

The content of this volume is informed by a major GSD exhibition guest curated by Ken Tadashi Oshima in fall 2012 entitled "Tectonic Visions between Land and Sea: The Works of Kiyonori Kikutake." All of these activities speak to the historical resonance and contemporary excitement that is present in the study of Japanese architecture and urbanism. At the GSD, we will continue to promote this enriching exploration into Japan's consistently influential design culture.

Mohsen Mostafavi

View of GSD Kikutake exhibition.

KIYONORI KIKUTAKE
BETWEEN LAND AND SEA

Edited by Ken Tadashi Oshima

Harvard University, Graduate School of Design

Design: Integral Lars Müller / Lars Müller and Natascha Kuhn
Lithography: Ast & Fischer, Wabern, Switzerland
Paper: Allegro 170 g/m²
Printing and binding: Kösel, Altusried-Krugzell, Germany

Lars Müller Publishers
Zurich, Switzerland
www.lars-mueller-publishers.com

ISBN 978-3-03778-432-7

Printed in Germany

CREDITS

Arai Masao: 17, 137 left, right.
Baan, Iwan: 6, 11, 66, 129, 215.
Central Research Institute of Electric Power Industry: 36, 37.
DAAS: 180, 206, 207.
Endo Shokan: 80 right.
Harvard University Graduate School of Design (photography by Adam Kellie): 49 left, 61 left, 76 left, 122, 123, 134, 135, 164, 165, 172, 173, 196 left, 198.
Hatakeyama Naoya: 65 upper left, upper right.
Hirayama Chūji: 32 left.
Kawasumi Akio: 22 right, 33, 60, 124, 126, 127 right, 128.
Kikutake Yuki and Masanori: 28, 38, 53 upper right, 90, 92, 106, 160, 168, 184, 186, 188, 189, 194, 199 left, 201 right, 204.
Kikutake Architects: 10, 29, 41, 76 right, 77, 108, 130, 132, 133, 140, 141, 146–49, 154–55, 159, 162–63, 170–71, 179, 190–93, 196–97, 200, 202, 210.
Kikutake Kiyonori: 32 right.
Kochi Prefecture, Ishimoto Yasuhiro Photo Center, 136.
Kuan, Seng: 39.
Mitsubishi Heavy Industries: 205.
Miyagi Prefecture Sightseeing Section: 64 left.
Mori Art Museum-Echelle-1: 199.
Mulligan, Mark: 74, 75, 78, 79, 82, 83, 84, 85, 86.
Oshima, Ken Tadashi: 12, 14, 15, 18, 19, 20, 21, 22 left, 23, 25 bottom, 52 right, 55 left, 53 bottom, 61 right, 156 left.
Oyama Takashi: 55 right, 63 right, 68, 80 left, 82 right, 138, 142, 143, 166, 174, 175.
Murai Osamu: 52 left, 56, 62 left, 127 right, 150–151, 156 bottom, 157, 167, 197 left.
Shikada Kenichiro: 125.
Shiratori Yoshio: 25 top right, left.
Taira Toshio: 13.
Tange Associates: 41.
Yoda Sadakazu: 80 right.

KIKUTAKE WRITINGS

"Sky House," *Japan Architect,* vol. 34 (January–February 1959), 107.

"Marine City," *Kokusai kenchiku*, vol. 26, no. 2 (February 1959), 36–39.

"Tower-Shaped Community," *Kokusai kenchiku*, vol. 26, no. 1 (February 1959), 12–19.

"The Great Shrine of Izumo," originally published in English in *World Architecture,* no. 2 (1965), 12–21 [19]. Revised complete version of the text published as Kikutake Kiyonori, *Taisha kenchikuron ka kata katachi* (Tokyo: Shōkokusha, 1969).

"The Order of Things One Can See: Floors and Columns," Kikutake Kiyonori, *Taisha kenchikuron ka kata katachi* (Tokyo: Shōkokusha, 1969), 116–129.

"New Form and Old Tradition," reprinted in *Arts and Architecture*, vol. 81, no. 12 (December 1964), 14–17, and in *Kenchiku* (October 1965), 28.